HSPT PREP BOOK 2024 CATHOLIC SCHOOLS

The Complete Study Guide with 2 Full-Length Practice Exams and 800+ Practice Questions

Grady Roser

TABLE OF CONTENTS

INTRODUCTION

Welcome to the *HSPT Prep Book 2024-2025 for Catholic Schools: The Complete Study Guide with 2 Full-Length Practice Exams and 800+ Practice Questions.* If you're reading this, you're likely preparing for one of the most important exams you'll take during your academic career—the High School Placement Test (HSPT). This book has been crafted specifically for students applying to Catholic high schools, helping you navigate the complexities of the HSPT while building confidence, mastering content, and developing the test-taking strategies necessary to succeed.

Preparing for an exam like the HSPT might seem overwhelming at first, especially when you realize that this test can play a pivotal role in your admission to your preferred Catholic high school. The good news is that with the right tools and dedication, you can overcome the challenges and achieve a high score. This book is designed to be that tool, giving you everything you need in one place.

The *HSPT Prep Book 2024-2025* is more than just a guide; it's a comprehensive roadmap. From a detailed breakdown of each section to two full-length practice exams, this guide has been curated to cover everything that could appear on the exam, ensuring that you're fully prepared when test day arrives. Whether you're a first-time test-taker looking to familiarize yourself with the format or a student seeking to improve your score, this book will guide you step by step through the process.

How to Use This Book

One of the most important things to do before you start studying is to understand how to best use this guide. A comprehensive resource is only as effective as your approach to using it. We've structured this book to take you from basic concepts to advanced strategies, with detailed reviews and plenty of practice along the way. Here's how you can make the most of this study guide.

Step-by-Step Breakdown of Chapters

Each chapter of this book has been carefully organized to cover one of the key subtests that make up the HSPT: Verbal Skills, Quantitative Skills, Reading, Mathematics, and Language. You'll find that every section offers a comprehensive review of the content, strategies for answering questions, and practice problems to help reinforce what you've learned.

For instance, in the **Verbal Skills** section, you'll be introduced to concepts such as synonyms, antonyms, and analogies. In each case, you'll not only learn what the questions look like but also how to think through the problems strategically. Similarly, the **Quantitative Skills** section will walk you through number sequences, geometric and non-geometric comparisons, and computations—breaking down these complex topics into manageable parts.

Don't rush through the material. The key to mastering the HSPT is taking the time to thoroughly review each section, practice regularly, and understand your strengths and weaknesses. Skimming won't give you the depth of understanding needed to perform well on test day. Instead, focus on mastering each section before moving on to the next.

Timing and Practice

This book also emphasizes **timed practice**—an essential part of preparing for the HSPT. Each of the five sections has specific timing requirements, and practicing under these time constraints is crucial for success. You'll want to use a timer as you go through the practice questions, ensuring that you can pace yourself efficiently on the real exam.

Here's the breakdown of the sections and their timing:

- **Verbal Skills**: 60 questions in 18 minutes

- **Quantitative Skills**: 52 questions in 30 minutes

- **Reading**: 62 questions in 25 minutes

- **Mathematics**: 64 questions in 45 minutes

- **Language**: 60 questions in 25 minutes

In addition to practicing the individual subtests, this book includes **two full-length practice exams** that mimic the actual test format and timing. These exams will give you a chance to test your skills, assess your progress, and become comfortable with the HSPT's pacing.

Actionable Tip: As you complete each chapter, note the types of questions you find most challenging. Use this information to guide your practice sessions, focusing extra time and attention on areas where you need improvement. The goal is to turn your weaknesses into strengths by the time you take the full-length practice exams.

The Role of Review and Feedback

After completing each section's review and practice problems, you'll find **detailed explanations** for each question. It's important to review these explanations, even for the questions you answered correctly. Understanding why a particular answer is right (and why the other options are wrong) will deepen your knowledge and help you avoid similar mistakes in the future.

Each practice exam at the end of this book comes with an answer key and an **explanation section**. When you take the practice tests, simulate the real testing environment by sticking to the timing and avoiding distractions. Afterward, use the explanations to identify any gaps in your knowledge and revisit the relevant sections for a refresher.

Building Your Study Plan

It's not enough to just dive into the material randomly. A structured study plan is crucial for getting the most out of your preparation. Depending on how much time you have before test day, you'll want to divide your study sessions across the different sections, focusing more time on areas where you struggle. This book provides you with a **study planner** in the appendix, which can be tailored to fit your schedule, whether you have a few months or just a few weeks before the test.

As a general rule, here's a suggested study timeline:

- **3–6 months before the test**: Start by focusing on understanding the concepts in each section. Spend time reviewing the foundational material in Verbal Skills, Quantitative Skills, and Reading, and gradually incorporate practice problems.

- **1–3 months before the test**: Shift your focus to timed practice. By this stage, you should be able to complete practice questions within the allotted time. Begin taking the full-length practice tests and focus on reviewing your errors.

- **1–3 weeks before the test**: Focus on fine-tuning your skills. Review key concepts, work on any remaining weak areas, and make sure you're comfortable with the timing of each subtest.

By following a structured plan, you'll maximize your chances of success on test day.

What to Expect on the HSPT

Now that you understand how to use this book, let's take a closer look at the HSPT itself. The HSPT is designed to assess both your **cognitive skills** and your **academic achievement**, providing Catholic high schools with a comprehensive overview of your abilities. The test covers five main areas:

1. **Verbal Skills**: This section tests your ability to work with words, relationships between words, and logical reasoning. You'll need to be familiar with synonyms, antonyms, analogies, and verbal classifications.

2. **Quantitative Skills**: The quantitative section challenges your number sense, requiring you to solve problems involving sequences, comparisons, and basic computations. This section focuses less on complex mathematical concepts and more on your ability to reason with numbers.

3. **Reading**: The reading section is split into comprehension and vocabulary. You'll be asked to read passages and answer questions based on your understanding of the text. You'll also need to demonstrate your ability to define words based on their context.

4. **Mathematics**: In the mathematics section, you'll encounter a broad range of topics, from basic arithmetic to more advanced concepts such as algebra and geometry. This section tests both your computational skills and your problem-solving abilities.

5. **Language**: Finally, the language section assesses your grammar, punctuation, spelling, and overall writing mechanics. You'll be asked to correct sentences, identify errors, and demonstrate your understanding of proper usage.

Each of these sections is timed, so **time management** will be a crucial part of your test-day strategy. The entire HSPT lasts about 2.5 hours, and you'll need to maintain focus and pace yourself to ensure you have time to answer all the questions.

Key Study Strategies for Success

Preparing for the HSPT isn't just about reviewing content and memorizing facts—it's about implementing strategic study methods that maximize your learning efficiency and ensure you're ready for every type of question the test might throw at you. Effective study habits not only boost your confidence but also enhance your ability to retain information and perform under pressure. This section will guide you through essential study strategies tailored specifically for the HSPT, helping you build a solid foundation and excel on test day.

Create a Structured Study Schedule

The foundation of any successful exam preparation lies in creating and sticking to a well-organized study plan. With the HSPT covering five distinct subtests, it's important to allocate your study time wisely, ensuring that you dedicate ample time to each area. A well-structured schedule ensures you cover all sections, reinforces your learning, and prevents last-minute cramming, which is often ineffective.

1. **Assess Your Strengths and Weaknesses**: Before diving into a study plan, take a diagnostic test or a few practice questions from each subtest to assess where you currently stand. This will help you identify the areas where you need the most improvement. For example, if you find the math section particularly challenging but breeze through verbal skills, you'll want to devote more study time to mathematics.

2. **Divide and Conquer**: Break your study plan down into manageable chunks. Start by studying individual sections—Verbal Skills, Quantitative Skills, Reading, Mathematics, and Language— and move on to practice questions for each subtest. Don't try to tackle too much at once. Focus on one section at a time, but rotate through different subtests regularly to keep your preparation balanced.

3. **Set Realistic Goals**: Ensure that your study plan includes daily or weekly goals. For example, aim to complete a certain number of practice questions or review a specific set of vocabulary words each day. Avoid overwhelming yourself with unrealistic expectations—small, consistent progress will add up over time.

4. **Include Breaks and Rest Days**: While it's important to dedicate significant time to your HSPT preparation, overloading yourself with too many study hours in a single day can lead to burnout. Be sure to schedule short breaks during study sessions (about 5-10 minutes after every 45 minutes of study) and incorporate rest days to recharge.

5. **Track Your Progress**: As you work through the material, track your performance on practice questions and subtests. This will help you gauge whether you're improving and allow you to adjust your study plan accordingly. If you notice that you're consistently missing a certain type of question—such as analogy questions in Verbal Skills—take extra time to focus on that area.

Master Time Management

The HSPT is not only about knowing the material—it's also about completing the test within the allotted time. With nearly 300 questions to answer in a little over two hours, mastering time management is crucial. Developing effective pacing strategies will ensure that you have enough time to answer all the questions without feeling rushed or panicked.

1. **Practice Under Timed Conditions**: Whenever you practice, use a timer to simulate real test conditions. This will help you become comfortable with the time limits for each subtest and train you to work at the right pace. For example, in the Verbal Skills section, you'll have about 18 minutes to answer 60 questions, which averages to about 18 seconds per question. This means you'll need to quickly assess each question and eliminate incorrect answers to move through the section efficiently.

2. **Use the Process of Elimination**: When you encounter a difficult question, especially in sections like Verbal Skills or Quantitative Skills, use the process of elimination to narrow down your options. Eliminating even one or two incorrect answers increases your chances of guessing correctly, and it can help you save time by preventing you from overthinking the question.

3. **Skip and Return**: If you find yourself stuck on a particularly challenging question, don't waste too much time trying to figure it out. Skip it, mark it, and move on to the next question. Once you've completed the easier questions, go back and tackle the more difficult ones. This ensures that you maximize your score by answering all the questions you know before running out of time.

4. **Pacing Yourself in the Math Section**: The Mathematics section tends to be the longest (64 questions in 45 minutes), and it's easy to get bogged down in complex calculations. It's important to practice pacing in this section, focusing on answering the questions you find easiest first. Save more time-consuming problems, like those involving word problems or geometry, for later.

Use Active Learning Techniques

Active learning involves engaging with the material in a way that promotes deeper understanding and retention, rather than passively reading or memorizing. Implementing active learning strategies can help reinforce difficult concepts and keep you engaged throughout your study sessions.

1. **Take Notes and Summarize**: As you work through each chapter of this book, take notes in your own words. Summarizing the key points helps to solidify your understanding. For example, when studying Verbal Skills, jot down the types of analogies you've encountered and how you solved them. Similarly, for the Mathematics section, note down formulas or strategies for solving particular types of problems.

2. **Teach the Material**: One of the most effective ways to learn is to teach the material to someone else. If you can explain a concept clearly, whether it's a grammar rule in the Language section or

a strategy for solving number sequences in Quantitative Skills, it means you've mastered it. Consider studying with a friend or family member, and take turns teaching each other the material.

3. **Use Flashcards**: Flashcards are an excellent tool for building vocabulary and reviewing key concepts, especially for sections like Verbal Skills and Reading, where understanding definitions and word relationships is critical. Create flashcards with common vocabulary words, prefixes, suffixes, and root words, and quiz yourself regularly.

4. **Practice Retrieval**: Rather than simply re-reading material, test your knowledge by recalling information from memory. This can be done through practice questions, writing summaries, or even explaining concepts aloud. Practicing retrieval helps you retain information better and strengthens your ability to recall it during the exam.

Simulate Test Conditions

One of the most valuable steps you can take during your HSPT preparation is to simulate the actual test environment. Taking full-length practice tests under timed conditions not only builds endurance but also helps you become familiar with the test format, reducing anxiety on the actual exam day.

1. **Take Practice Tests Regularly**: This book provides two full-length practice tests that mirror the actual HSPT. These practice tests are designed to replicate the timing, structure, and difficulty level of the real exam. Set aside a quiet, uninterrupted time to take the test in one sitting, just as you will on test day. This will help you build the stamina needed to focus for the full 2.5 hours.

2. **Review Your Mistakes**: After completing a practice test, take the time to review your mistakes and understand why you got certain questions wrong. Were you rushing? Did you misinterpret the question? Understanding your errors will help you avoid making the same mistakes on the actual exam.

3. **Develop a Test Day Routine**: As test day approaches, start developing a routine that you can follow on the morning of the HSPT. This includes getting a good night's sleep, eating a healthy breakfast, and arriving at the test site early. Practicing this routine in advance will help you feel calm and prepared on the actual test day.

Incorporate Relaxation Techniques

Test anxiety is common, but it can also hinder your performance if not managed properly. Incorporating relaxation techniques into your study routine can help you stay calm and focused, both during your preparation and on test day.

1. **Mindful Breathing**: Practicing mindful breathing can help reduce stress and improve focus. Take a few moments before each study session to practice deep breathing, inhaling through your nose and exhaling slowly through your mouth. This technique can also be used during the exam if you start to feel overwhelmed.

2. **Visualization**: Visualization is a powerful tool that athletes and high-achievers use to prepare for big events. Spend a few minutes each day visualizing yourself successfully completing the HSPT. Imagine yourself calmly working through the questions, staying focused, and finishing on time. This mental rehearsal can boost your confidence and reduce test-day jitters.

3. **Positive Affirmations**: Replace negative thoughts (e.g., "I'm going to fail" or "I'm not good at math") with positive affirmations. Remind yourself of the progress you've made and the effort you've put into your preparation. Simple affirmations like "I'm prepared and ready for this test" can make a big difference in your mindset.

Frequently Asked Questions About the HSPT

As you prepare for the HSPT, it's natural to have questions about what to expect and how the test will impact your application to Catholic high schools. In this section, we've compiled answers to some of the most frequently asked questions to help clarify any uncertainties and ensure that you're fully prepared for the exam.

What is the HSPT, and Why is it Important?

The High School Placement Test (HSPT) is a standardized exam administered by Catholic high schools across the United States as part of the admissions process for incoming 9th graders. The exam is designed to assess both cognitive skills and academic achievement, giving schools a comprehensive picture of each student's strengths and areas for growth. While the test is important for admissions decisions, it can also play a role in merit-based scholarships and course placement within the school.

The HSPT is made up of five sections:

- Verbal Skills

- Quantitative Skills

- Reading

- Mathematics

- Language

These sections cover a wide range of topics, from vocabulary and logic to math and grammar. Students have approximately 2.5 hours to complete the test, and scores are often reported as percentiles, comparing each student's performance to that of other test-takers.

How Is the HSPT Scored?

The HSPT is scored differently from other standardized tests, such as the SAT or ACT. Instead of a raw score (the total number of correct answers), students receive a percentile ranking, which indicates how they performed compared to other students. For example, if you score in the 85th percentile, it means you performed better than 85% of other students who took the test.

In addition to overall percentiles, schools often break down the scores by subtest (Verbal, Quantitative, Reading, Mathematics, and Language). This allows schools to see which areas students excel in and which areas might need improvement.

It's important to note that there is no official "passing" or "failing" score on the HSPT. Each school sets its own admissions criteria, so what constitutes a "good" score can vary from one institution to another. However, students who score in the 75th percentile or higher are generally considered competitive applicants for most Catholic high schools.

When and Where Can I Take the HSPT?

The HSPT is typically administered during the fall or early winter of a student's 8th-grade year. Each Catholic high school sets its own test dates, so you'll need to contact the schools you're applying to for specific information about when the test is offered. Many schools administer the HSPT on their campuses, though some schools may offer alternative testing locations for students who live far away or have scheduling conflicts.

It's important to register for the test well in advance, as spots can fill up quickly. Some schools may also offer practice exams or diagnostic tests to help students prepare before taking the actual HSPT.

Can I Take the HSPT More Than Once?

Most Catholic high schools only allow students to take the HSPT once. However, some schools offer multiple test dates, giving students the option to choose the date that works best for them. It's a good idea to contact the admissions office of the school you're applying to and ask about their specific policies regarding HSPT retakes.

If your school does allow multiple attempts, be sure to space out your test dates to allow enough time for additional study and practice. Taking the test too close together may not give you enough time to improve your skills between attempts.

What Should I Bring on Test Day?

On the day of the HSPT, it's important to arrive prepared. Here's a checklist of items to bring with you:

- **#2 pencils**: Make sure you bring several sharpened pencils, as you'll be filling in answers on a bubble sheet.
- **Erasers**: A clean, effective eraser is essential for correcting mistakes.

- **Registration confirmation**: Bring any documents required by the school to confirm your registration for the test.

- **Water bottle**: Staying hydrated during the test is important, but be sure to follow the school's rules about when and where you can drink water.

- **Snacks**: If the school allows snacks during breaks, bring something light and energizing, like a granola bar or piece of fruit.

- **Watch**: Many schools don't allow students to have cell phones in the testing room, so bring a simple watch to keep track of time during each section.

Be sure to dress comfortably and in layers, as the testing room may be cooler or warmer than expected.

What Happens After the Test?

After completing the HSPT, your results will be sent to the schools you applied to, typically within a few weeks. Each school will then use the scores as part of their admissions process, alongside other factors such as grades, recommendations, and extracurricular activities.

In some cases, you may also receive a copy of your test results, either directly from the school or from the test provider. If you have any questions about how your scores will be reported or used, it's a good idea to contact the admissions office at your prospective high school.

By following the study strategies outlined in this chapter and utilizing the comprehensive review and practice materials in this book, you'll be well-prepared to tackle the HSPT and achieve your academic goals. Remember, preparation is key, and the effort you put into studying will pay off on test day.

PART 1: EXAM OVERVIEW AND TEST-TAKING STRATEGIES

Chapter 1: Introduction to the HSPT

Overview of the HSPT for Catholic Schools

The High School Placement Test (HSPT) serves as a critical gateway for students seeking admission into Catholic high schools across the United States. Administered annually, this standardized test is designed to evaluate a student's cognitive abilities and academic skills. The test assesses five key areas: Verbal Skills, Quantitative Skills, Reading, Mathematics, and Language. For Catholic schools, the HSPT plays a significant role in determining both admissions and academic placement, offering schools a clear metric to gauge a student's readiness for high school-level coursework.

What is the HSPT?

The HSPT is administered by the Scholastic Testing Service (STS), a nationally recognized organization that specializes in creating standardized exams tailored to the needs of private schools. Catholic high schools use the HSPT to evaluate applicants not only on academic proficiency but also on cognitive reasoning skills. Unlike state-administered public school exams, the HSPT focuses on a wide range of subjects and reasoning abilities, providing Catholic schools with a comprehensive understanding of a student's potential for academic success.

Why is the HSPT Important for Catholic Schools?

Catholic schools take a holistic approach to education, often emphasizing moral, spiritual, and academic development. However, the HSPT provides a quantitative measure that allows these schools to maintain rigorous academic standards. For many schools, HSPT scores serve as a key determinant for admission. Schools may also use these scores to award scholarships and to decide class placements for incoming freshmen.

For students, excelling on the HSPT is not only about gaining admission but can also open the door to academic scholarships and advanced placement in higher-level courses. In highly competitive Catholic schools, students with top percentile scores are often considered for honors or accelerated learning tracks, which can significantly impact their high school experience and future college applications.

Differences Between the HSPT and Other Entrance Exams

Many students applying to private high schools may encounter several different entrance exams, including the Independent School Entrance Examination (ISEE) and the Secondary School Admission Test (SSAT). However, the HSPT is distinct from these exams in several ways. While the ISEE and SSAT are used by a range of independent schools, the HSPT is designed specifically for Catholic high schools. The content is tailored to reflect the broad educational focus of Catholic schools, with an emphasis on foundational academic skills.

One of the key differences lies in the structure and content of the tests. The HSPT's focus on cognitive reasoning sets it apart, emphasizing not just what students have learned in middle school but also how they think and process information. This aligns with Catholic schools' desire to nurture both intellectual and ethical growth. Moreover, while other tests such as the SSAT may include essay components or subject-specific questions, the HSPT focuses entirely on multiple-choice questions, allowing for a more uniform and objective scoring process.

Another key distinction is the format of the HSPT. It is designed to be completed within a strict time limit—typically two and a half hours—forcing students to demonstrate both knowledge and efficiency. This makes time management skills essential for success, a theme we will explore in detail later in this chapter.

The Role of the HSPT in the Admissions Process

Catholic schools typically incorporate HSPT scores into a broader admissions process that includes letters of recommendation, previous school records, and sometimes interviews. However, the weight of the HSPT in admissions decisions can be significant. Many schools establish a baseline score for admissions, and students who fall below this threshold may not be considered for acceptance.

In some cases, high HSPT scores can offset weaker areas of a student's application. For example, a student with less than stellar grades in middle school might still gain admission to a competitive Catholic high school if their HSPT scores demonstrate strong cognitive abilities and academic potential. Likewise, students who perform well on the HSPT may qualify for merit-based scholarships, which can ease the financial burden of private school tuition.

How the HSPT Has Evolved

The HSPT has been in use for decades, and over time, it has evolved to meet the changing needs of Catholic schools. Originally, the test focused primarily on traditional academic subjects such as reading, writing, and mathematics. However, recent updates have incorporated more advanced reasoning and problem-solving components, reflecting a growing emphasis on critical thinking skills in high school education.

Additionally, the format of the test has become more standardized, with rigorous quality controls to ensure fairness and accuracy. The test's multiple-choice format has remained consistent, but the range of questions has expanded to cover a broader array of cognitive skills. For example, students are now expected to demonstrate proficiency in both basic mathematical operations and more complex algebraic reasoning. This ensures that the test remains challenging and relevant in a modern educational context.

Understanding the HSPT's role in Catholic school admissions is crucial for both students and parents. This standardized test not only influences admissions decisions but also plays a key role in determining academic placement and scholarship eligibility. As we move into the next section, we will dive deeper into the structure of the HSPT, breaking down each of the five subtests and offering strategies to manage your time effectively during the exam.

Subtest Structure and Time Management

Successfully navigating the HSPT requires not only a strong understanding of academic content but also the ability to manage time effectively. The HSPT consists of five subtests: Verbal Skills, Quantitative Skills, Reading, Mathematics, and Language. Each of these subtests is timed separately, and students must complete the entire test in approximately two and a half hours. While that may seem like a generous amount of time, the pressure of answering nearly 300 questions means that time management is critical to achieving a high score.

The Five Subtests of the HSPT

Each of the five subtests measures different skills, and understanding the format and expectations of each is essential for maximizing your performance. Let's break down each subtest in detail.

1. **Verbal Skills Subtest**

   o The Verbal Skills section is designed to assess your ability to understand and use language effectively. It includes questions on synonyms, antonyms, analogies, verbal classifications, and logic. This subtest consists of 60 questions to be answered in 18 minutes, which means you'll need to move quickly.

   o **Key Strategies**: The best approach is to quickly eliminate obviously incorrect answer choices. This will allow you to focus on narrowing down the remaining options. For analogy questions, identifying the relationship between the two words in the prompt can help you find the correct answer more efficiently.

2. **Quantitative Skills Subtest**

   o The Quantitative Skills subtest focuses on numerical reasoning and includes questions on sequences, comparisons, and computations. You'll have 30 minutes to answer 52 questions. This subtest requires a balance of speed and accuracy, as the questions range from simple arithmetic to more complex reasoning problems.

   o **Key Strategies**: For sequence questions, identifying patterns early can save time. When faced with comparison or computation problems, it's often helpful to work through the easier questions first, leaving the more complex ones for later.

3. **Reading Subtest**

   o The Reading subtest consists of 62 questions, which must be completed in 25 minutes. This section is divided between reading comprehension questions and vocabulary-in-context questions. You'll be asked to read several passages and answer questions that test your understanding of main ideas, supporting details, and vocabulary.

   o **Key Strategies**: Practice reading passages under timed conditions. Skimming passages for main ideas before reading the questions can help you locate key information more quickly.

4. **Mathematics Subtest**

- The Mathematics subtest includes 64 questions that must be answered in 45 minutes. Topics range from basic arithmetic to algebra, geometry, and problem-solving. The difficulty of the questions increases as you progress through the test, so it's important to maintain a steady pace.

- **Key Strategies**: As with the Quantitative Skills subtest, start with the easier questions and work your way up to the more difficult ones. Be mindful of the time, but don't rush through calculations, as even minor mistakes can cost you points.

5. **Language Subtest**

- The Language subtest measures your grammar, spelling, and punctuation skills. It consists of 60 questions, which you must complete in 25 minutes. This section covers capitalization, usage, spelling, and sentence structure.

- **Key Strategies**: Brush up on grammar rules before the test. For spelling and usage questions, it's helpful to trust your instincts. If you've been reading and writing regularly, your brain is already familiar with the correct forms, even if you don't consciously realize it.

Effective Time Management Strategies

Time management is perhaps the most crucial skill for excelling on the HSPT. With nearly 300 questions to answer in just over two hours, every second counts. Here are some proven strategies to help you manage your time effectively during the test:

1. **Prioritize Easy Questions**: Start by answering the questions you find easiest. These will likely take less time to complete and will give you a confidence boost. Once you've answered the easier questions, you can go back and tackle the more difficult ones.

2. **Use the Process of Elimination**: For multiple-choice questions, eliminating obviously incorrect answers can increase your chances of choosing the correct one. Even if you're unsure of the answer, narrowing down your choices gives you a better shot at guessing correctly.

3. **Keep an Eye on the Clock**: Time yourself during practice tests so you can develop an internal sense of how much time has passed. During the actual test, check the clock periodically, but don't obsess over it. If you're running out of time, make educated guesses rather than leaving questions blank.

4. **Skip and Return**: If a question stumps you, don't spend too much time on it. Mark it and move on. Once you've completed the rest of the subtest, go back to the questions you skipped. This ensures that you don't waste valuable time on one question when you could be answering others.

5. **Practice Under Timed Conditions**: The best way to improve your time management skills is to practice taking tests under timed conditions. Simulate the testing environment by setting a timer and working through practice questions or full-length tests. This will help you get accustomed to the pace of the actual HSPT.

Pacing Strategies for Each Subtest

Each subtest of the HSPT has its own unique time constraints, and it's important to develop pacing strategies for each. Here's a breakdown of how much time you should ideally spend on each question:

- **Verbal Skills**: 18 minutes for 60 questions means you have approximately 18 seconds per question. Move quickly, but take care to avoid careless mistakes.

- **Quantitative Skills**: With 30 minutes for 52 questions, you have about 35 seconds per question. Be efficient, especially with simpler computation problems.

- **Reading**: You'll have 25 minutes for 62 questions, or roughly 24 seconds per question. Practice reading passages quickly and answering questions accurately to improve your speed.

- **Mathematics**: The longest subtest, you'll have 45 minutes for 64 questions, which gives you about 42 seconds per question. Don't rush through calculations, but don't linger too long on difficult problems either.

- **Language**: With 25 minutes for 60 questions, you'll need to move at a pace of about 25 seconds per question. Brush up on grammar rules ahead of time so you can answer these questions more quickly.

Conclusion of Subtopic

Mastering the structure and time management of the HSPT is just as important as knowing the academic content. By understanding the format of each subtest and practicing timed questions, you'll be well-prepared to handle the pressure of the exam. In the next section, we'll explore how the HSPT is scored and how to interpret your results, so you can better understand what your scores mean and how they'll impact your high school admissions process.

Understanding Test Scoring and Percentiles

The scoring system of the HSPT is one of the most crucial aspects of the test that both students and parents need to understand. Unlike regular classroom tests, where raw scores are often used to determine performance, the HSPT uses percentile rankings to compare your results with those of other students across the country. These percentile scores are then used by schools to make important decisions about admissions, scholarships, and academic placements.

How is the HSPT Scored?

The HSPT consists of five subtests: Verbal Skills, Quantitative Skills, Reading, Mathematics, and Language. Each subtest is scored separately, and students receive a raw score, which is the total number of correct answers. This raw score is then converted into a scaled score, which ranges from 200 to 800. Finally, the scaled scores are used to calculate percentile rankings.

The percentile score is a measure of how well you performed compared to other students who took the same test. For example, if you scored in the 90th percentile, it means that you performed better than 90% of the students who took the test. It's important to note that percentile scores are not the same as raw scores or percentages. A percentile score of 90 does not mean you answered 90% of the questions correctly; it means you performed better than 90% of other test-takers.

Understanding Percentiles

Percentile rankings are one of the most important metrics used by schools when evaluating HSPT results. These rankings allow schools to compare students from different schools, regions, and backgrounds in a standardized way. While raw scores tell you how many questions you answered correctly, percentile rankings give you a clearer picture of how your performance stacks up against other students.

For example, let's say you answered 250 out of 298 questions correctly. While this raw score might give you a general sense of how well you did, your percentile score will provide more context. If the test was particularly difficult and most students answered fewer than 250 questions correctly, your percentile score might be quite high, even though your raw score wasn't perfect.

Conversely, if the test was easier and many students answered more than 250 questions correctly, your percentile score might be lower, despite your strong raw score. This is why percentile scores are often considered more important than raw scores—they provide a more accurate comparison of your performance relative to your peers.

The Importance of Percentile Rankings

Catholic high schools place a great deal of emphasis on percentile rankings when making admissions decisions. While raw scores are still important, percentile rankings give schools a better understanding of how a student performed compared to others in the same cohort. Students who score in the top percentiles are more likely to be admitted to competitive Catholic high schools and may also be eligible for merit-based scholarships.

It's worth noting that different schools may have different expectations when it comes to HSPT scores. Some schools may require students to score in the top 10% to be considered for admission, while others may accept students with lower scores, particularly if they excel in other areas of their application. Understanding how your percentile score compares to the expectations of your target schools is crucial for planning your next steps.

Common Misconceptions About HSPT Scoring

Many students and parents have misconceptions about how the HSPT is scored and what the results mean. One of the most common misconceptions is that a percentile score of 50 is a failing grade. In reality, a percentile score of 50 means that you performed better than half of the students who took the test. For many schools, a percentile score in the 50th to 75th range is considered solid, particularly if the student's overall application is strong.

Another misconception is that all students are expected to score in the top percentiles. While it's true that many Catholic high schools prioritize high scores, not all schools have the same admissions criteria. Some schools take a more holistic approach, considering not only HSPT scores but also factors like grades, extracurricular activities, and letters of recommendation.

Strategies for Improving Your Percentile Score

If you're aiming to improve your HSPT scores, it's important to focus on strategies that will boost your performance across all five subtests. Here are some tips for improving your percentile rankings:

1. **Practice Regularly**: The best way to improve your scores is to practice regularly. Take full-length practice tests under timed conditions to simulate the actual test. This will help you become more familiar with the format and improve your time management skills.

2. **Focus on Weak Areas**: After taking practice tests, identify your weakest areas and focus on improving them. If you struggle with math, spend extra time reviewing mathematical concepts and solving practice problems. If reading comprehension is challenging, practice reading passages and answering questions under timed conditions.

3. **Use Process of Elimination**: For multiple-choice questions, use the process of elimination to narrow down your options. Even if you're unsure of the correct answer, eliminating obviously incorrect answers can increase your chances of guessing correctly.

4. **Stay Calm and Focused**: Test anxiety can negatively impact your performance, so it's important to stay calm and focused during the test. Take deep breaths, pace yourself, and remember that it's okay to skip difficult questions and come back to them later.

5. **Review Your Mistakes**: After completing practice tests, review your mistakes carefully. Understanding why you answered a question incorrectly will help you avoid making the same mistake on the actual test. Many practice tests provide detailed explanations for incorrect answers, so take advantage of these resources.

How Test Scores Impact Admissions and Scholarships

In addition to determining admissions, HSPT scores can also impact scholarship opportunities. Many Catholic high schools offer merit-based scholarships to students who score in the top percentiles. These scholarships can significantly reduce the cost of tuition and make private education more affordable for families.

If you're hoping to qualify for a scholarship, it's important to set specific goals for your HSPT performance. Research the scholarship requirements at your target schools and aim to score in the top percentile range. Keep in mind that some schools may offer tiered scholarships, with higher awards going to students with higher scores.

Understanding how the HSPT is scored and how percentile rankings work is crucial for navigating the admissions process. By focusing on improving your performance across all five subtests and using the strategies outlined in this section, you'll be well-prepared to achieve a high score and maximize your chances of admission and scholarship opportunities.

Chapter 2: Preparing for the HSPT

The High School Placement Test (HSPT) is a significant milestone for students aiming to attend Catholic high schools. Proper preparation is the key to ensuring that you walk into the exam room feeling confident and ready. This chapter focuses on how to effectively prepare for the HSPT, offering detailed strategies and practical advice on studying, staying calm, and mastering the test format. We will explore the best study tips and techniques, how to reduce test anxiety, the importance of practice exams, and how to create a personalized study schedule that fits your needs. Let's dive into each of these essential elements to make sure you are fully prepared to excel on your HSPT.

Study Tips and Techniques

Preparing for the HSPT requires more than just opening a book and reading through the material. You need to engage actively with the content, understand how to apply strategies for each section, and work on building endurance for the timed nature of the exam. In this section, we'll explore practical study techniques that will help you get the most out of your preparation time and set you on the path toward success.

1. Break the Material into Manageable Chunks

One of the most common mistakes students make when preparing for an exam like the HSPT is trying to tackle too much information at once. The HSPT covers a broad range of topics, including verbal skills, quantitative skills, reading comprehension, mathematics, and language. Trying to master all these areas in one go is overwhelming and counterproductive. Instead, break the material into smaller, manageable chunks.

For example, set aside a day to focus solely on vocabulary or analogies in the Verbal Skills section. On another day, you might focus entirely on fractions, decimals, and percents for the Mathematics section. By dividing your study sessions into focused, smaller tasks, you'll retain more information and feel less overwhelmed.

2. Set Specific Study Goals

Each study session should have a clear objective. For instance, if you are working on reading comprehension, your goal might be to understand how to identify main ideas and details in a passage. If you are working on math, your goal might be to master solving algebraic equations. Having specific goals for each session will keep you on track and ensure that you make measurable progress.

3. Active Learning Techniques

Engage with the material actively rather than passively reading through it. This means using methods like summarizing what you've learned in your own words, teaching the material to someone else, or creating flashcards for tricky concepts. Active learning techniques, such as testing yourself on key definitions or walking through math problems out loud, help reinforce what you've learned and improve retention.

4. Create Visual Aids

Many students find that creating visual aids, such as charts, graphs, or concept maps, helps them understand and remember complex material. For instance, when studying vocabulary, you can create a word web that links new words with their synonyms, antonyms, and usage in sentences. For math, drawing diagrams or plotting out problem-solving steps can help solidify your understanding of geometric and algebraic concepts.

5. Use Memory Aids and Mnemonics

Mnemonic devices are a fantastic way to remember complex or abstract information. For example, if you're struggling to remember the order of operations in math, you can use the mnemonic "PEMDAS" (Parentheses, Exponents, Multiplication, Division, Addition, and Subtraction). Developing these memory aids helps make studying more engaging and makes it easier to recall information on test day.

6. Study in Short, Frequent Sessions

Research shows that studying in shorter, more frequent sessions is far more effective than cramming for long hours in one sitting. Try the "Pomodoro Technique" — 25 minutes of focused studying followed by a 5-minute break. After four sessions, take a longer break (15-30 minutes). This method keeps your brain fresh and helps prevent burnout. Consistency is key, so aim to study a little bit every day, rather than having long gaps between study sessions.

7. Focus on Weak Areas

When preparing for the HSPT, it's natural to spend more time on the areas you find difficult. However, it's equally important not to ignore the sections where you excel. First, identify your weak areas by taking a diagnostic test or one of the full-length practice tests included in this book. Use the results to determine where you need to focus your efforts. If, for example, you struggle with reading comprehension but excel in mathematics, dedicate more time to reading while still maintaining your math skills.

8. Practice Active Reading

For the reading comprehension section, practice active reading techniques. This involves underlining or highlighting key points in the passage, summarizing paragraphs as you read, and identifying the main idea and supporting details. Reading slowly and thoughtfully during practice sessions will help you absorb more information and improve your comprehension skills.

9. Balance Review and Practice

While it's essential to review the content, don't forget the importance of hands-on practice. After reviewing the material for each section, immediately follow it with practice questions or exercises. This not only reinforces what you've learned but also gives you insight into the types of questions that will appear on the test.

10. Make Use of Flashcards

Flashcards are particularly effective for subjects like vocabulary and mathematical formulas. Write down a word or concept on one side of the card and its definition or explanation on the other. As you go through the cards, quiz yourself on each one. Flashcards are portable and easy to use, making them a convenient tool for reviewing during breaks or downtime.

11. Stay Organized

An organized study space leads to an organized mind. Set up a designated study area that is free of distractions and has all the materials you need, including your HSPT prep book, practice tests, highlighters, and a notebook for taking notes. Keep your study materials organized in folders or binders, and track your progress by checking off topics as you master them.

12. Group Study Sessions

Studying with a group can be beneficial, especially if you have friends who are also preparing for the HSPT. Group study sessions allow you to quiz each other, explain concepts in different ways, and motivate one another. However, be mindful to stay focused on the task at hand, as group sessions can sometimes lead to distractions. Set clear goals for the session, such as completing a set of practice questions or reviewing a particular section together.

13. Reward Yourself

To stay motivated throughout your study sessions, create a reward system. After completing a challenging task or reaching a study milestone, reward yourself with something you enjoy, whether it's a short break, a snack, or some downtime. Positive reinforcement helps keep you motivated and energized for the next study session.

Reducing Test Anxiety and Staying Focused

Test anxiety can undermine even the best preparation, making it difficult to perform well on exam day. In this section, we'll explore strategies for managing anxiety and staying focused before and during the HSPT. Learning how to calm your nerves and maintain focus is just as important as knowing the material itself.

1. Understand the Source of Anxiety

Before you can manage test anxiety, it's essential to understand where it comes from. Test anxiety is often rooted in fear — fear of failure, fear of not living up to expectations, or fear of the unknown. By identifying what specifically makes you anxious, you can take steps to address it. For example, if you're worried about running out of time during the exam, focus on practicing timed sections in your study sessions. If you're concerned about specific content areas, spend extra time reviewing those topics.

2. Practice Relaxation Techniques

Relaxation techniques, such as deep breathing, progressive muscle relaxation, or visualization, can help calm your mind and body. Deep breathing is one of the easiest and most effective techniques. Take a slow, deep breath in through your nose, hold it for a count of three, then exhale slowly through your mouth. Repeat this a few times until you feel more relaxed. You can practice this technique during your study sessions and use it on test day if you start to feel anxious.

3. Maintain a Positive Mindset

Your mindset plays a significant role in how you approach the exam. Instead of focusing on the possibility of failure, focus on your preparation and how far you've come. Remind yourself of the hard work you've put in and the progress you've made. Visualization can also be a helpful tool. Picture yourself successfully completing the exam, feeling confident and calm.

4. Create a Calm Environment

Your study environment has a direct impact on your anxiety levels. Study in a quiet, comfortable space where you can focus without distractions. Avoid studying in environments that are too noisy, cluttered, or chaotic, as these can increase your stress levels. You can also make your study space more inviting by adding personal touches, such as a calming scent or a comfortable chair.

5. Stay Physically Active

Physical activity is an excellent way to reduce stress and clear your mind. Even a short walk outside can help reduce anxiety and improve focus. Exercise releases endorphins, which are natural mood boosters, and helps reduce the physical symptoms of stress, such as muscle tension or headaches.

6. Build a Healthy Routine

Establishing a healthy routine in the weeks leading up to the HSPT is crucial for managing stress. Make sure you are getting enough sleep each night, eating well-balanced meals, and staying hydrated. Sleep, in particular, is vital for memory retention and overall cognitive function. Avoid staying up late cramming the night before the test, as this can increase anxiety and reduce your ability to perform well on test day.

7. Set Realistic Expectations

One way to alleviate test anxiety is by setting realistic expectations for yourself. While aiming for a high score is admirable, putting too much pressure on yourself can lead to unnecessary stress. Understand that the HSPT is just one component of your high school admissions process, and while it's important, it's not the sole determinant of your future success. Give yourself permission to make mistakes and remember that no one is perfect.

8. Take Practice Tests Under Realistic Conditions

One of the best ways to reduce test anxiety is to simulate the actual testing environment during your practice sessions. Take practice tests under timed conditions, in a quiet space, and with no distractions. By familiarizing yourself with the test format and timing, you'll feel more comfortable and confident when the real test day arrives. The more you practice in a realistic setting, the less intimidating the test will seem.

9. Focus on What You Can Control

On test day, there will be things you cannot control, such as the specific questions that appear on the test or the behavior of other students in the exam room. Instead of worrying about these factors, focus on what you *can* control — your preparation, your mindset, and your strategies for answering questions. When you focus on what you can control, you'll feel more empowered and less anxious.

10. Avoid Comparisons

It's natural to compare yourself to other students, but doing so can increase anxiety and make you feel inadequate. Remember that everyone has their strengths and weaknesses, and everyone's preparation journey is different. Focus on your own progress and don't worry about how others are preparing or performing.

The Importance of Practice Tests

Practice tests are one of the most crucial tools in your preparation arsenal for the HSPT. They not only help you assess your knowledge and understanding of the material but also give you valuable experience with the test format, timing, and question types. By simulating the real test environment, practice tests help build your confidence and reduce test-day anxiety. In this section, we will explore why practice tests are so important, how to use them effectively, and the benefits they provide throughout your HSPT preparation journey.

1. Familiarizing Yourself with the Test Format

One of the primary advantages of taking practice tests is that they familiarize you with the format of the HSPT. The HSPT consists of five subtests: Verbal Skills, Quantitative Skills, Reading Comprehension, Mathematics, and Language Skills. Each section has its own set of question types, time limits, and scoring criteria. Without practice, you may find the test format unfamiliar and intimidating on the actual test day.

When you take a practice test, you become accustomed to the layout of each section, the types of questions you'll encounter, and the pace at which you'll need to work. For example, the Verbal Skills section includes questions on synonyms, antonyms, analogies, and verbal logic, while the Mathematics section covers topics like algebra, geometry, and number operations. Familiarizing yourself with these different question types during practice will make the actual test feel less daunting.

Additionally, practice tests help you develop a sense of how much time to allocate to each question. Since the HSPT is a timed test, it's essential to learn how to pace yourself to ensure you complete all sections within the allotted time. The more practice tests you take, the better you'll become at managing your time effectively.

2. Building Endurance for the Timed Test

The HSPT is a lengthy test that requires sustained concentration and focus over a period of more than two hours. Many students are unaccustomed to taking such long exams, which can lead to fatigue and a decline in performance toward the end of the test. By taking full-length practice tests, you'll build the stamina needed to maintain your focus and energy throughout the entire exam.

It's important to take practice tests under realistic conditions, including timing yourself and working in a quiet, distraction-free environment. This will help you simulate the actual test experience and prepare your mind and body for the mental endurance required on test day. Over time, you'll develop the ability to stay focused and perform well, even during the later sections of the test.

3. Identifying Strengths and Weaknesses

One of the most valuable aspects of practice tests is their ability to reveal your strengths and weaknesses. After completing a practice test, take the time to carefully review your answers and analyze your performance in each section. Pay attention to the types of questions you answered correctly and those you struggled with.

By identifying your weak areas, you can tailor your study plan to focus on the subjects or question types that need improvement. For example, if you consistently struggle with analogy questions in the Verbal Skills section, you can devote more time to practicing analogies and reviewing strategies for answering those questions. On the other hand, if you perform well in the Mathematics section, you may only need occasional review to maintain your proficiency.

Keep track of your scores on each practice test to monitor your progress over time. As you continue to take practice tests and review your results, you should see improvement in your weak areas and an overall increase in your confidence and performance.

4. Improving Test-Taking Strategies

In addition to testing your knowledge, practice tests allow you to experiment with different test-taking strategies. For example, you may find that answering all the easier questions first and then returning to the more challenging ones helps you maximize your score. Alternatively, you might discover that you perform better when you tackle the sections in the order they're presented.

Another important strategy to practice is eliminating incorrect answer choices. On multiple-choice tests like the HSPT, it's often possible to narrow down the options by eliminating answers that are clearly wrong. By practicing this technique on sample questions, you'll become more efficient at identifying the correct answer, even when you're unsure.

Practice tests also give you the opportunity to fine-tune your approach to pacing. As you take more practice tests, you'll develop a sense of how much time to spend on each question and how to avoid getting stuck on difficult questions. This is particularly important in sections with strict time limits, such as the Quantitative Skills or Reading Comprehension subtests.

5. Reducing Test Anxiety

One of the most significant benefits of practice tests is their ability to reduce test anxiety. Test anxiety often stems from fear of the unknown or a lack of familiarity with the test format. The more practice tests you take, the more comfortable and confident you'll feel on the actual test day.

Practice tests help desensitize you to the pressure of a timed exam by allowing you to experience the same conditions in a lower-stakes environment. Over time, you'll become more accustomed to the pacing, timing, and question types, making the real test feel like just another practice session. This familiarity can significantly reduce test-day jitters and improve your overall performance.

6. Enhancing Time Management Skills

Time management is a critical skill for success on the HSPT. Each section of the test is timed, and students often struggle to complete all the questions within the allotted time. By taking timed practice tests, you'll learn how to manage your time effectively and ensure that you finish each section before time runs out.

As you take practice tests, pay attention to how much time you spend on each question and each section. If you find that you consistently run out of time, consider adjusting your pacing. For example, you might want to set a specific time limit for each question or prioritize answering easier questions first.

In addition, practice tests can help you develop strategies for dealing with time pressure. For instance, if you're running out of time on a particular section, you can practice quickly scanning the remaining questions and answering the ones you're most confident about. This strategy can help you maximize your score, even when time is tight.

7. Measuring Progress

Taking regular practice tests allows you to track your progress and see how much you've improved over time. After each test, review your scores and compare them to your previous results. Look for patterns in your performance, such as improvement in certain sections or consistency in your weak areas.

Tracking your progress can also boost your motivation. As you see your scores increase and your performance improve, you'll gain confidence in your abilities and feel more prepared for the real test. This sense of progress can help keep you focused and motivated throughout your study journey.

8. Simulating Test Day Conditions

One of the most important aspects of practice tests is their ability to simulate the actual test day conditions. By taking full-length practice tests in a quiet, timed environment, you'll get a sense of what to expect on the real test day. This can help reduce the element of surprise and make you feel more comfortable when it's time to take the actual HSPT.

Try to mimic the test day experience as closely as possible when taking practice tests. Find a quiet place to work, set a timer for each section, and avoid distractions. The more realistic your practice sessions are, the better prepared you'll be for the actual test.

9. Building Confidence

Confidence is key to performing well on any standardized test, and practice tests are an excellent way to build that confidence. The more practice you get, the more comfortable you'll become with the test format, the types of questions, and the time limits. As your familiarity with the test increases, so will your confidence in your ability to succeed.

Each time you complete a practice test, remind yourself of the progress you've made and the skills you've developed. Over time, you'll build a sense of self-assurance that will carry you through the actual test day.

10. Practicing Under Pressure

Finally, practice tests help you get used to the pressure of performing under timed conditions. Many students struggle with the stress of answering questions quickly and accurately within a limited time frame. By taking practice tests, you'll learn how to stay calm and focused, even when the clock is ticking.

Practice tests give you the opportunity to practice performing under pressure, which is a valuable skill for any timed exam. The more you practice, the better you'll become at managing your time, answering questions efficiently, and staying composed under stress.

Planning Your Study Schedule

Creating a well-structured study schedule is one of the most important steps in preparing for the HSPT. A good study plan ensures that you cover all the necessary material, practice effectively, and build up your stamina for test day. In this section, we'll walk you through the process of developing a personalized study schedule that fits your needs and maximizes your chances of success on the HSPT.

1. Start Early and Be Consistent

The key to effective HSPT preparation is starting early and maintaining consistency. Ideally, you should begin studying at least three to six months before your scheduled test date. This gives you ample time to review each section, practice with sample questions, and take multiple full-length practice tests.

Consistency is crucial when it comes to studying for a standardized test. Instead of cramming all your study time into the week before the exam, spread your study sessions out over several months. Studying a little bit each day is far more effective than trying to absorb all the material at once.

When planning your study schedule, aim for shorter, more frequent study sessions. For example, you might study for one to two hours each day, focusing on different sections of the test each time. This approach prevents burnout and allows you to retain more information.

2. Set Clear Goals for Each Study Session

Every study session should have a clear goal in mind. Instead of sitting down to "study for the HSPT," break your study sessions into specific tasks. For example, you might dedicate one session to reviewing vocabulary words, another to practicing algebra problems, and another to reading comprehension exercises.

Setting specific goals for each study session keeps you focused and ensures that you're making progress. As you complete each task, check it off your study plan to keep track of your accomplishments.

3. Prioritize Weak Areas

When creating your study schedule, it's important to prioritize the areas where you need the most improvement. Start by taking a diagnostic test or a full-length practice test to identify your strengths and weaknesses. Once you know which sections you struggle with, devote more time to reviewing and practicing those topics.

For example, if you find that you struggle with the Verbal Skills section, allocate more study time to vocabulary, analogies, and verbal logic. On the other hand, if you excel in the Mathematics section, you may only need occasional review sessions to maintain your proficiency.

Keep in mind that while it's important to focus on your weak areas, you should still review all sections of the test. Even if you feel confident in one area, regular practice will help reinforce your skills and ensure that you're fully prepared for the HSPT.

4. Mix Review with Practice

A successful study schedule balances content review with hands-on practice. After reviewing a section of the test, follow it up with practice questions to reinforce what you've learned. For example, after reviewing the rules of grammar, practice identifying and correcting errors in sample sentences.

Practice is essential for building your confidence and improving your performance. The more practice questions you complete, the more familiar you'll become with the types of questions on the HSPT and the strategies needed to answer them.

Be sure to include full-length practice tests in your study schedule as well. Aim to take at least two to three full-length tests in the weeks leading up to the exam. These practice tests will help you build stamina, improve your pacing, and identify any remaining areas that need improvement.

5. Break Study Sessions into Manageable Chunks

It's important to avoid overwhelming yourself by studying for too long in one session. Instead, break your study sessions into manageable chunks. For example, you might study for 25-30 minutes, then take a 5-10 minute break before continuing. This technique, known as the Pomodoro Technique, helps improve focus and prevent burnout.

Breaking your study sessions into smaller chunks also allows you to focus more effectively on the material. By studying in short, concentrated bursts, you'll retain more information and feel less fatigued.

6. Use a Study Planner or Calendar

To stay organized and on track, use a study planner or calendar to map out your study sessions. Write down the topics you plan to cover each day and set specific goals for each session. For example, you might write, "Monday: Review algebra and practice 20 math problems" or "Wednesday: Take a practice test and review results."

Having a visual representation of your study plan will help you stay accountable and ensure that you're covering all the necessary material. It also allows you to track your progress and make adjustments as needed.

Chapter 3: Test Day Strategies

What to Expect on Test Day

Test day can feel like an overwhelming event, especially when you've spent weeks, or even months, preparing for it. However, with the right mindset and preparation, you can approach it with confidence. In this section, we'll break down everything you should expect on test day—from the moment you wake up to when you finally put your pencil down after the last question. Understanding what to expect will eliminate the fear of the unknown and help you perform at your best.

Arriving at the Testing Center

The first thing to know about test day is that punctuality is crucial. Schools administering the HSPT have strict policies about start times, and arriving late could result in a significant disadvantage or even disqualification from taking the test. Therefore, plan to arrive at the testing center at least 30 minutes before the scheduled start time.

This extra time will give you a buffer in case of any unexpected delays, such as traffic, or difficulty finding the location. It also provides you with the opportunity to settle in, find your seat, and become familiar with the environment. Knowing where the bathrooms are, locating the clock, and getting comfortable with your surroundings can help reduce anxiety and make you feel more at ease.

As you walk into the testing center, expect to check in with a proctor. You will likely need to present a form of identification and your registration confirmation, so ensure that these items are packed and ready to go the night before. After checking in, the proctor will likely direct you to your seat. Depending on the school, the seating arrangement might be alphabetical or assigned at random. Make sure to bring only approved materials (such as #2 pencils, erasers, and your ID) and leave everything else (phones, books, etc.) outside the testing area.

The Testing Environment

The environment in which the HSPT is administered can vary from school to school, but it is typically held in a classroom setting. Desks will be spaced out to prevent distractions, and the room will likely be quiet except for the occasional sound of pencils scratching on paper or chairs shifting.

One important aspect of test day is the presence of the proctor or test administrator. They will give you instructions before each section, manage time, and ensure that the test proceeds smoothly. Listen carefully to their instructions; although you have likely prepared extensively for the test and are familiar with the format, the proctor's guidance will ensure that you are following the correct procedures. Misunderstanding instructions can lead to mistakes, even if you know the material.

Expect the proctor to enforce strict rules about time. They will tell you when to begin each section and when to stop. It is crucial to follow these instructions exactly, as continuing to work after time is called can result in penalties. To help with time management, most testing rooms will have a clock visible to all students, but it is still wise to bring your own watch (a simple analog or digital one, not a smartwatch) to keep track of your progress.

Breaks and Timing

The HSPT consists of multiple subtests, each with its own allotted time. Typically, the test will be divided into verbal skills, quantitative skills, reading, mathematics, and language, with a few minutes of break time between sections. Breaks are short—usually around five minutes—so make the most of them. During these breaks, it is essential to stand up, stretch, and move around to keep your blood circulating. Physical movement helps reduce fatigue and keeps your mind sharp for the next section.

You should also use this time to grab a quick snack if allowed. Light, easily digestible snacks such as granola bars, fruit, or nuts can help maintain your energy levels without making you feel sluggish. Remember, hydration is just as important. Bringing a bottle of water and taking small sips during breaks will keep you hydrated, but avoid drinking too much to prevent frequent trips to the restroom.

It's also crucial to use the restroom during these breaks. While you may feel nervous or eager to stay focused on the test, taking a quick break to visit the restroom will prevent distractions during the test itself. Remember, you won't be allowed to leave the testing room once a section begins, so it's better to be proactive.

The Structure of the Test

The HSPT is divided into five main subtests: Verbal Skills, Quantitative Skills, Reading, Mathematics, and Language. Each section varies in length and the number of questions, but on average, you'll spend about 2.5 hours completing the entire exam. Understanding the structure of the test beforehand will help you pace yourself and reduce surprises on test day.

- **Verbal Skills**: This section typically includes questions that test your ability to reason using words, such as analogies, synonyms, antonyms, and logic-based questions. You will have 18 minutes to complete this section, which consists of approximately 60 questions.

- **Quantitative Skills**: The quantitative portion assesses mathematical reasoning without heavy calculations. You'll encounter sequences, comparisons, and basic computations. This section allows 30 minutes for around 52 questions.

- **Reading**: Expect a mix of comprehension questions and vocabulary questions. You'll be tasked with reading passages and answering questions about the main ideas, details, and the meaning of words in context. This section usually consists of about 62 questions and is timed at 25 minutes.

- **Mathematics**: This section will test your knowledge of basic math skills, including algebra, geometry, and word problems. It consists of approximately 64 questions, and you'll have 45 minutes to complete it.

- **Language**: The final subtest evaluates your grammar, punctuation, and spelling skills. It includes around 60 questions and allows 25 minutes for completion.

Once you understand the pacing of the test, you'll know what to expect as you move from one section to the next. This will help you manage your time effectively during each subtest and minimize feelings of being rushed or overwhelmed.

The Role of the Proctor

The proctor is your guide on test day. They are there to maintain order, manage time, and ensure that the exam is conducted fairly. While the proctor is present to help, their primary responsibility is to enforce the rules, so it's important to understand what you can and cannot do during the test. For example, once the proctor calls time for a section, you must immediately stop writing, even if you're mid-sentence.

If you have any questions or need clarification during the exam, the proctor is your go-to person. However, remember that they cannot help you with any questions related to test content. Their role is to manage logistics, such as distributing materials, keeping time, and answering procedural questions.

Essential Test-Taking Tips

Successfully navigating the HSPT is not just about knowing the material—it's also about how you approach the test itself. This section covers a wide range of tips that will help you manage your time, avoid common pitfalls, and stay focused from start to finish. These strategies are designed to maximize your performance and give you the best chance of achieving a high score.

Time Management is Key

One of the most important aspects of taking any standardized test is managing your time effectively. Each subtest on the HSPT is strictly timed, and running out of time can mean leaving easy points on the table. To avoid this, you need a clear plan for pacing yourself through each section.

- **Know the Time Allotments**: Familiarize yourself with the amount of time you have for each subtest. For instance, the Mathematics section allows 45 minutes for 64 questions, which means you should aim to spend less than a minute on each question. On the other hand, the Verbal Skills section gives you just 18 minutes to answer 60 questions, so you will need to move even more quickly through this section.

- **Practice with a Timer**: Before test day, take several timed practice tests to get used to the pace of the HSPT. When you practice with a timer, you will become more aware of how long it takes you to answer certain types of questions. This will help you avoid spending too much time on any one question on test day.

- **Use the Process of Elimination**: When you encounter a question that you don't know the answer to right away, use the process of elimination to narrow down your options. Even if you're not sure of the correct answer, eliminating obviously incorrect choices increases your chances of guessing correctly.

Focus on Accuracy Before Speed

While it's essential to manage your time effectively, accuracy should always be your top priority. A quick answer is only helpful if it's also the right answer. If you rush through the test trying to answer every question quickly, you increase the risk of making careless mistakes. Here are some strategies to ensure that you balance speed with accuracy:

- **Read Each Question Carefully**: Don't skim the questions, even if you're feeling pressured for time. Misreading a question can lead to incorrect answers, even if you know the material. Take a deep breath, read the question thoroughly, and then choose your answer.

- **Double-Check Your Work**: If you finish a section early, use the extra time to go back and double-check your answers. Focus on the questions that seemed difficult or confusing the first time around. However, resist the urge to second-guess yourself too much—trust your instincts unless you have a clear reason to change an answer.

- **Skip and Return**: Don't spend too long on any one question. If you find yourself stuck on a particularly difficult problem, skip it and move on to the next one. You can always come back to it later if you have time. The key is to keep moving and ensure that you answer as many questions as possible within the time limit.

Effective Guessing Strategies

One of the most important things to remember about the HSPT is that there's no penalty for guessing. This means you should never leave a question blank. If you're unsure of an answer, use the process of elimination to narrow down your options, and then make an educated guess. Here's how you can approach guessing strategically:

- **Eliminate Wrong Answers First**: Even if you don't know the correct answer, you can often eliminate one or two choices that are clearly wrong. This will increase your odds of guessing correctly. For example, if you're guessing between two remaining options, you have a 50% chance of getting the answer right.

- **Stick to a Pattern**: If you're truly stuck and can't eliminate any answer choices, it's a good idea to stick to a consistent guessing strategy. For instance, if you always guess "B" when you're unsure, you won't waste time debating between multiple choices. Statistically, this won't hurt your score, and it will save you valuable time.

- **Don't Overthink It**: If you've narrowed down the answer choices and made an educated guess, don't spend too much time second-guessing yourself. Often, your first instinct is the correct one. Move on to the next question and keep your momentum going.

The Importance of Staying Focused

Maintaining your focus during the HSPT is easier said than done. With so many questions and such a strict time limit, it's easy to feel overwhelmed or distracted. However, staying focused is critical to your success. Here are some tips for staying sharp throughout the test:

- **Take It One Question at a Time**: Don't think about the entire test at once—this can feel overwhelming and lead to stress. Instead, focus on one question at a time. Concentrate on the question in front of you, and don't worry about how many are left.

- **Block Out Distractions**: In a testing environment, there are bound to be distractions—whether it's the sound of someone shifting in their seat or the proctor walking around the room. Train yourself to block out these distractions and focus solely on the test. If you find your mind wandering, take a deep breath and bring your attention back to the task at hand.

- **Take Micro-Breaks**: While you can't physically leave your seat during the test, you can take micro-breaks to help refresh your mind. Every 10-15 minutes, take a deep breath, stretch your hands or neck, and refocus. These short pauses can help prevent mental fatigue and keep you sharp throughout the exam.

Handling Test Day Stress and Timing

Test day stress is a common experience for most students. It's natural to feel nervous or anxious before and during a high-stakes exam like the HSPT, especially when it plays a critical role in high school admissions. However, understanding how to manage that stress and the clock can make a significant difference in your performance. In this section, we'll explore practical strategies for staying calm, focused, and in control of your time.

Recognizing the Signs of Test Day Stress

First, it's essential to recognize the signs of test day stress so that you can take steps to manage it. Stress can manifest in different ways for different people, but some common symptoms include:

- **Physical Symptoms**: These might include sweating, a racing heart, feeling lightheaded, or even having an upset stomach. These are your body's natural reactions to stress, but they can be managed with the right techniques.

- **Mental Symptoms**: Test anxiety can cause your mind to race or go blank. You might feel like you're forgetting everything you studied or find it hard to focus on the questions in front of you. These mental barriers can be just as challenging as physical symptoms.

- **Emotional Symptoms**: Stress can also take an emotional toll, making you feel overwhelmed, frustrated, or even defeated before the test begins. This is often a result of putting too much pressure on yourself to perform perfectly.

Pre-Test Stress Management Techniques

Managing test day stress starts long before you walk into the testing center. Incorporating relaxation techniques and stress-reducing strategies into your routine in the days leading up to the test can significantly reduce anxiety. Here are some ways to manage your stress before test day:

- **Establish a Routine**: Having a consistent pre-test routine can help reduce anxiety because it provides a sense of control. In the days leading up to the test, establish a routine that includes adequate sleep, healthy eating, and light exercise. The night before the test, pack your materials and go to bed at a reasonable hour.

- **Visualization**: Visualize yourself going through the test calmly and confidently. Picture yourself walking into the test center, sitting down, and answering the questions with ease. Visualization is a powerful tool that can help reduce anxiety by reinforcing positive outcomes in your mind.

- **Relaxation Techniques**: Practice deep breathing exercises or meditation in the days before the test. Deep breathing helps to calm the body and mind by reducing the physiological symptoms of stress, such as a racing heart or shallow breathing.

- **Positive Affirmations**: Remind yourself of your hard work and preparation. Repeat positive affirmations like, "I am prepared for this test," or "I can do this," to build confidence and combat negative thoughts.

Managing Stress During the Test

Even with the best pre-test preparation, it's natural to feel some level of stress on test day. However, knowing how to manage that stress while you're taking the exam is critical. Here are some techniques to keep your stress levels in check during the test:

- **Use Deep Breathing**: If you start to feel overwhelmed, take a few slow, deep breaths. Focus on inhaling deeply through your nose, holding the breath for a moment, and then exhaling slowly through your mouth. This will help calm your nerves and lower your heart rate.

- **Stay Positive**: Avoid negative self-talk during the test. If you come across a challenging question, instead of thinking, "I can't do this," remind yourself that you've prepared well and that one tough question doesn't define your success.

- **Pace Yourself**: Don't rush through the test. Take each question one at a time, and remind yourself that there is enough time to complete the test if you stay focused and use your time wisely.

PART 2: COMPREHENSIVE SUBJECT REVIEWS AND PRACTICE QUESTIONS

Chapter 4: Mastering Verbal Skills

Verbal skills play a critical role in the HSPT, as they measure not only a student's vocabulary but also their ability to think critically and reason logically through language. In this chapter, we'll dive deep into mastering key areas of the verbal section, focusing on **synonyms and antonyms**, **analogies**, and **verbal logic and classifications**. By the end of this chapter, you will have a thorough understanding of the question types you'll face, along with practical strategies for answering them efficiently. Each section is followed by practice questions designed to reinforce your learning and allow you to apply what you've studied. Let's get started with **synonyms and antonyms**—a crucial part of the verbal skills subtest.

Synonyms and Antonyms

Understanding Synonyms and Antonyms

In the HSPT verbal section, synonym and antonym questions test your ability to understand words and their meanings. Synonyms are words that have similar meanings, while antonyms are words that have opposite meanings. Recognizing these relationships helps gauge your vocabulary breadth and your ability to decipher context and nuance.

Synonyms questions will ask you to select the word most similar in meaning to a given word. On the other hand, **antonym** questions will ask you to choose the word that is the opposite of the given word. These questions are about more than memorization; they test your ability to distinguish subtle differences between words and phrases. The trick lies in having a broad vocabulary and understanding the various shades of meaning that different words convey.

Key Strategy: Root Words, Prefixes, and Suffixes A great starting point in tackling synonyms and antonyms is understanding **roots, prefixes, and suffixes**. Many words in English share common roots, which give clues to their meaning. For example, the root "bene" (from Latin) means "good." Therefore, words like "beneficial," "benevolent," and "benign" all carry positive connotations. When encountering an unfamiliar word, breaking it down into its root and affixes can often help you narrow down its meaning.

Context is Everything In synonym and antonym questions, context is crucial. For example, consider the word "bright." Depending on the context, "bright" could mean intelligent, vivid, or shiny. In a question asking for a synonym, the correct answer might change depending on the context provided. If the sentence reads, "Her bright ideas always impressed her teachers," then "intelligent" would be the best synonym. However, if the sentence reads, "The sun was bright that afternoon," then "shiny" or "luminous" would be more appropriate. For antonym questions, it's equally important to think about the context in which the word is used, as the opposite of "bright" could be "dull," "dim," or "unintelligent," depending on the usage.

Common Synonym and Antonym Mistakes One common mistake is assuming that words are either perfect synonyms or perfect antonyms. In reality, very few words have exact equivalents. Most synonym pairs have slight differences, making it essential to consider nuances. Likewise, antonyms can vary. The opposite of "hot" could be "cold," "cool," or even "tepid," depending on the context. In the HSPT, careful attention to the subtleties in meaning will give you an edge.

Building a Strong Vocabulary The best preparation for synonym and antonym questions is building a strong vocabulary. You can do this through a combination of reading, writing, and study. Keep a vocabulary journal where you jot down new words you come across. Reading a variety of texts—fiction, nonfiction, articles, and essays—will expose you to a broader range of vocabulary, helping you expand your word bank. Focus on commonly tested words and review lists like the one provided in this book's appendix.

Another tip is to learn words in **families**. For instance, once you learn the word "benevolent," you can expand your vocabulary by learning other words with the same root, like "benign," "benefactor," and "beneficiary." Similarly, if you learn the antonym "malevolent," you can extend your study to related words like "malignant" and "malefactor."

Sample Synonym and Antonym Questions

1. Which word is the best synonym for **abundant**?

   o (A) scarce

   o (B) plentiful

   o (C) heavy

   o (D) brief

Answer: (B) plentiful. "Abundant" and "plentiful" are nearly identical in meaning.

2. Which word is the best antonym for **pessimistic**?

   o (A) cheerful

   o (B) realistic

   o (C) cautious

   o (D) melancholy

Answer: (A) cheerful. The opposite of a pessimistic (negative) outlook is a cheerful (positive) one.

Exercise: Practice Synonym and Antonym Recognition Take the following words and write both a synonym and antonym for each:

1. **Generous**

2. **Fickle**

3. **Sparse**

4. **Affectionate**

5. **Inevitable**

This exercise will help you get comfortable identifying both synonyms and antonyms, an essential skill for this section of the HSPT.

Analogies: Relationships Between Words

Understanding Analogies

Analogies test your ability to recognize relationships between words, phrases, and ideas. On the HSPT, analogies typically follow this format:

- **A** is to **B** as **C** is to **D**.

Your job is to determine the relationship between the first pair of words and apply that same relationship to the second pair. Analogies can test many types of relationships: synonyms, antonyms, cause and effect, part to whole, function, and degree, among others.

Key Strategy: Identify the Relationship The first step in solving analogies is to clearly identify the relationship between the first two words. Consider this example:

- **Bird** is to **wing** as **fish** is to ____ .

To solve this analogy, you need to recognize that a wing is a part of a bird. Applying that relationship to the second pair, the correct answer would be "fin," since a fin is a part of a fish.

It's essential to articulate the relationship clearly in your mind or even out loud. If you're unsure, try creating a sentence that defines the relationship. For instance, for the analogy **tree** is to **forest** as **student** is to **class**, you could say, "A tree is a part of a forest, just like a student is a part of a class."

Common Types of Analogies Here are some of the most common analogy types you'll encounter on the HSPT:

1. **Synonym/Antonym Analogies**: These analogies test your understanding of synonyms and antonyms. For example:

   o **Brave** is to **courageous** as **frightened** is to ____ .

   o The answer would be "scared," since brave and courageous are synonyms, and frightened and scared are synonyms.

2. **Part to Whole**: These analogies focus on relationships where one word is a part of the other. For example:

- o **Finger** is to **hand** as **toe** is to _____.

- o The correct answer is "foot," since a finger is part of a hand and a toe is part of a foot.

3. **Cause and Effect**: These analogies describe cause-and-effect relationships. For example:

   - o **Rain** is to **flood** as **sun** is to _____.

   - o The answer is "drought," because rain can cause floods, and a lack of rain (or sun) can cause a drought.

4. **Function or Purpose**: In these analogies, the first word describes the function of the second word. For example:

   - o **Scissors** are to **cutting** as **pen** is to _____.

   - o The answer is "writing," since scissors are used for cutting and pens are used for writing.

5. **Degree of Intensity**: These analogies describe relationships based on degree or extent. For example:

   - o **Warm** is to **hot** as **cool** is to _____.

   - o The answer is "cold," because hot is a more intense version of warm, just as cold is a more intense version of cool.

Strategies for Tackling Analogies

- • **Eliminate Wrong Answers**: If you can't immediately identify the correct answer, try eliminating choices that clearly don't fit. This will narrow down your options and increase your chances of selecting the correct answer.

- • **Practice Recognizing Relationships**: The more familiar you are with different types of relationships, the easier it will be to spot them during the test. Practice categorizing different relationships as you study.

Sample Analogy Questions

1. **Hammer** is to **carpenter** as **scalpel** is to:

   - o (A) doctor

   - o (B) artist

   - o (C) gardener

   - o (D) teacher

Answer: (A) doctor. A hammer is a tool used by a carpenter, just as a scalpel is a tool used by a doctor.

2. **Puppy** is to **dog** as **kitten** is to:

   - o (A) bird

- o (B) cat

- o (C) cub

- o (D) lion

Answer: (B) cat. A puppy grows into a dog, and a kitten grows into a cat.

Exercise: Creating Your Own Analogies Try creating five analogies of your own using the categories listed above. This exercise will help you think creatively about relationships between words, a critical skill for mastering analogy questions.

Verbal Logic and Classifications

Understanding Verbal Logic

Verbal logic questions in the HSPT are designed to test your ability to reason through language-based problems. These questions may include scenarios that present a series of true statements, and your task is to determine whether a third statement is true, false, or uncertain based on the information provided. Verbal logic questions rely on deductive reasoning and your ability to process relationships and consequences based on given information.

Unlike analogy or synonym questions, verbal logic requires you to draw conclusions from logical connections, often without the luxury of familiar words or clear definitions. Instead, you'll need to focus on relationships between ideas or objects, assessing how one idea leads to another.

Common Types of Verbal Logic Questions

1. **True, False, or Uncertain**: These are the most common types of verbal logic questions. You will be given two true statements, followed by a third statement. Your job is to determine whether the third statement is true, false, or uncertain based on the information from the first two.

Example:

- o Statement 1: All dogs are mammals.

- o Statement 2: All mammals are warm-blooded.

- o Third statement: All dogs are warm-blooded.

Based on the first two statements, the third statement is **true**.

2. **Syllogism**: These questions involve drawing logical conclusions from premises. A syllogism follows a format where two premises lead to a conclusion. You need to evaluate whether the conclusion logically follows from the premises.

Example:

- o Premise 1: All flowers need sunlight.

     ◦ Premise 2: Roses are flowers.

     ◦ Conclusion: Roses need sunlight.

The conclusion is **true**, as it logically follows from the premises.

  3. **Conditional Logic**: This type of verbal logic is based on "if-then" relationships. You may be asked to determine what happens if a certain condition is true or to evaluate the result of a specific condition.

Example:

     ◦ If it rains, then the match will be canceled.

     ◦ If the match is canceled, then the stadium will be empty.

     ◦ Based on these two statements, if it rains, what can be concluded about the stadium?

Answer: The stadium will be empty, because rain leads to the match being canceled, which in turn leads to an empty stadium.

Approach to Verbal Logic Questions

  1. **Read Carefully**: Verbal logic questions require you to process relationships between statements with precision. Read each statement slowly and carefully, making sure to understand the connections between them before trying to solve the question.

  2. **Map the Relationship**: In your mind (or on scratch paper if allowed), map out the relationships between the statements. This helps you see the logical sequence clearly, which in turn makes it easier to draw conclusions.

  3. **Look for Keywords**: Pay attention to keywords that indicate relationships, such as **all**, **some**, **none**, **if**, **then**, **because**, and **therefore**. These words are critical to understanding the logical connections between statements.

  4. **Avoid Assumptions**: Stick strictly to the information provided in the statements. Verbal logic questions are designed to trap you into making assumptions that are not supported by the information given. Only conclude what is directly supported by the facts.

Classifications: Grouping Based on Relationships

In addition to logic-based questions, the HSPT also tests your ability to classify words based on shared characteristics. Classification questions ask you to find the word or object that doesn't belong in a group, or alternatively, to find the relationship that ties a group together.

Types of Classification Questions

  1. **Odd One Out**: In these questions, you are given four words or objects, three of which belong together, and one that doesn't. Your task is to identify the odd one out based on a specific shared trait between the other three.

Example:

- o Apple, banana, carrot, orange.

- o Answer: Carrot. The other three are fruits, while a carrot is a vegetable.

2. **Category Match**: In these questions, you are asked to identify the category to which a set of items belongs.

Example:

- o Fork, spoon, knife.

- o What is the shared category? Answer: Utensils.

Strategies for Classification Questions

1. **Identify the Shared Characteristic**: When tackling classification questions, first look for a common characteristic that three of the words or objects share. This could be based on function (tools), category (animals), or characteristics (colors, shapes).

2. **Eliminate Obvious Differences**: If you're unsure about the shared characteristic, look for the item that is most obviously different from the others. Often, this will help you identify the correct answer.

3. **Don't Overthink**: Classification questions are usually straightforward. Don't overanalyze the answers, as these questions typically have one clear and logical solution.

Sample Verbal Logic and Classification Questions

1. Which of the following statements is **true**?

- o (A) All birds can fly.

- o (B) Penguins are birds.

- o (C) Penguins can fly.

Answer: (B) Penguins are birds. This is a true statement, while the others are false.

2. Which of the following does not belong?

- o (A) Triangle

- o (B) Circle

- o (C) Square

- o (D) Rectangle

Answer: (B) Circle. All the other shapes have straight sides, while the circle does not.

Exercise: Practice Verbal Logic and Classifications Review the following statements and classify them based on the shared characteristics. What is the common feature, and which item doesn't belong?

1. **Dog, cat, horse, fish**

2. **Teacher, engineer, doctor, painter**

3. **Shirt, jeans, shoes, scarf**

This practice will enhance your skills in identifying logical relationships and grouping items based on shared characteristics.

Practice Questions

Now that you have a thorough understanding of the various verbal skills tested on the HSPT, it's time to apply your knowledge. In this section, you will find practice questions that cover **synonyms and antonyms**, **analogies**, and **verbal logic and classifications**. These questions are designed to mimic the format and difficulty level of the actual HSPT, giving you an opportunity to test your skills under exam-like conditions.

As you work through these questions, remember the strategies we've discussed in this chapter. Focus on understanding the relationships between words, eliminating wrong answers, and using context to your advantage.

Synonyms and Antonyms Practice Questions

1. Which word is the best synonym for **elated**?

   - (A) discouraged
   - (B) thrilled
   - (C) neutral
   - (D) tired

Answer: (B) thrilled. "Elated" means extremely happy or excited, just like "thrilled."

2. Which word is the best antonym for **diligent**?

   - (A) careless
   - (B) hard-working
   - (C) attentive
   - (D) thorough

Answer: (A) careless. "Diligent" means being careful and thorough, so its opposite is "careless."

Analogy Practice Questions

1. **Ocean** is to **saltwater** as **lake** is to:

   - (A) pond
   - (B) freshwater
   - (C) fish
   - (D) river

Answer: (B) freshwater. Just as an ocean contains saltwater, a lake typically contains freshwater.

2. **Pianist** is to **piano** as **guitarist** is to:

   - (A) instrument
   - (B) drums
   - (C) guitar
   - (D) music

Answer: (C) guitar. A pianist plays the piano, just as a guitarist plays the guitar.

Verbal Logic Practice Questions

1. Statement 1: All mammals have fur. Statement 2: Dogs are mammals. Conclusion: All dogs have fur.

Is the conclusion **true**, **false**, or **uncertain**?

Answer: **True.** Based on the first two statements, all dogs have fur.

2. Statement 1: Some birds can fly. Statement 2: Penguins are birds. Conclusion: Penguins can fly.

Is the conclusion **true**, **false**, or **uncertain**?

Answer: **False.** Penguins are birds, but they cannot fly.

Detailed Answer Explanations

This section provides detailed explanations for each of the practice questions above. It's important to not only check whether you got the answer correct but also to understand why the correct answer is right. Learning from both your mistakes and your successes will help solidify your grasp of the material.

Synonyms and Antonyms

1. **Elated** means overjoyed or thrilled, which is why the correct answer is **(B) thrilled**. The other options don't capture the same intensity of emotion.

2. **Diligent** refers to being careful and hardworking, so its opposite is **(A) careless**. The other options are either synonyms or irrelevant.

Analogies

1. The analogy compares **ocean** (saltwater) to **lake** (freshwater), making **(B) freshwater** the correct answer. The other choices do not describe the content of the body of water.

2. A **pianist** plays the **piano**, and similarly, a **guitarist** plays the **guitar**, so the correct answer is **(C) guitar**.

Verbal Logic

1. Based on the statements, the conclusion that **all dogs have fur** is **true**, because dogs are mammals and all mammals have fur.

2. While penguins are birds, the second statement does not imply

that they can fly, so the conclusion
is **false**.

Chapter 5: Quantitative Skills Review

The Quantitative Skills section of the HSPT is designed to assess your ability to reason mathematically. This section requires a thorough understanding of numerical relationships, sequences, comparisons, and computations. Success in this area is not just about solving math problems but being able to recognize patterns, make comparisons, and use mathematical reasoning to arrive at the correct answer quickly and efficiently.

In this chapter, we will delve into the essential components of quantitative skills, ensuring that you are well-prepared for each type of question you will encounter. We'll cover the core concepts of sequences and patterns, comparisons and mathematical reasoning, and computations and problem-solving. After each section, you'll have the opportunity to practice with HSPT-style questions and review detailed answer explanations.

Understanding Sequences and Patterns

Sequences and patterns form the backbone of many quantitative reasoning questions on the HSPT. These questions assess your ability to identify the rule governing a series of numbers or figures and apply that rule to predict the next element in the sequence. This type of problem tests both your understanding of numerical progression and your ability to think logically about relationships between numbers.

Types of Sequences

In the HSPT, sequences generally fall into a few key categories, each with its own set of rules. Let's explore these categories:

1. **Arithmetic Sequences**: An arithmetic sequence is a series of numbers in which each term after the first is obtained by adding a constant difference. For example:

2,5,8,11,14,...

In this case, the common difference is 3. To find the next number in the sequence, simply add 3 to the last term. Thus, the next term would be 17. The rule for arithmetic sequences is:

$a_n = a_1 + (n - 1) \times d$

- *Where:*
    - a_n is the nth term
    - a_1 is the first term
    - n is the position of the term in the sequence
    - d is the common difference

2. Geometric Sequences:

- In a geometric sequence, each term is obtained by multiplying the previous term by a constant factor.
- *Example:*

3, 6, 12, 24, 48,...

- The constant multiplier in this case is 2
- *Formula:*

$a_n = a_1 \times r^{(n-1)}$

- *Where:*
    - a_n is the nth term
    - a_1 is the first term
    - r is the common ratio
    - n is the term number

3. Fibonacci Sequences:

- One of the most famous sequences in mathematics is the Fibonacci sequence, where each number is the sum of the two preceding numbers.

- The Fibonacci sequence begins like this:

0, 1, 1, 2, 3, 5, 8, 13,...

- While the Fibonacci sequence doesn't appear frequently on standardized tests, understanding its concept helps sharpen your pattern recognition skills.

Recognizing Patterns in Sequences

The key to solving sequence problems is recognizing the rule that governs the progression. Here's how to approach sequence questions:

1. **Identify the Pattern**: Look at the relationship between the terms. Is there a consistent addition, subtraction, multiplication, or division? Try to discern if it's an arithmetic, geometric, or other type of sequence.

2. **Check the Difference or Ratio**: For arithmetic sequences, calculate the difference between successive terms. For geometric sequences, divide one term by the previous term to identify the common ratio.

3. **Apply the Rule**: Once you've identified the pattern, apply it to find the next term in the sequence.

Examples

1. Example 1:

7, 10, 13, 16, ...

Solution: This is an arithmetic sequence where the common difference is 3. Adding 3 to 16 gives us 19, so the next term in the sequence is 19.

2. Example 2:

5, 15, 45, 135, ...

Solution: This is a geometric sequence where the common ratio is 3. Multiplying 135 by 3 gives us 405, so the next term is 405.

3. Example 3:

4, 9, 16, 25, ...

Solution: This sequence represents the squares of consecutive integers. The next number in the sequence would be $6^2 = 36$.

Advanced Pattern Recognition

Some sequence problems may involve more complex patterns that don't fit neatly into arithmetic or geometric rules. For example:

2, 4, 8, 14, 22, ...

In this sequence, the pattern is not immediately obvious. However, by examining the differences between terms:

- 4 - 2 = 2
- 8 - 4 = 4
- 14 - 8 = 6
- 22 - 14 = 8

You'll notice that the differences between terms increase by 2 each time. The next difference should be 10, so adding 10 to 22 gives the next term: 32.

Tips for Tackling Sequence Problems

1. **Look for Simplicity:** Start by checking whether the sequence fits an arithmetic or geometric pattern before considering more complex patterns.

2. **Practice Mental Math:** Being able to quickly add, subtract, multiply, and divide will save time and help you stay focused during the test.

3. **Don't Overcomplicate:** Sometimes the pattern may be more straightforward than it first appears. Trust your instincts and apply the simplest rule first.

Comparisons and Mathematical Reasoning

In the Quantitative Skills section, you'll also encounter problems that require comparing numbers or mathematical expressions. These problems test your ability to apply mathematical reasoning to assess whether one quantity is greater, less, or equal to another.

Understanding Comparisons

Comparisons involve evaluating mathematical expressions to determine their relationships. These questions typically follow a format where you are asked to compare two or more expressions and choose the correct relationship (greater than, less than, or equal to). The key to mastering comparison questions is to quickly and accurately simplify the expressions involved.

1. Numerical Comparisons: Numerical comparison problems may ask you to compare two or more numbers. Such as:

- 45 vs. 67
- 3/4 vs. 5/8
- sin(2/5) vs. 1/5

2. Algebraic Comparisons: Comparisons can also involve algebraic expressions like:

- 2x + 4 vs. 3x - 4
- x - 2 vs. 2x + 4
- 2x + 4 > 2x - 1
- 5x - 7 = 3x + 11

Common Comparison Question Types

1. **Direct Comparison:** These questions ask you to compare two numbers, fractions, or decimals.

2. **Variable-Based Comparisons:** These comparisons require you to evaluate algebraic expressions for variable.

Approaching Comparison Problems

1. **Simplify Expressions:** When comparing expressions, always try to simplify them as much as possible. This might involve performing arithmetic operations or factoring.

2. **Use Estimation:** If you're dealing with complex fractions or large numbers, approximate the values to help you compare easier.

3. **Plug in Values:** If you're unsure with algebraic expressions, substitute specific values for the variables to make comparisons easier.

4. **Look for Shortcuts:** Sometimes, you can compare the size of numbers or expressions without performing the full calculation. Use estimation or look for key relationships.

Examples

1. Example 1: Compare 1.25 x 32 and 12 ÷ 4

- Solution 1: Compute: 1.25 x 32 = 40 and 12 ÷ 4 = 3. Since 40 > 3, the correct comparison is >

- Solution 2: Substitute for ÷ : To avoid both operations, when 12 ÷ 4 = 3

1.25 x 32 > 12 ÷ 4 is 1.25 x 32 > 3

2. Example 2: Compare 3(2) + 7 and 10 + 7

- Solution: Compute both expressions

- 3(2) + 7 -> 6 + 7 -> 13

- 10 + 7 -> 17

- Since both expressions equal 17, the correct comparison is = when x = 2

Strategies for Success

1. **Work Efficiently:** Time is critical on the HSPT, so use efficient strategies like estimation and simplifying expressions whenever possible

2. **Be Precise:** Always check your work to ensure that you haven't made careless mistakes when comparing numbers or expressions

3. **Look for Clues:** Sometimes, comparison problems include subtle clues in the structure of the question. Pay attention to the wording and any relationships between the numbers or expressions.

Computations and Problem Solving

The heart of the Quantitative Skills section lies in computations and problem-solving questions. These questions test your ability to perform basic arithmetic operations, solve word problems, and apply logical reasoning to find solutions.

Core Arithmetic Operations

Most computation questions will require you to perform one or more of the following operations:

1. **Addition**: Be sure to line up numbers by place value and carry over correctly.

2. **Subtraction**: Like addition, subtraction requires careful attention to place value. Borrowing from the next column can often be tricky, so practice this skill.

3. **Multiplication**: Multiply multi-digit numbers carefully, ensuring that each step is lined up correctly.

4. **Division**: Long division requires practice, especially when dealing with multi-digit divisors or decimals.

Common Computation Types

1. **Basic Arithmetic:** Computation questions may simply ask you to perform basic arithmetic. For example:

$345 + 678 + 457 = ?$

Solution: Add the numbers together: $345 + 678 + 457 = 1480$

2. **Word Problems:** Computation problems often appear in the form of word problems. These questions require you to translate a written problem into a mathematical equation and then solve it.

3. **Order of Operations:** Computations problems on the HSPT often require you to follow the order of operations (PEMDAS/BODMAS), which dictates the order in

which you perform calculations: Parentheses/Brackets, Exponents/Orders, Multiplication and Division (from left to right), Addition and Subtraction (from left to right). For example:

$3 + 6 \div (5 - 2) \times 4 - 7 = ?$

Solution: First, solve inside the parentheses:

$3 + 6 \div 3 \times 4 - 7 = ?$

Next, perform multiplication and division from left to right:

$3 + 2 \times 4 - 7 = ?$

$3 + 8 - 7 = ?$

Finally, add and subtract:

$11 - 7 = 4$

Approaching Computation Problems

1. **Understand the Question:** For word problems, make sure you fully understand what is being asked before you start solving. Identify key information and the operation(s) needed to solve the problem

2. **Show Your Work:** Even though the HSPT is a multiple-choice, writing out your work can help you avoid careless mistakes and make it easier to check your answers.

3. **Use Estimation When Possible:** To make some computations quicker, try to large numbers, decimals, or fractions to values that are easier to work with.

4. **Double-Check Your Work:** It is easy to make small mistakes in computations, so always go back and review your work if time permits.

Examples

Example 1: A farmer has 350 apples and sells 1/5 of them. How many apples does he have left?

Solution: This is a simple subtraction problem.

- $350 \div 5 = 70$

- $350 - 70 = 280$

So the farmer has 280 apples left.

Example 2: Solve: $2 (18 - 3) \div 3 + 12 = ?$

Solution: First, solve the division inside the parentheses:

$2 (15) \div 3 + 12 = ?$

Then, multiply by 2:

$30 \div 3 + 12 = ?$

Finally, add 12:

$10 + 12 = 22$

Tips for Success

1. **Practice Mental Math:** Being able to perform basic arithmetic quickly and accurately will save valuable time on the HSPT.

2. **Write Down Key Steps:** Even while the math seems simple, writing down the key steps can help prevent mistakes.

3. **Pace Yourself:** Don't spend too much time on any one computation problem. If you find yourself stuck, move on and come back to it later.

Practice Questions

Now that we've reviewed the core quantitative skills, let's put your knowledge to the test with some practice questions. Remember to apply the strategies and tips from the previous sections to solve these problems efficiently and accurately.

Question 1: Sequences

What is the next number in the sequence?

3, 7, 11, 15, ...

A) 17 B) 19 C) 20 D) 23

Answer: The sequence increases by 4 each time. The next number is $15 + 4 = 19$. The correct answer is B.

Question 2: Comparisons

Which of the following is greater?

A) 25 x 3 B) 100 ÷ 4

Answer: 25 x 3 = 75, and 100 ÷ 4 = 25. Therefore, A is greater than B.

Question 3: Sequences

Find the missing number in the sequence: 2, 5, 10, 17, ... ?

A) 20 B) 26 C) 23 D) 32

Answer: To solve this, observe the pattern of differences between the numbers.

- 5 - 2 = 3
- 10 - 5 = 5
- 17 - 10 = 7

The differences are increasing by 2 each time. The next difference should be 7 + 2 = 9. Adding 9 to 17 gives us 26. Thus, the missing number is 26. The correct answer is **B**.

Question 4: Comparisons

Which is greater?

A) 2^5 B) 5 x 3 + 10 ÷ 2

Answer: First, calculate 2^5.

$2^5 = 32$

Next, calculate 5 x 3 + 10 ÷ 2

5 x 3 + 10 ÷ 2 15 + 5 = 20

Since 32 is greater than 20, the correct answer is **A**.

Question 5: Computations

A train travels 60 miles in 1 hour and 20 minutes. What is the average speed of the train in miles per hour?

A) 45 mph B) 50 mph C) 55 mph D) 60 mph

Answer: First, convert 1 hour and 20 minutes to hours.

1 hour 20 minutes = 1 + 20/60 = 1 + 1/3 = 4/3 hours

Now, use the formula for average speed:

Speed = Distance / Time

Speed = 60 miles / (4/3 hours) = 60 * 3 / 4 = 45 mph.

The correct answer is **A**.

Question 6: Sequences

What is the next term in the sequence? 4, 8, 16, 32....

A) 40 B) 48 C) 64 D) 36

Answer: This is a geometric sequence where each term is multiplied by 2. To find the next term:

32 x 2 = 64.

The correct answer is **C**

Question 7: Computations

If a rectangle has a length of 8 inches and a width of 5 inches, what is its perimeter?

A) 13 inches B) 40 inches C) 26 inches D) 30 inches

Answer: The formula for the perimeter of a rectangle is:

Perimeter = 2 × (Length + Width)

Substitute the given values:

Perimeter = 2 × (8 + 5) = 2 × 13 = 26 inches.

Detailed Answer Explanations

Let's take a closer look at how these practice questions were solved to reinforce your understanding of the concepts covered in this chapter. Each explanation breaks down the approach step-by-step, helping you recognize the methods and strategies used.

Question 1 Explanation: Sequences

The sequence given is:

3, 7, 11, 15, ...

This is an arithmetic sequence where the common difference is 4. Each term is found by adding 4 to the previous term. Therefore:

The correct answer is **C**.

Question 8: Comparisons

Compare the two expressions:

A) ⅝ B) 0.85

Answer: Convert ⅝ to a decimal

⅝ = 0.625

Now compare the two decimals

0.625 vs. 0.85

0.85 > 0.625

The correct answer is **B**.

15 + 4 = 19.

The correct answer is **B**.

Question 2 Explanation: Comparisons

The two expressions to compare are:

2^5 and $100 \div 4$.

Start by solving each expression.

$2^5 = 32$

and

$100 \div 4 = 25$

Clearly, 32 is greater than 25, so the correct answer is **A**

Question 3 Explanation: Sequences

The sequence was a bit more complex because it didn't follow a simple arithmetic or geometric rule. Instead, it involved an increasing difference between the terms. By calculating the differences, we found:

- $5 - 2 = 3$
- $10 - 5 = 5$
- $17 - 10 = 7$

The differences were increasing by 2 each time. The next difference should be:

- $7 + 2 = 9$

Thus, adding 9 to 17 gives:

- $17 + 9 = 26$.

The correct answer is B.

Question 4 Explanation: Comparisons

The two expressions given were:

2^5 and $5 \times 3 + 10 \div 2$.

Start by solving each:

$5 \times 3 + 10 \div 2 = 15 + 5 = 20$

$2^5 = 32$

Clearly, 32 is greater than 20, so the correct answer is A.

Question 5 Explanation: Computations

To solve this word problem, we needed to find the average speed. The total distance was given as 60 miles, and the time was 1 hour and 20 minutes, which we converted to hours:

1 hour 20 minutes = $1 + \frac{1}{3}$ hours = $4/3$ hours.

The formula for speed is:

Speed = Distance / Time

Substitute the values:

Speed = $60 / (4/3) = 60 * (3/4) = 45$ mph.

The correct answer is A.

Question 6 Explanation: Sequences

This was a simple geometric sequence where each term is multiplied by 2. The sequence is:

4, 8, 16, 32,...

To find the next term:

$32 \times 2 = 64$.

The correct answer is C.

Question 7 Explanation: Computations

To find the perimeter of a rectangle, use the formula:

Perimeter = $2 \times$ (Length + Width).

Substitute the values for length and width:

Perimeter = 2 × (8 + 5) = 2 × 13 = 26 inches.

The correct answer is C.

Question 8 Explanation: Comparisons

This question compared two values:

7/8 and 0.85

First, convert 7/8 to a decimal:

7/8 = 0.875

Now compare:

0.875 > 0.85

The correct answer is A.

This chapter has covered all of the key concepts and strategies needed to excel in the **Quantitative Skills** section of the HSPT. We've explored sequences and patterns, comparisons, and computations, with each topic followed by detailed practice questions to help you solidify your understanding.

The most important takeaway is to approach each problem methodically. Whether you're solving a sequence, comparing numbers, or performing calculations, practicing these skills regularly will help you improve both your speed and accuracy on test day. Keep practicing with the strategies outlined here, and you'll be well on your way to mastering the Quantitative Skills section!

Chapter 6: Improving Reading Skills

In this chapter, we will focus on improving your reading skills to help you excel in the reading section of the HSPT. Reading comprehension is a crucial part of the exam, and understanding how to effectively approach reading passages will significantly improve your ability to answer questions correctly and efficiently. We will cover how to approach reading passages, identify main ideas and details, answer inference and vocabulary questions, and provide extensive practice questions along with detailed answer explanations.

How to Approach Reading Passages

Reading comprehension can be intimidating, especially when faced with multiple reading passages that cover a variety of topics. The key to success in this section is developing a strategy that allows you to read efficiently while retaining the most important information. This will help you manage your time and ensure that you have enough energy to tackle the subsequent questions.

1. Skim the Passage First

The first step when approaching a reading passage is to skim it. This doesn't mean reading every word carefully—instead, you should quickly scan the passage to get a general sense of its structure and content. Pay particular attention to:

- The first and last sentences of each paragraph

- Any headings or subheadings

- Words in bold or italics, if present

- Any unusual punctuation, such as dashes or parentheses, which might indicate additional information

Skimming helps you understand the overall flow of the passage, which will be helpful when answering questions later. You're not trying to memorize details at this stage—just get a sense of what the passage is about.

2. Identify Key Sections

As you skim, note any sections that seem particularly important. These might include:

- The introduction, where the author presents their main argument or purpose

- The conclusion, where the author summarizes their ideas

- Any lists, examples, or data that might be referenced in the questions

By identifying key sections, you'll have a mental map of where important information is located. This will save time when you need to refer back to the passage to answer questions.

3. Understand the Structure of the Passage

Passages are often organized in predictable ways. Common structures include:

- **Chronological order**: Events or ideas are presented in the order in which they occurred.

- **Problem and solution**: The author presents a problem and then offers a solution.

- **Compare and contrast**: The author compares two or more ideas, events, or perspectives.

- **Cause and effect**: The author discusses the causes of a particular event or outcome.

Understanding the structure will help you anticipate the types of questions you might be asked and where in the passage you might find the answers.

4. Read the Questions First

Before you dive into reading the passage in detail, quickly read through the questions. This may seem counterintuitive, but it's an important strategy. By knowing what the questions are asking, you can focus on finding the relevant information as you read the passage. Look for keywords in the questions that you can keep in mind as you read.

For example, if a question asks about the main idea, you'll want to focus on the passage's overall message. If a question asks about specific details, like a date or a person's name, you'll know to keep an eye out for that information.

5. Active Reading

Once you have skimmed the passage, identified key sections, and read the questions, it's time to engage in **active reading**. Active reading means reading with the intention of understanding and retaining the information. As you read, make mental notes of the following:

- The author's main argument or purpose

- How the passage is organized (chronologically, by cause and effect, etc.)

- Key points and details that seem important or might be relevant to the questions

- Any shifts in tone or perspective, such as a change from neutral to critical or from positive to negative

Active reading is different from passive reading, where you simply read the words without engaging with the content. By being an active reader, you'll retain more information and find it easier to answer questions.

6. Take Notes as You Read

Taking notes as you read can be incredibly helpful, especially for longer or more complex passages. You don't need to write down everything—just jot down a few keywords or phrases that will help you remember the main points. You can also underline or highlight key information if your test booklet allows it.

For example, if the passage mentions several important dates, write them in the margin or underline them so you can easily find them when answering questions. Similarly, if the author makes a particularly strong argument or presents an important piece of evidence, make a note of it.

7. Manage Your Time

Time management is crucial on the HSPT, especially during the reading section. You'll need to balance reading the passage carefully with answering the questions in a timely manner. A good rule of thumb is to spend no more than half of your time reading the passage, leaving the other half for answering questions.

For example, if you have 25 minutes for the reading section and you're faced with a long passage, aim to spend about 12 minutes reading and 12 minutes answering questions. If the passage is shorter, adjust your time accordingly. Always keep an eye on the clock, but don't rush. Accuracy is more important than speed, and careful reading will save you time in the long run by reducing the need to re-read sections of the passage.

8. Stay Calm and Focused

It's easy to feel overwhelmed during the reading section, especially if the passage is on a topic you're not familiar with or particularly interested in. However, it's important to stay calm and focused. Remember that the questions are testing your ability to read and comprehend, not your prior knowledge of the subject matter.

If you find yourself getting stuck on a particular sentence or paragraph, take a deep breath and move on. You can always come back to it later. Sometimes, the answer to a difficult question will become clearer after you've read the entire passage or answered other questions.

9. Practice Makes Perfect

Like any other skill, improving your reading comprehension requires practice. The more passages you read and questions you answer, the more comfortable you'll become with the format and the types of questions you'll encounter on the HSPT.

Try to read a variety of materials, such as articles, essays, and short stories, to broaden your reading experience. Focus on identifying the main ideas and details, and practice answering questions about what you've read. Over time, you'll find that your reading speed and comprehension improve, making the HSPT reading section less intimidating.

Identifying Main Ideas and Details

One of the most important skills you'll need for the reading section of the HSPT is the ability to identify the main idea of a passage and the supporting details. The main idea is the central point or message that the author is trying to convey, while the supporting details are the pieces of information that help explain or reinforce the main idea.

1. Understanding the Main Idea

The main idea is often expressed directly in the passage, especially in shorter, more straightforward passages. It's usually found in one of two places:

- The **first sentence** of the passage, where the author introduces their main argument or purpose

- The **last sentence** of the passage, where the author summarizes their argument or provides a conclusion

Sometimes, the main idea is not stated explicitly but must be inferred from the overall content of the passage. In these cases, pay attention to the **big picture**—what is the passage mainly about? What is the author trying to tell you? Look for patterns or recurring themes that suggest the main idea.

For example, if a passage discusses the history of space exploration, the main idea might be about the technological advancements that made space travel possible. If a passage is about climate change, the main idea might be the impact of human activity on the environment.

2. Finding Supporting Details

Once you've identified the main idea, the next step is to find the supporting details. These are the pieces of information that help explain, illustrate, or reinforce the main idea. Supporting details can include:

- **Facts**: Specific pieces of information that are objectively true, such as dates, statistics, or historical events.

- **Examples**: Specific instances or case studies that illustrate the main idea.

- **Explanations**: Clarifications or elaborations that help the reader understand the main idea more fully.

- **Quotations**: Words or phrases taken from another source that support the author's argument.

Supporting details are often scattered throughout the passage, so you may need to go back and re-read certain sections to find them. Pay attention to transitional words and phrases like "for example," "in addition," or "as a result," which often signal the presence of supporting details.

3. Differentiating Between Main Ideas and Details

It's important to differentiate between the main idea and the supporting details. The main idea is the central point of the passage, while the details are the pieces of information that support that point. Think of the main idea as the "big picture" and the details as the smaller pieces that help you see that picture more clearly.

For example, in a passage about the importance of exercise, the main idea might be that regular physical activity is essential for maintaining good health. The supporting details might include facts about how exercise improves cardiovascular health, examples of different types of exercise, and explanations of how exercise can reduce stress.

4. Identifying Main Ideas in Complex Passages

In longer or more complex passages, the main idea might not be immediately obvious. The author may present multiple arguments or points of view, making it harder to pin down the central message. In these cases, look for **repeated themes** or ideas that are emphasized throughout the passage.

For example, if a passage discusses both the benefits and the drawbacks of a particular technology, the main idea might be that the technology has both positive and negative aspects. If a passage presents multiple perspectives on a political issue, the main idea might be that the issue is complex and requires careful consideration of all viewpoints.

5. Practice Identifying Main Ideas and Details

The best way to improve your ability to identify main ideas and details is to practice. As you read passages, try to summarize the main idea in your own words. Then, go back and find the supporting details that help explain or reinforce that idea.

For each passage, ask yourself the following questions:

- What is the passage mainly about?

- What is the author trying to tell me?

- What information does the author provide to support their main argument?

As you practice, you'll find it easier to quickly identify the main idea and the supporting details, which will help you answer reading comprehension questions more accurately.

Answering Inference and Vocabulary Questions

Inference questions are a common type of reading comprehension question on the HSPT. These questions ask you to make an educated guess or draw a conclusion based on the information presented in the passage. Vocabulary questions, on the other hand, test your understanding of the meaning of words as they are used in context.

1. Understanding Inference Questions

Inference questions require you to go beyond the literal meaning of the text and make a logical conclusion based on the information provided. These questions often begin with phrases like:

- "What can be inferred from the passage?"

- "Which of the following is most likely true based on the passage?"

- "What does the author imply in the passage?"

To answer an inference question, you need to consider what the author **suggests** without directly stating it. This involves reading between the lines and using your understanding of the passage to draw a reasonable conclusion.

For example, if a passage describes a character who is constantly checking their phone and avoiding eye contact during a conversation, you might infer that the character is nervous or distracted, even though the author doesn't explicitly say so.

2. Strategies for Answering Inference Questions

When answering inference questions, follow these steps:

1. **Read the question carefully**: Make sure you understand exactly what is being asked. Look for keywords like "infer," "imply," or "suggest."

2. **Refer back to the passage**: Reread the relevant section of the passage to see if it provides any clues that will help you make an inference.

3. **Eliminate incorrect answer choices**: Use the process of elimination to narrow down your options. If an answer choice is too far-fetched or contradicts the information in the passage, cross it off.

4. **Make an educated guess**: Based on the information in the passage, choose the answer that seems most reasonable and logical.

Inference questions can be tricky, but with practice, you'll become better at recognizing the subtle clues that lead to the correct answer.

3. Understanding Vocabulary Questions

Vocabulary questions test your understanding of how words are used in context. These questions often ask you to define a word or phrase based on how it is used in the passage. For example:

- "What does the word 'inevitable' mean as used in the passage?"

- "Which of the following best describes the meaning of the word 'resilient' in the passage?"

To answer vocabulary questions, it's important to pay attention to the **context** in which the word is used. Even if you're not familiar with the word, you can often figure out its meaning by looking at the surrounding sentences and how the word fits into the overall meaning of the passage.

4. Strategies for Answering Vocabulary Questions

When answering vocabulary questions, follow these steps:

1. **Identify the word in the passage**: Find the word in question and read the sentence in which it appears. Then, read the sentences before and after to get a sense of the context.

2. **Consider the tone and meaning of the passage**: Think about the overall tone and message of the passage. This can help you determine whether the word has a positive, negative, or neutral connotation.

3. **Eliminate incorrect answer choices**: If you know that a word has a positive connotation, you can eliminate any answer choices with negative meanings.

4. **Use word roots, prefixes, and suffixes**: If you're familiar with the root of the word or any prefixes or suffixes, use that knowledge to help you determine its meaning.

With regular practice, you'll become more comfortable answering vocabulary questions, even when you encounter unfamiliar words.

Practice Questions

The following practice questions will help you apply the skills you've learned in this chapter. Read each passage carefully and answer the accompanying questions.

Passage 1

The history of aviation is one of triumph and innovation. From the Wright brothers' first powered flight in 1903 to the development of supersonic jets, humankind has always been fascinated by the idea of flight. Early aviators faced numerous challenges, including limited technology, unpredictable weather, and a lack of funding. However, their perseverance paved the way for the modern aviation industry, which now connects people and cultures around the world.

1. What is the main idea of the passage? a. The history of aviation is full of challenges. b. The Wright brothers were the first to fly. c. Aviation has connected people and cultures. d. The aviation industry has grown over time.

2. What can be inferred about early aviators? a. They were motivated by a desire for fame. b. They faced many obstacles but persevered. c. They had advanced technology at their disposal. d. They relied on government funding.

3. What does the word "triumph" mean as used in the passage? a. Failure b. Success c. Conflict d. Journey

Passage 2

Climate change is one of the most pressing issues of our time. Rising global temperatures have led to melting ice caps, more frequent extreme weather events, and shifts in ecosystems. Scientists agree that human activity, particularly the burning of fossil fuels, is a major contributor to climate change. However, there is still hope for mitigating its effects through sustainable practices, such as reducing carbon emissions and protecting natural habitats.

1. What is the main idea of the passage? a. Climate change is caused by natural forces. b. Human activity is a major contributor to climate change. c. Scientists are divided on the causes of climate change. d. The effects of climate change cannot be mitigated.

2. What can be inferred from the passage about the author's perspective on climate change? a. The author believes that climate change is not a serious issue. b. The author is hopeful that its effects can be mitigated. c. The author thinks that the effects of climate change are inevitable. d. The author believes that scientists are unsure about the causes of climate change.

3. What does the word "mitigating" mean as used in the passage? a. Worsening b. Ignoring c. Reducing d. Delaying

---

Detailed Answer Explanations

Let's go over the detailed answer explanations for the practice questions above to help you understand how to approach each question and why certain answers are correct or incorrect.

Passage 1

1. **Answer: c. Aviation has connected people and cultures.**

o **Explanation**: The passage discusses the history of aviation and highlights the ways in which it has connected people and cultures around the world. While the passage does mention challenges, the main idea is about the overall impact of aviation, not just the difficulties faced by early aviators.

2. **Answer: b. They faced many obstacles but persevered.**

   o **Explanation**: The passage mentions that early aviators encountered challenges such as limited technology and unpredictable weather, but it also emphasizes their perseverance. There is no indication that they were motivated by fame or had access to advanced technology.

3. **Answer: b. Success.**

   o **Explanation**: The word "triumph" is used in the context of describing the history of aviation, which is portrayed as a story of success and innovation. Therefore, the best synonym for "triumph" in this context is "success."

Passage 2

1. **Answer: b. Human activity is a major contributor to climate change.**

   o **Explanation**: The passage explicitly states that human activity, particularly the burning of fossil fuels, is a major contributor to climate change. While the passage does discuss the effects of climate change, the main focus is on human activity as the cause.

2. **Answer: b. The author is hopeful that its effects can be mitigated.**

   o **Explanation**: The passage concludes by mentioning that there is hope for mitigating the effects of climate change through sustainable practices. This indicates that the author is optimistic about the possibility of reducing the impact of climate change.

3. **Answer: c. Reducing.**

   o **Explanation**: The word "mitigating" is used in the context of discussing how the effects of climate change can be lessened through sustainable practices. Therefore, the best synonym for "mitigating" is "reducing."

73

Chapter 7: Mathematics Review

Number Operations and Computations

In this section, we'll begin by reviewing one of the most fundamental aspects of mathematics: number operations and computations. A solid understanding of basic arithmetic operations is essential for success on the HSPT. You will encounter questions that involve addition, subtraction, multiplication, division, and the use of negative numbers, decimals, and exponents. Mastering these operations will enable you to approach more complex problems with confidence.

Addition and Subtraction

Addition and subtraction are the building blocks of all arithmetic. These operations form the basis for much of the problem-solving you will do, not just on the HSPT, but in mathematics throughout your education. In addition and subtraction, the numbers being combined are called "operands," while the process itself is straightforward:

- **Addition** involves combining numbers to increase their total. For example:

$23 + 15 = 38$

Here, the two operands are 23 and 15, and the result is 38.

- **Subtraction** involves finding the difference between two numbers. For example:

$45 - 12 = 33$

In this case, 45 is the "minuend," 12 is the "subtrahend," and 33 is the result, also called the "difference."

Both operations can be applied to whole numbers, decimals, and fractions. It is critical to note that when subtracting, the order of the numbers matters, unlike addition where the order of operands can be reversed (commutative property). This is not the case for subtraction. Let's look at an example that illustrates subtraction with decimals:

15.7 - 8.2 = 7.5

In problems involving negative numbers, be mindful of the operation signs. Subtracting a negative number is equivalent to adding the positive equivalent of that number. For instance:

7 - (-5) = 7 + 5 = 12

Practice identifying and simplifying problems that involve negative numbers, as they are common in the HSPT quantitative section.

Multiplication and Division

Multiplication is repeated addition, while division is the process of finding how many times one number is contained within another. Both operations are fundamental in more complex problem-solving scenarios, such as those involving exponents or algebra.

- **Multiplication:**

When multiplying two numbers, each is referred to as a factor, and their product is the result of the multiplication. For example:

6 x 8 = 48

The two factors, 6 and 8, produce the product 48.

Multiplication is commutative, meaning you can change the order of the numbers without changing the result:

8 x 6 = 48

When working with decimals, the principle remains the same, but you must adjust the decimal place in the result. Consider:

3.5 x 4 = 14.0

Here, the decimal placement in the result depends on the position of the decimal points in the operands.

- **Division:**

Division is the inverse of multiplication. When dividing, you split a number into equal parts. The number being divided is the "dividend," and the number you are dividing by is the "divisor." For example:

$56 \div 8 = 7$

In this case, 56 is the dividend, 8 is the divisor, and 7 is the quotient.

Division, unlike multiplication, is not commutative. Dividing in the reverse order changes the result:

$8 \div 56 = 0.142857$

When dealing with decimal numbers in division, it is important to align the decimal points properly and move them as necessary to simplify the problem. For example:

$15.6 \div 3 = 5.2$

In both multiplication and division, it is essential to remember the rules for dealing with negative numbers. If one operand is negative and the other is positive, the result will be negative. If both are negative, the result will be positive:

- Multiplying two negatives: $(-4) \times (-5) = 20$

- Dividing two negatives: $(-40) \div (-8) = 5$

As you work through practice questions, ensure you are comfortable with both operations, including cases where negative numbers or decimals are involved.

Order of Operations (PEMDAS)

One of the most important rules in arithmetic is the order of operations. When solving problems that involve multiple operations (such as addition, subtraction, multiplication, and division), it is essential to follow the correct order to arrive at the right answer. The order of operations is governed by the acronym PEMDAS, which stands for:

- **Parentheses:** First, perform the operations inside parentheses.

- **Exponents:** Next, solve any exponents.

- **M**ultiplication and **D**ivision: Then, multiply or divide from left to right.

- **A**ddition and **S**ubtraction: Lastly, add or subtract from left to right.

Let's break this down with an example:

$3 + 6 \times (5 + 4) \div 3\char`\^2$

- First, solve the expression inside the parentheses:

$3 + 6 \times (9) \div 3\char`\^2$

- Next, handle the exponent:

$3 + 6 \times 9 \div 9$

- Then, perform multiplication and division from left to right:

$3 + 54 \div 9 = 3 + 6$

- Finally, add the remaining numbers:

$3 + 6 = 9$

Following the correct order of operations is crucial, especially on a timed test like the HSPT, where a single mistake could cost valuable points.

Exponents and Roots

Exponents are shorthand for repeated multiplication. For example, 2^4 means multiplying 2 by itself four times:

- $2^4 = 2 \times 2 \times 2 \times 2 = 16$

Some key rules to remember for exponents:

- Multiplying powers with the same base: Add the exponents.

  - $3^2 \times 3^3 = 3^{2+3} = 3^5 = 243$

- Dividing powers with the same base: Subtract the exponents.

  - $6^5 \div 6^2 = 6^{5-2} = 6^3 = 216$

77

- Raising a power to a power: Multiply the exponents.

    ○ $(2^3)^2 = 2^{3 \times 2} = 2^6 = 64$

Inversely, roots (especially square roots) are the opposite of exponents. Finding the square root of a number means identifying which number multiplied by itself equals the original number. For example:

- $\sqrt{64} = 8$ since $8 \times 8 = 64$

Understanding exponents and roots is crucial for algebra, which we will cover in the upcoming sections.

Practice with Mixed Operations

Many problems on the HSPT will involve more than one operation. It's essential to apply the order of operations correctly while maintaining accuracy with individual computations. Let's look at an example:

$(5 + 2^2) \times 3 - 8 \div 2$

1. First, solve the exponent: $(5 + 4) \times 3 - 8 \div 2$

2. Next, handle the operations inside the parentheses: $9 \times 3 - 8 \div 2$

3. Then, perform multiplication and division from left to right: $27 - 4 = 23$

Accuracy is key, especially in timed situations. Practice problems like these regularly to ensure you're comfortable with handling multiple operations under pressure.

Fractions, Decimals, Percents, and Ratios

In this section, we will dive into a key aspect of the HSPT mathematics section: fractions, decimals, percents, and ratios. These concepts are interrelated, and mastering them is essential for success on the test. Understanding how to convert between these forms and apply them in various problem-solving situations is crucial.

Understanding Fractions

A fraction represents a part of a whole and consists of two parts:

- **Numerator**: The number above the line, indicating how many parts are being considered.

- **Denominator**: The number below the line, indicating how many equal parts the whole is divided into.

For example:

3/4

This fraction means that three out of four equal parts are being considered. The denominator tells us the whole has been divided into four parts, and the numerator indicates that three of those parts are being used.

Types of Fractions

- **Proper Fractions**: Fractions where the numerator is smaller than the denominator, e.g., $\frac{3}{5}$.

- **Improper Fractions**: Fractions where the numerator is larger than or equal to the denominator, e.g., 7/4.

- **Mixed Numbers**: A whole number combined with a proper fraction, e.g., $2\frac{1}{3}$.

Operations with Fractions

You will frequently encounter fraction operations on the HSPT. Here's how to handle each type:

- **Addition and Subtraction of Fractions**:

To add or subtract fractions, you must have a common denominator. If the denominators are different, you need to find the least common denominator (LCD) before performing the operation.

For example:

$\frac{1}{3} + \frac{1}{4}$

First, find the LCD of 3 and 4, which is 12. Convert each fraction:

$\frac{1}{3} = \frac{4}{12} , \frac{1}{4} = \frac{3}{12}$

Now, add the fractions:

$4/12 + 3/12 = 7/12$

Subtraction follows the same process. For example:

$5/6 - 1/4$

The LCD of 6 and 4 is 12, so:

$5/6 = 10/12$, $1/4 = 3/12$

Now subtract:

$10/12 - 3/12 = 7/12$

- **Multiplication of Fractions**: Multiplying fractions is simpler. You multiply the numerators and the denominators:

- $3/5 \times 2/3 = (3 \times 2) / (5 \times 7) = 6/35$

- **Division of Fractions**: To divide fractions, multiply the first fraction by the reciprocal of the second:

- $4/5 \div 2/3 = 4/5 \times 3/4 = 12/10 = 6/5$

You can also express the answer as a mixed number if needed:

$6/5 = 1 \frac{1}{5}$

Simplifying Fractions

Always simplify fractions by dividing both the numerator and the denominator by their greatest common factor (GCF). For example:

$18/24$

The GCF of 18 and 24 is 6, so:

$18/24 = (18 \div 6) / (24 \div 6) = 3/4$

Decimals: A Deeper Look

What are Decimals?

Decimals provide an alternative way to represent fractions, particularly those with denominators that are powers of 10 (like 10, 100, 1000, etc.).

- 1/10 is equivalent to 0.1

- 1/100 translates to 0.01

Converting Between Fractions and Decimals

Fraction to Decimal

Divide the fraction's numerator (top number) by its denominator (bottom number).

- $3/4 = 3 \div 4 = 0.75$

Some fractions lead to repeating decimals:

- $1/3 = 0.3333...$ (the 3s continue infinitely)

Decimal to Fraction

1. The decimal becomes the numerator.

2. The denominator is a power of 10, based on the decimal's place value.

3. Simplify the fraction if possible.

- $0.75 = 75/100 = 3/4$

Repeating decimals require a bit more thought:

- $0.6666... = 2/3$

Math with Decimals

Basic operations ($+$, $-$, $\times$, $\div$) work similarly to whole numbers, but the decimal point needs attention.

Addition & Subtraction

Align the decimal points vertically.

- $3.25 + 2.7 = 5.95$

Multiplication

1. Multiply as if they were whole numbers.

2. Count the total decimal places in both original numbers.

3. Place the decimal in the answer, counting from the right.

- $2.5 \times 3.4 = 8.50$

Division

1. Shift the divisor's decimal to make it a whole number.

2. Shift the dividend's decimal the same number of places.

3. Divide as usual.

- $7.2 \div 0.4 = 72 \div 4 = 18$

Percentages: A Special Kind of Fraction

Understanding Percents

Think of a percent as a fraction out of 100. It shows a portion relative to a whole.

- 50% means 50/100, which simplifies to 1/2 (half)

Conversions Galore

Percent to Fraction

1. Put the percent number over 100.

2. Simplify.

- 75% = 75/100 = 3/4

Fraction to Percent

1. Divide numerator by denominator.

2. Multiply by 100.

3. Add the % symbol

- $3/4 = 0.75 \times 100 = 75\%$

Decimal to Percent

Multiply by 100 and add %.

- $0.85 \times 100 = 85\%$

Percent to Decimal

Divide by 100.

- $85\% = 0.85$

Solving Percent Problems

Common questions fall into these categories:

1. **Finding a percentage of a number**
   - "What is 20% of 150?"
   - Convert percent to decimal, then multiply: $0.20 \times 150 = 30$

2. **Determining the percentage one number represents of another**
   - "30 is what percent of 150?"
   - Divide, then multiply by 100: $(30/150) \times 100 = 20\%$

3. **Finding the original number when given a percentage**
   - "20% of what number is 30?"
   - Set up an equation: $0.20 \times x = 30$
   - Solve for x: $x = 30 / 0.20 = 150$

Ratios & Proportions: Comparing Quantities

Ratios: The Basics

A ratio compares two quantities. It has multiple formats:

- Fraction: a/b

- Colon: a:b

- Words: a to b

Simplifying

Divide both parts of the ratio by their greatest common factor.

- 12:16 simplifies to 3:4 (both are divisible by 4)

Equivalence

Two ratios are equivalent if they simplify to the same value.

- 4/6 and 2/3 are equivalent (both simplify to 2/3)

Proportions: Equal Ratios

A proportion is an equation stating two ratios are equal.

Solving

Cross-multiply and solve for the unknown.

- $2/3 = x/9$

- Cross-multiply: $2 \times 9 = 3 \times x$

- Simplify: $18 = 3x$

- Solve for x: $x = 18 / 3 = 6$

Algebra and Word Problems

Algebra forms an integral part of the HSPT math section. It involves using variables to represent unknowns and solving for them. Mastering algebra allows you to solve more complex mathematical problems, and word problems are a way to test your ability to apply algebra in real-world situations.

Introduction to Algebra

Algebra is often considered one of the most abstract forms of mathematics, but it is essentially the art of solving problems using variables. These variables represent unknown quantities that can be solved by performing operations like addition, subtraction, multiplication, and division. For example:

x + 7 = 12

In this equation, x is the unknown, and our goal is to solve for x. To do this, we perform the inverse operation of adding 7, which is subtracting 7:

x = 12 - 7 x = 5

This is the most basic form of algebra, but the principles remain the same for more complex equations and expressions.

Key Concepts in Algebra

Let's review some fundamental concepts and operations you'll encounter in algebra questions on the HSPT.

- Variables: Letters (like x or y) that represent unknown values. In equations, our goal is to solve for these variables.

- Constants: Numbers that have fixed values, like 2, -5, or 10. Constants don't change in an equation.

- Expressions: A combination of variables, constants, and operations. For example, 3x + 2 is an expression.

- Equations: An equation shows the equality between two expressions. For example, 3x + 2 = 11 is an equation.

Solving Linear Equations

Linear equations are equations where the variable has an exponent of 1 (e.g., x^1) and the graph of the equation is a straight line. A typical linear equation looks like this:

2x + 3 = 11

To solve it, follow these steps:

1. Isolate the variable by performing inverse operations. Subtract 3 from both sides: 2x = 8

2. Solve for the variable by dividing both sides by 2: x = 8 / 2 = 4

This method can be applied to a wide variety of linear equations.

Working with Inequalities

Inequalities are similar to equations, but instead of an equal sign, they use inequality symbols:

- $<$ (less than)

- $\leq$ (less than or equal to)

- (greater than)

- $\geq$ (greater than or equal to)

For example:

$2x + 3 > 7$

To solve inequalities, follow the same steps as solving an equation:

Subtract 3 from both sides: $2x > 4$

Divide by 2: $x > 2$

Remember, if you multiply or divide both sides of an inequality by a negative number, you must reverse the inequality sign. For example:

$-3x \leq 9$

Divide by -3:

$x \geq -3$

Inequalities appear frequently on the HSPT, so practice solving them thoroughly.

Solving Systems of Equations

Sometimes, you'll encounter systems of equations, where two or more equations must be solved simultaneously. These are typically linear equations and can be solved using one of three methods:

- Substitution: Solve one equation for one variable, then substitute that value into the other equation. For example:

$y = 2x + 3$ $3x + y = 10$

Substitute $y = 2x + 3$ into the second equation:

$3x + (2x + 3) = 10$

Simplify and solve for x:

$5x + 3 = 10$ $5x = 7$ $x = 7/5$

- Elimination: Add or subtract the equations to eliminate one variable, then solve for the other variable. For example:

$2x + y = 10$ $x - y = 3$

Add the two equations:

$(2x + y) + (x - y) = 10 + 3$

This eliminates y, leaving:

$3x = 13$

Solve for x:

$x = 13/3$

- Graphing: Solve the system of equations by graphing each equation on a coordinate plane. The point where the lines intersect represents the solution.

Introduction to Word Problems

Word problems test your ability to apply algebraic methods to real-world scenarios. On the HSPT, you will likely encounter word problems that involve various mathematical concepts, such as ratios, percentages, distances, and rates.

Steps for Solving Word Problems

1. **Read the problem carefully**: Understand what is being asked and identify the relevant information.

2. **Identify the unknown**: Assign a variable to the unknown quantity you are solving for.

3. **Set up an equation**: Use the information given in the problem to write an algebraic equation involving the unknown.

4. **Solve the equation**: Use algebraic methods to solve for the variable.

5. **Check your answer**: Make sure your solution makes sense in the context of the problem.

Common Types of Word Problems

1. Distance-Rate-Time Problems

These problems use the formula:

Distance = Rate × Time

For example: "Jane travels 150 miles in 3 hours. What is her average speed?"

Using the formula:

Rate = Distance / Time = 150 miles / 3 hours = 50 mph

2. Work Problems

Work problems involve tasks that are completed over time. Use the formula:

Work Done = Rate of Work × Time

For example: "Tom can paint a room in 4 hours. If both Tom and Jerry work together, and Jerry can paint the same room in 6 hours, how long will it take them to paint the room together?"

To solve this, we add their rates of work. Tom's rate is 1/4 (since he can paint one room in 4 hours), and Jerry's rate is 1/6. Together, they work at a rate of:

1/4 + 1/6 = 3/12 + 2/12 = 5/12

So, it will take them:

12/5 hours = 2.4 hours

3. Mixture Problems

Mixture problems involve combining two or more substances with different concentrations to form a mixture. For example: "How many liters of a 30% saline solution must be added to 10 liters of a 50% saline solution to get a mixture that is 40% saline?"

Let x be the amount of 30% solution added. The total amount of salt in the solution is 0.30x from the 30% solution and 0.50 × 10 from the 50% solution. The total volume is x + 10. We set up the equation:

$0.30x + 0.50 \times 10 = 0.40(x + 10)$

Simplifying:

$0.30x + 5 = 0.40x + 4$ $5 - 4 = 0.40x - 0.30x$ $1 = 0.10x$ $x = 1 / 0.10 = 10$ liters

So, you need to add 10 liters of the 30% solution.

Practice Questions

Let's test what you've learned with a few practice questions:

- Solve for x: $3x + 5 = 20$

- Solve the system of equations: $2x + y = 5$ $x - y = 1$

- Solve the inequality: $-2x + 3 \leq 7$

- A train travels 60 miles per hour. How long will it take to travel 180 miles?

- If a mixture of 10% juice is combined with a mixture of 25% juice, how many liters of each should be used to get 20 liters of a 15% juice mixture?

Detailed Answer Explanations

- $3x + 5 = 20$

Subtract 5 from both sides:

$3x = 15$

Divide by 3:

$x = 5$

- Solve the system of equations:

Using substitution or elimination, we find:

$x = 2, y = 1$

- Inequality:

$-2x + 3 \leq 7$

Subtract 3 from both sides:

$-2x \leq 4$

Divide by -2 and reverse the inequality:

$x \geq -2$

- Time:

Time = 180 / 60 = 3 hours

- Mixture Problem:

Solve using the formula for mixture problems, where x is the amount of the 10% juice solution and 20 - x is the amount of 25% juice.

Geometry: Shapes, Properties, and Formulas

Geometry is a crucial section of the HSPT, focusing on the properties and relationships between points, lines, surfaces, and solids. This section covers everything from basic shapes like triangles and circles to more advanced concepts like the Pythagorean Theorem and volume formulas for 3D objects. Mastering geometry requires both memorization of key formulas and an understanding of how to apply them to solve problems.

Basic Geometric Shapes and Their Properties

Before diving into more complex topics, it's essential to understand the basic properties of common geometric shapes.

Points, Lines, and Angles

- **Point**: A point indicates a position but has no size or shape.

- **Line**: A straight, continuous arrangement of infinitely many points extending in both directions without end.

- **Ray**: A part of a line that starts at a point and extends infinitely in one direction.

- **Line Segment**: A portion of a line bounded by two endpoints.

Angles: An **angle** is formed when two rays meet at a common endpoint (called the vertex). Angles are measured in degrees (°), and there are several types:

- **Acute Angle**: Less than 90°.

- **Right Angle**: Exactly 90°.

- **Obtuse Angle**: Greater than 90° but less than 180°.

- **Straight Angle**: Exactly 180°.

When two lines intersect, they form angles. If the lines are perpendicular, they form four 90° (right) angles.

Types of Triangles

Triangles are a fundamental shape in geometry, defined by three sides and three angles. The sum of the interior angles of any triangle is always 180°. The HSPT often tests your knowledge of different types of triangles and their properties:

- **Equilateral Triangle**: All three sides and angles are equal. Each angle measures 60°.

- **Isosceles Triangle**: Has two equal sides and two equal angles.

- **Scalene Triangle**: All sides and angles are different.

- **Right Triangle**: One angle is a right angle (90°), and the Pythagorean Theorem applies.

Pythagorean Theorem

The Pythagorean Theorem is a key formula used with right triangles. It states that in a right triangle, the square of the length of the hypotenuse (the side opposite the right angle) is equal to the sum of the squares of the other two sides:

$a^2 + b^2 = c^2$

Where c is the hypotenuse and a and b are the lengths of the other two sides.

For example, if one leg of the triangle is 3 units, the other leg is 4 units, and you need to find the hypotenuse:

$3^2 + 4^2 = c^2$ $9 + 16 = c^2$ $25 = c^2$ $c = 5$

Quadrilaterals and Their Properties

A **quadrilateral** is any four-sided polygon. Here are some common types:

1. **Square**: All sides are equal, and all angles are 90°.

2. **Rectangle**: Opposite sides are equal, and all angles are 90°.

3. **Parallelogram**: Opposite sides are parallel and equal in length, and opposite angles are equal.

4. **Rhombus**: All sides are equal, and opposite angles are equal. It is essentially a slanted square.

5. **Trapezoid**: Only one pair of sides is parallel.

Each of these shapes has its own area formula, which we will review in the next section.

Formulas for Perimeter and Area

Knowing how to calculate the perimeter and area of basic shapes is fundamental for solving HSPT geometry problems. Here are the key formulas:

Square:

- Perimeter: $P = 4s$ (where s is the length of one side)
- Area: $A = s^2$

Rectangle:

- Perimeter: $P = 2l + 2w$ (where l is the length and w is the width)
- Area: $A = l \times w$

Triangle:

- Perimeter: $P = a + b + c$ (sum of all sides)
- Area: $A = \frac{1}{2} \times$ base $\times$ height

Parallelogram:

- Perimeter: $P = 2a + 2b$ (sum of opposite sides)
- Area: $A =$ base $\times$ height

Trapezoid:

- Area: $A = \frac{1}{2} \times (b_1 + b_2) \times h$ (where b_1 and b_2 are the lengths of the parallel sides, and h is the height)

Circles: Circumference and Area

A circle is defined by all points in a plane that are equidistant from a center point. To solve circle-related questions on the HSPT, you must know two essential formulas:

1. **Circumference:** The distance around a circle. The formula is:

    o $C = 2\pi r$ or $C = \pi d$

    o   Where r is the radius, and d is the diameter (twice the radius).

2. **Area:** The space enclosed by the circle. The formula is:

- $A = \pi r^2$

For example, if the radius of a circle is 7 units, the area is:

- $A = \pi \times 7^2 = \pi \times 49 \approx 153.94$ square units

Three-Dimensional Shapes and Volume

The key concepts to know include surface area and volume.

Cubes:

- A cube has six square faces, all of equal size. The formulas for surface area and volume are:
    - Surface Area: $SA = 6s^2$
    - Volume: $V = s^3$

Rectangular Prisms:

- A rectangular prism is like a 3D rectangle or box. The formulas are:
    - Surface Area: $SA = 2lw + 2lh + 2wh$
    - Volume: $V = l \times w \times h$

Cylinders:

- A cylinder is a 3D shape with two parallel circular bases. The formulas are:
    - Surface Area: $SA = 2\pi r^2 + 2\pi rh$
    - Volume: $V = \pi r^2 h$

Spheres:

- A sphere is a perfectly round 3D object. The formulas are:
    - Surface Area: $SA = 4\pi r^2$
    - Volume: $V = \frac{4}{3}\pi r^3$

Cones:

- A cone has a circular base and a pointed top (apex). The formulas are:
    - Surface Area: $SA = \pi r^2 + \pi r l$ (where l is the slant height)
    - Volume: $V = \frac{1}{3}\pi r^2 h$

Practice Questions

Let's reinforce these concepts with practice questions:

1. **Find the area of a triangle** with a base of 10 units and a height of 6 units.

2. **Calculate the circumference of a circle** with a radius of 4 units.

3. **Find the volume of a cube** with side lengths of 5 units.

4. **Calculate the surface area of a cylinder** with a radius of 3 units and a height of 7 units.

5. **Determine the area of a trapezoid** with bases of 8 and 10 units and a height of 5 units.

Detailed Answer Explanations

Area of a triangle:

- We use the formula: $A = 1/2 \times base \times height$
- Plug in the given values: $A = 1/2 \times 10 \times 6$
- Calculate: $A = 30$ square units

Circumference of a circle:

- We use the formula: $C = 2\pi r$
- Plug in the given value: $C = 2 \times \pi \times 4$
- Approximate π as 3.14159 and calculate: $C \approx 25.13$ units

Volume of a cube:

95

- We use the formula: $V = s^3$

- Plug in the given value: $V = 5^3$

- Calculate: V = 125 cubic units

Surface area of a cylinder:

- We use the formula: $SA = 2\pi r^2 + 2\pi rh$

- Plug in the given values: $SA = 2 \times \pi \times 3^2 + 2 \times \pi \times 3 \times 7$

- Approximate π as 3.14159 and calculate: $SA \approx 188.4954$ square units

Area of a trapezoid:

- We use the formula: $A = 1/2 \times (b_1 + b_2) \times h$

- Plug in the given values: $A = 1/2 \times (8 + 10) \times 5$

- Calculate: A = 45 square units

Practice Questions

Question Set 1: Number Operations and Computations

Simplify the expression:

$5 \times (8 + 2) - 3^2$

Find the value of x:

7x - 5 = 30

Evaluate the expression:

3(6 + 4) / 2 - 5

Solve the inequality:

$-2x + 8 \geq 14$

Find the product:

$(-4) \times (6) \times (-2)$

Question Set 2: Fractions, Decimals, Percents, and Ratios

Convert 7/8 into a decimal.

What is 25% of 240?

Find the missing term in the proportion:

2/3 = 4/x

Simplify the fraction:

45/60

Convert 0.65 into a percent.

Question Set 3: Algebra and Word Problems

Solve the system of equations:

$2x + y = 7$

$x - y = 3$

If a car travels 60 miles per hour for 3.5 hours, how far does it travel?

A rectangle has a length that is 4 units more than twice its width. If the perimeter is 56 units, find the dimensions of the rectangle.

Find the value of y:

$3(y - 2) = 4y + 6$

A train leaves a station and travels at 45 miles per hour. Another train leaves the same station an hour later traveling at 60 miles per hour. How long will it take the second train to catch up to the first train?

Question Set 4: Geometry

Find the area of a circle with a radius of 5 units.

Determine the perimeter of a triangle with side lengths of 7, 10, and 12 units.

Calculate the surface area of a cube with side lengths of 6 units.

Find the volume of a rectangular prism with a length of 8 units, a width of 5 units, and a height of 4 units.

Determine the area of a trapezoid with bases of 6 and 8 units and a height of 5 units.

Detailed Answer Explanations

After solving the practice questions, review these detailed explanations to ensure you fully understand each concept.

Question Set 1: Number Operations and Computations

1. Simplify the expression:

- $5 \times (8 + 2) - 3\textasciicircum2$

- **Order of Operations (PEMDAS):** Parentheses, Exponents, Multiplication and Division (from left to right), Addition and Subtraction (from left to right).

- **Step 1: Parentheses**
  - $5 \times (10) - 3\textasciicircum2$

- **Step 2: Exponents**
  - $5 \times 10 - 9$

- **Step 3: Multiplication**
  - $50 - 9$

- **Step 4: Subtraction**
  - 41

2. Find the value of x:

- 7x - 5 = 30
- **Goal:** Isolate 'x' on one side of the equation.
- **Step 1: Add 5 to both sides**
  - 7x = 35
- **Step 2: Divide both sides by 7**
  - x = 5

3. Evaluate the expression:

- 3(6 + 4) / 2 - 5
- **Step 1: Parentheses**
  - 3(10) / 2 - 5
- **Step 2: Multiplication**
  - 30 / 2 - 5
- **Step 3: Division**
  - 15 - 5
- **Step 4: Subtraction**
  - 10

4. Solve the inequality:

- -2x + 8 ≥ 14
- **Goal:** Isolate 'x' on one side of the inequality.
- **Step 1: Subtract 8 from both sides**
  - -2x ≥ 6

- **Step 2: Divide both sides by -2 (Remember to flip the inequality sign when dividing/multiplying by a negative number)**
  - x ≤ -3

5. Find the product:

- (-4) × (6) × (-2)
- **Multiplying numbers with different signs:**
  - Positive × Negative = Negative
  - Negative × Negative = Positive
- **Step 1:**
  - 24 × (-2)
- **Step 2:**
  - -48

Question Set 2: Fractions, Decimals, Percents, and Ratios

1. Convert 7/8 into a decimal:

- Divide the numerator (7) by the denominator (8).
- 7 ÷ 8 = 0.875

2. What is 25% of 240?

98

- Percent means "out of one hundred"

- 25% = 0.25

- Multiply the decimal equivalent of the percent by the given number.

- 0.25 × 240 = 60

3. **Find the missing term in the proportion:**

- 2/3 = 4/x

- **Cross-multiplication:** Multiply the numerator of the first fraction by the denominator of the second fraction, and vice versa.

- 2x = 12

- Divide both sides by 2 to isolate 'x'

- x = 6

4. **Simplify the fraction:**

- 45/60

- **Find the greatest common divisor (GCD) of 45 and 60, which is 15.**

- Divide both numerator and denominator by 15.

- (45 ÷ 15) / (60 ÷ 15) = 3/4

5. **Convert 0.65 into a percent:**

- Multiply the decimal by 100 and add the percent symbol (%).

- 0.65 × 100 = 65%

Question Set 3: Algebra and Word Problems

1. Solve the system of equations:

- 2x + y = 7 and x - y = 3

- **Substitution Method:**

  1. Solve one of the equations for one variable in terms of the other.

  2. Substitute this expression into the other equation.

  3. Solve for the remaining variable.

  4. Substitute the value back into either of the original equations to find the other variable.

- **Step 1: Solve the second equation for x**

  ○ x = y + 3

- **Step 2: Substitute into the first equation**

  ○ 2(y + 3) + y = 7

- **Step 3: Simplify and solve for y**

  ○ 2y + 6 + y = 7

- $3y + 6 = 7$
- $3y = 1$
- $y = 1/3$
- **Step 4: Substitute back to find x**
  - $x = (1/3) + 3$
  - $x = 10/3$

2. Distance problem:

- Distance = Rate × Time
- Rate = 60 mph
- Time = 3.5 hours
- Distance = $60 \times 3.5 = 210$ miles

3. Perimeter of a rectangle:

- Perimeter = 2(length + width)
- Let width = x
- Length = $2x + 4$
- Perimeter = 56
- **Set up the equation and solve for x (width)**
  - $2(x + 2x + 4) = 56$
  - $2(3x + 4) = 56$
  - $6x + 8 = 56$
  - $6x = 48$
  - $x = 8$

- **Find the length**
  - Length = $2(8) + 4 = 20$
- **Dimensions:**
  - Width = 8 units
  - Length = 20 units

4. Solving for y:

- $3(y - 2) = 4y + 6$
- **Step 1: Expand both sides (Distributive Property)**
  - $3y - 6 = 4y + 6$
- **Step 2: Subtract 3y from both sides**
  - $-6 = y + 6$
- **Step 3: Subtract 6 from both sides**
  - $-12 = y$

5. Train problem:

- Let 't' represent the time it takes the second train to catch up.
- Distance traveled by the first train = $45(t + 1)$ (It has a 1-hour head start)
- Distance traveled by the second train = 60t

- When the second train catches up, the distances traveled by both trains are equal.

- **Set up the equation and solve for t**

  - $45(t + 1) = 60t$

  - $45t + 45 = 60t$

  - $15t = 45$

  - $t = 3$

- It takes the second train 3 hours to catch up.

Question Set 4: Geometry

1. Area of a circle:

- $A = \pi r^2$, where r is the radius.

- Radius (r) = 5 units

- $A = \pi \times 5^2$

- $A = 25\pi$ square units

- $A \approx 78.54$ square units (using $\pi \approx 3.14$)

2. Perimeter of a triangle:

- Perimeter = Sum of all sides

- $P = 7 + 10 + 12 = 29$ units

3. Surface area of a cube:

- $SA = 6s^2$, where 's' is the side length.

- Side (s) = 6 units

- $SA = 6 \times 6^2$

- $SA = 6 \times 36$

- $SA = 216$ square units

4. Volume of a rectangular prism:

- $V = l \times w \times h$, where l is length, w is width, and h is height

- l = 8 units, w = 5 units, h = 4 units

- $V = 8 \times 5 \times 4$

- $V = 160$ cubic units

5. Area of a trapezoid:

- $A = 1/2 \times$ (sum of parallel sides) $\times$ height

- Parallel sides: 6 units and 8 units

- Height = 5 units

- $A = 1/2 \times (6 + 8) \times 5$

- $A = 1/2 \times 14 \times 5$

- $A = 35$ square units

Chapter 8: Mastering Language Skills

When it comes to acing the HSPT, mastering language skills is not only crucial but can also significantly boost your overall score. This chapter is designed to equip you with all the necessary tools to excel in the language subtest. From grammar and usage rules to the finer points of punctuation, capitalization, and spelling, we will cover each aspect in great depth. The subtest is not just about knowing the rules but also understanding how to apply them effectively in various contexts, which is why this chapter is packed with practice questions and detailed answer explanations to ensure you're fully prepared.

Grammar and Usage Rules

Grammar and usage rules form the foundation of effective communication. On the HSPT, this section tests your ability to identify and correct errors in sentence structure, subject-verb agreement, tense usage, and more. Having a strong command of grammar ensures that you can construct sentences that are not only correct but also clear and concise.

1. Subject-Verb Agreement

One of the most common grammatical errors students make is failing to match the subject with the correct verb form. On the HSPT, you'll be asked to identify sentences where the subject and verb do not agree in number. The rule is simple: singular subjects take singular verbs, and plural subjects take plural verbs. However, tricky sentence structures and phrases can obscure this rule, leading to mistakes.

For example:

Incorrect: The team of players are winning the game.
Correct: The team of players is winning the game.

In the incorrect sentence, the verb "are" does not match the singular subject "team." Even though "players" is plural, the main subject is "team," which is singular, so the correct verb should be "is."

Common Pitfalls:

- **Phrases between the subject and verb**: Words that come between the subject and verb do not change the number of the subject.

  - **Example**: The list of books is on the shelf. ("List" is the subject, not "books.")

- **Indefinite pronouns**: Words like "everyone," "nobody," and "each" are singular.

  - **Example**: Everyone needs to bring his or her own lunch. ("Everyone" is singular.)

Practice Tip: When in doubt, isolate the subject and the verb. Ignore any additional descriptive phrases that come between them to ensure they agree in number.

2. Pronoun-Antecedent Agreement

Pronouns are used to replace nouns to avoid repetition. However, when using a pronoun, it must agree in number and gender with the noun it replaces (antecedent). This is another rule often tested on the HSPT.

Incorrect: Every student must bring their own book.
Correct: Every student must bring his or her own book.

In this example, "student" is singular, so the pronoun must be singular as well. "Their" is incorrect because it is a plural pronoun.

Common Pitfalls:

- **Collective nouns**: Words like "jury," "team," or "class" are singular when acting as a unit, but can be plural when acting as individuals.

  - **Example**: The jury has reached its verdict. (Singular because the jury is acting as one body.)

- o **Example**: The jury have expressed their individual opinions. (Plural because the jury members are acting independently.)

- **Ambiguous antecedents**: If it's unclear which noun a pronoun refers to, clarity must be improved.

  - o **Example**: When Susan and Maria finished their exams, she left the room. (Who left, Susan or Maria?)

  - o **Revised**: When Susan and Maria finished their exams, Susan left the room.

3. Verb Tenses

Verb tenses tell us when an action takes place, and using the correct tense is essential for clear communication. On the HSPT, you'll encounter sentences where you must choose the appropriate verb tense.

Simple Tenses:

- **Present**: I walk to school every day.

- **Past**: I walked to school yesterday.

- **Future**: I will walk to school tomorrow.

Perfect Tenses:

- **Present Perfect**: I have walked to school many times. (Action began in the past and may continue.)

- **Past Perfect**: I had walked to school before it started raining. (Action completed before another past action.)

- **Future Perfect**: I will have walked to school by the time the bus arrives. (Action will be completed before a future event.)

Common Pitfalls:

- **Shifts in tense**: Avoid switching tenses within the same sentence unless there is a clear reason for the change.

- o **Incorrect**: She was playing soccer when she hears the news. (Mixed tenses.)

- o **Correct**: She was playing soccer when she heard the news. (Both verbs are in the past tense.)

4. Parallelism

Parallel structure (or parallelism) involves using the same pattern of words to show that two or more ideas have the same level of importance. Parallelism is often tested in sentences that list items or actions.

Incorrect: She enjoys reading, to jog, and watching TV.
Correct: She enjoys reading, jogging, and watching TV.

In the incorrect sentence, the verbs "reading" and "watching" are gerunds, but "to jog" is an infinitive. For the sentence to be parallel, all verbs must be in the same form.

Practice Tip: When dealing with lists or comparisons, ensure that the elements are in the same grammatical form.

Sentence Structure and Composition

Mastering sentence structure is essential for communicating your ideas clearly and effectively. The HSPT tests your ability to construct sentences that are not only grammatically correct but also stylistically sound.

1. Types of Sentences

Understanding the different types of sentences is the first step to mastering sentence structure.

- **Simple Sentence**: Contains one independent clause.

  - o **Example**: The dog barked.

- **Compound Sentence**: Contains two or more independent clauses joined by a coordinating conjunction (for, and, nor, but, or, yet, so).

- o **Example**: The dog barked, and the cat ran away.
- **Complex Sentence**: Contains one independent clause and at least one dependent clause.
  - o **Example**: When the dog barked, the cat ran away.
- **Compound-Complex Sentence**: Contains two or more independent clauses and at least one dependent clause.
  - o **Example**: When the dog barked, the cat ran away, but the mouse stayed still.

Common Pitfalls:

- **Comma splices**: A comma splice occurs when two independent clauses are joined by a comma without a coordinating conjunction.
  - o **Incorrect**: The dog barked, the cat ran away.
  - o **Correct**: The dog barked, and the cat ran away. (Or separate into two sentences: The dog barked. The cat ran away.)
- **Run-on sentences**: These occur when two or more independent clauses are joined without punctuation or conjunctions.
  - o **Incorrect**: The dog barked the cat ran away.
  - o **Correct**: The dog barked. The cat ran away.

2. Sentence Variety

Good writing uses a mix of sentence types to keep the reader engaged. On the HSPT, you'll be tested on your ability to recognize and revise sentences for better variety.

Example: The teacher explained the lesson. The students listened carefully. The lesson was interesting.
Revision: The teacher explained the lesson, and the students listened carefully because the lesson was interesting.

In this example, the revision combines sentences for smoother flow and better readability.

3. Combining Sentences

Combining sentences is a key skill tested in the language section. Often, two short, choppy sentences can be combined into one more sophisticated sentence.

Example: The boy ran to the store. He needed milk.
Revision: The boy ran to the store because he needed milk.

By combining the two sentences, the second sentence becomes a dependent clause, making the sentence more complex and informative.

4. Fragments and Complete Sentences

A complete sentence contains at least one independent clause—a subject and a verb that expresses a complete thought. A sentence fragment, on the other hand, is an incomplete sentence that cannot stand on its own.

Fragment: Running down the street.
Complete Sentence: She was running down the street.

Fragments often lack a subject, verb, or both, and must be revised to form a complete sentence.

Common Pitfalls:

- **Starting with a conjunction**: Words like "and," "but," or "because" should not start a sentence unless the sentence is complete.
    - **Incorrect**: Because he was late. (Fragment.)
    - **Correct**: Because he was late, he missed the bus.

Capitalization, Punctuation, and Spelling

Capitalization, punctuation, and spelling errors are often easy to overlook, but they can significantly impact the clarity and professionalism of your writing. This section will ensure you know how to apply these rules correctly and consistently on the HSPT.

1. Capitalization Rules

Capitalization is essential for proper nouns, the beginning of sentences, and specific titles. Let's review the most important capitalization rules.

- **Beginning of Sentences**: Every sentence must begin with a capital letter.

    o **Example**: The quick brown fox jumps over the lazy dog.

- **Proper Nouns**: Always capitalize names of people, places, organizations, and specific titles.

    o **Example**: John attended Harvard University.

- **Titles**: Capitalize major words in titles but not articles, prepositions, or conjunctions unless they are the first word of the title.

    o **Example**: The Great Gatsby.

Common Pitfalls:

- **Common vs. proper nouns**: Be sure to capitalize proper nouns (specific names) but not common nouns (general names).

    o **Incorrect**: We visited the Eiffel tower.

    o **Correct**: We visited the Eiffel Tower.

2. Punctuation Rules

Correct punctuation ensures that your sentences convey the right meaning and are easy to read. Misplacing or omitting punctuation can lead to confusion or misinterpretation.

Commas

Commas are used to separate elements in a sentence and clarify meaning.

- **In a list**: Use commas to separate three or more items.

    o **Example**: I bought apples, bananas, and oranges.

- **Before conjunctions**: Use a comma before coordinating conjunctions (and, but, or) when they join independent clauses.

    o **Example**: I wanted to go to the store, but it was closed.

- **Introductory elements**: Use a comma after an introductory phrase.

  o **Example**: After the game, we went out for ice cream.

Semicolons

Semicolons join two closely related independent clauses or separate items in a complex list.

- **Example**: I wanted to go to the store; however, it was closed.

Practice Questions

Now that you have thoroughly reviewed the grammar, usage, sentence structure, and punctuation rules, it's time to put your knowledge to the test. The following practice questions are designed to mimic the types of questions you will encounter on the HSPT. After you finish answering the questions, be sure to check your answers in the "Detailed Answer Explanations" section to understand where you excelled and where you may need additional review.

Grammar and Usage Practice Questions

1. Which of the following sentences contains a subject-verb agreement error?

   o a) The dogs in the park are running freely.

   o b) The team of players is ready for the championship.

   o c) The group of students were excited about the field trip.

   o d) Each of the books is available in the library.

2. Choose the sentence where the pronoun agrees with its antecedent:

   o a) Neither Jack nor Jill brought their umbrella.

   o b) Each student must complete their homework by Friday.

   o c) Both Susan and Maria forgot to bring their books.

   o d) Everyone on the team must submit their permission slip.

3. Which of the following sentences correctly uses parallel structure?

o a) I enjoy reading books, to swim, and watching movies.

o b) She loves dancing, singing, and to paint.

o c) He is responsible for organizing events, coordinating volunteers, and writing reports.

o d) They plan to hike, running, and biking during their trip.

4. Identify the sentence with the incorrect verb tense:

o a) She was studying when her friends arrived.

o b) We had eaten dinner by the time the movie started.

o c) He is going to the store yesterday.

o d) They will be visiting their relatives next weekend.

5. Which of the following sentences contains a pronoun-antecedent error?

o a) The committee has finished their report.

o b) Every student must bring his or her textbook to class.

o c) Both James and Carla submitted their essays on time.

o d) The jury reached its decision quickly.

Sentence Structure and Composition Practice Questions

6. Which of the following is a sentence fragment?

o a) After the game ended, we went out for dinner.

o b) Because he was tired from the long hike.

o c) She worked hard to finish her project, and it was a success.

o d) I enjoy running, but I also like cycling.

7. Identify the sentence that uses a comma splice:

o a) The sun set behind the mountains, and the sky turned orange.

o b) The cat ran outside, she chased after it.

o c) We went to the store, and then we cooked dinner.

o d) He studied hard for the exam, and he passed with flying colors.

8. Choose the correct way to combine these sentences: "I finished my homework. I watched TV."

   o a) I finished my homework, and then I watched TV.

   o b) I finished my homework, TV was next.

   o c) I finished my homework; and I watched TV.

   o d) I finished my homework because I watched TV.

9. Which of the following is an example of correct parallelism?

   o a) She enjoys reading novels, to paint, and writing poetry.

   o b) The coach is responsible for training the players, creating game plans, and to supervise practices.

   o c) The store sells shoes, hats, and clothing.

   o d) I plan to go jogging, hiking, and to swim this weekend.

10. Identify the complete sentence:

   • a) Running through the park on a sunny day.

   • b) She loves reading mystery novels.

   • c) When the teacher entered the classroom.

   • d) If it rains tomorrow.

Capitalization, Punctuation, and Spelling Practice Questions

11. Which of the following sentences contains a capitalization error?

   • a) My family visited the Grand Canyon last summer.

   • b) We went to the movies on friday night.

   • c) She is reading "To Kill a Mockingbird" for her English class.

   • d) The mayor will attend the meeting.

12. Choose the sentence that correctly uses punctuation:

- a) We need to buy: apples, oranges, and bananas.

- b) I have finished my homework; now I can relax.

- c) He didn't know the answer, so he guessed, and got it right.

- d) The teacher asked, "Who is ready for the quiz"?

13. Which of the following sentences uses the correct form of the word?

- a) Their going to the park later.

- b) They're going to the park later.

- c) There going to the park later.

- d) Their going to the park later.

14. Which sentence correctly uses a semicolon?

- a) She studied for hours; because she wanted to ace the exam.

- b) The weather was beautiful; we decided to go for a hike.

- c) I went to the store; and I bought some groceries.

- d) He is always late to class; but he still manages to pass his exams.

15. Identify the sentence with correct spelling:

- a) The occurance of the event was surprising.

- b) She recieved an award for her work.

- c) His neice is very talented.

- d) I believe we will succeed.

Detailed Answer Explanations

In this section, you'll find detailed explanations for each of the practice questions provided above. Understanding why an answer is correct or incorrect is just as important as getting the right answer, so take the time to review these explanations carefully.

Grammar and Usage Answer Explanations

1. **Correct Answer: (c) The group of students were excited about the field trip.**

    o Explanation: "Group" is a collective noun and is singular, so the verb

112

should be "was," not "were."

2. **Correct Answer: (c) Both Susan and Maria forgot to bring their books.**

   o Explanation: "Both" refers to two people, so the plural pronoun "their" is correct.

3. **Correct Answer: (c) He is responsible for organizing events, coordinating volunteers, and writing reports.**

   o Explanation: All verbs are in the same form (gerunds), making the sentence parallel.

4. **Correct Answer: (c) He is going to the store yesterday.**

   o Explanation: The sentence mixes present and past tense. "Is going" should be "went" to match the past tense.

5. **Correct Answer: (a) The committee has finished their report.**

   o Explanation: "Committee" is a singular

noun, so the pronoun should be "its," not "their."

Sentence Structure and Composition Answer Explanations

6. **Correct Answer: (b) Because he was tired from the long hike.**

   o Explanation: This is a dependent clause and cannot stand alone as a complete sentence.

7. **Correct Answer: (b) The cat ran outside, she chased after it.**

   o Explanation: This is a comma splice. The two independent clauses should be separated by a period or a semicolon.

8. **Correct Answer: (a) I finished my homework, and then I watched TV.**

   o Explanation: The sentence correctly uses a coordinating conjunction to join two independent clauses.

9. **Correct Answer: (c) The store sells shoes, hats, and clothing.**

   o Explanation: All items in the list are nouns, making the sentence parallel.

113

10. **Correct Answer: (b) She loves reading mystery novels.**

   o Explanation: This is a complete sentence with both a subject and a verb, expressing a full thought.

Capitalization, Punctuation, and Spelling Answer Explanations

11. **Correct Answer: (b) We went to the movies on friday night.**

   o Explanation: "Friday" should be capitalized because it is the name of a day of the week.

12. **Correct Answer: (b) I have finished my homework; now I can relax.**

   o Explanation: The semicolon correctly joins two independent clauses.

13. **Correct Answer: (b) They're going to the park later.**

   o Explanation: "They're" is the contraction of "they are," which fits the context.

14. **Correct Answer: (b) The weather was beautiful; we decided to go for a hike.**

   o Explanation: The semicolon correctly separates two independent clauses.

15. **Correct Answer: (d) I believe we will succeed.**

   o Explanation: All words in this sentence are spelled correctly.

Mastering language skills for the HSPT is crucial for achieving a high score. By carefully reviewing grammar and usage rules, sentence structure, and punctuation, and by practicing consistently, you can ensure that you're fully prepared for the language subtest. Remember to use the strategies and rules outlined in this chapter as you work through the practice questions, and review the detailed explanations to strengthen your understanding.

PART 3: FULL-LENGTH PRACTICE EXAMS

Full-Length Practice Exam 1

Verbal Skills Subtest

Time Allowed: 16 minutes

Number of Questions: 60

Part 1: Synonyms (Questions 1-16)

Description: In this section, you will be presented with a word, followed by four answer choices. Your task is to select the word that is most similar in meaning to the given word.

Exhaust (a) Renew

(b) Deplete

(c) Increase

(d) Restore

Imminent (a) Certain

(b) Future

(c) Forthcoming

(d) Doubtful

Avid (a) Indifferent

(b) Eager

(c) Relaxed

(d) Casual

Detrimental (a) Helpful

(b) Harmful

(c) Delightful

(d) Neutral

Perpetual (a) Temporary

(b) Continuous

(c) Intermittent

(d) Occasional

Conventional (a) Radical

(b) Customary

(c) Innovative

(d) Foreign

Benevolent (a) Malicious

(b) Kind

(c) Selfish

(d) Greedy

Frivolous (a) Sensible

(b) Serious

(c) Unimportant

(d) Necessary

Adorn (a) Disfigure

(b) Decorate

(c) Abandon

(d) Expose

Inadvertent (a) Unintentional

(b) Intentional

(c) Necessary

(d) Scheduled

Futile (a) Hopeful

(b) Useless

(c) Productive

(d) Promising

Ominous (a) Fortunate

(b) Threatening

(c) Pleasing

(d) Clear

Lucid (a) Confusing

(b) Clear

(c) Cloudy

(d) Muddled

Conceal (a) Reveal

(b) Hide

(c) Announce

(d) Show

Inhibit (a) Encourage

(b) Prevent

(c) Promote

(d) Allow

Apathetic (a) Energetic

(b) Unconcerned

(c) Enthusiastic

(d) Interested

Part 2: Antonyms (Questions 17-30)

Description: In this section, you will be given a word, and your task is to select the word that has the opposite meaning from the given word.

Abundant (a) Scarce

(b) Plentiful

(c) Common

(d) Unlimited

Relinquish (a) Abandon

(b) Hold

(c) Release

(d) Submit

Subtle (a) Obvious

(b) Delicate

(c) Faint

(d) Refined

Vague (a) Clear

(b) General

(c) Uncertain

(d) Blurry

Commend (a) Praise

(b) Criticize

(c) Honor

(d) Compliment

Timid (a) Bold

(b) Cautious

(c) Fearful

(d) Nervous

Enhance (a) Diminish

(b) Improve

(c) Elevate

(d) Develop

Rigid (a) Flexible

(b) Strict

(c) Severe

(d) Solid

Solitary (a) Isolated

(b) Social

(c) Alone

(d) Single

Provoke (a) Incite

(b) Calm

(c) Irritate

(d) Annoy

Diligent (a) Lazy

(b) Hardworking

(c) Careful

(d) Persistent

Detest (a) Love

(b) Hate

(c) Avoid

(d) Resist

Innocuous (a) Harmful

(b) Safe

(c) Inoffensive

(d) Gentle

Obscure (a) Reveal

(b) Hide

(c) Conceal

(d) Cover

Part 3: Analogies (Questions 31-45)

Description: In this section, you will be given a pair of words and must determine the relationship between them. You will then choose another pair of words that has the same relationship.

Bridge is to river as tunnel is to: (a) Road

(b) Mountain

(c) Train

(d) Water

Glove is to hand as sock is to: (a) Foot

(b) Shoe

(c) Leg

(d) Finger

Oven is to bake as stove is to: (a) Heat

119

(b) Cook

(c) Fry

(d) Boil

Artist is to painting as chef is to: (a) Food

(b) Knife

(c) Recipe

(d) Cooking

Pencil is to write as scissors are to: (a) Cut

(b) Sharpen

(c) Paste

(d) Tear

Wing is to bird as fin is to: (a) Fish

(b) Bird

(c) Insect

(d) Plane

Key is to lock as password is to: (a) Vault

(b) Security

(c) Safe

(d) Door

Ear is to hear as eye is to: (a) See

(b) Watch

(c) Blink

(d) Light

Lawyer is to courtroom as teacher is to: (a) Book

(b) School

(c) Student

(d) Lecture

Dog is to bark as cat is to: (a) Hiss

(b) Growl

(c) Meow

(d) Purr

Battery is to energy as pen is to: (a) Paper

(b) Ink

(c) Write

(d) Pencil

Morning is to dawn as night is to: (a) Dusk

(b) Evening

(c) Midnight

(d) Twilight

Library is to books as museum is to: (a) Artifacts

(b) Learning

(c) Studies

(d) Statues

Pen is to ink as brush is to: (a) Paint

(b) Canvas

(c) Art

(d) Line

Page is to book as leaf is to: (a) Tree

(b) Bark

(c) Paper

(d) Branch

Part 4: Verbal Classifications (Questions 46-55)

Description: You will be given four words. Three of the words are related to one another in some way. You must identify the word that does not belong.

(a) Apple (b) Banana (c) Carrot (d) Orange

(a) Bus (b) Airplane (c) Bicycle (d) Car

(a) Desk (b) Chair (c) Book (d) Table

(a) Cat (b) Dog (c) Parrot (d) Tiger

(a) Doctor (b) Teacher (c) Engineer (d) Recipe

(a) Pencil (b) Marker (c) Crayon (d) Notebook

(a) Triangle (b) Square (c) Circle (d) Line

(a) Moon (b) Star (c) Sun (d) Comet

(a) Rose (b) Tulip (c) Grass (d) Daisy

(a) Violin (b) Guitar (c) Trumpet (d) Drum

Part 5: Verbal Logic (Questions 56-60)

Description: In this section, you will be presented with a series of statements. Based on the given information, you will decide whether the final statement is true, false, or uncertain.

All lions are animals. All animals have four legs. Therefore, all lions have four legs. (a) True

(b) False

(c) Uncertain

Some birds can fly. Penguins are birds. Therefore, penguins can fly. (a) True

(b) False

(c) Uncertain

All teachers are educated. Some educated people are doctors. Therefore, some teachers are doctors. (a) True

(b) False

(c) Uncertain

All squares have four sides. Some four-sided shapes are rectangles. Therefore, some squares are rectangles. (a) True

(b) False

(c) Uncertain

All pencils are writing tools. Some writing tools are pens. Therefore, some pencils are pens. (a) True

(b) False

(c) Uncertain

Quantitative Skills Subtest

Allocated Time: 30 Minutes

Total Questions: 52

Introduction: Quantitative Skills Subtest Overview

The Quantitative Skills section of the HSPT is designed to measure your ability to reason through mathematical and numerical problems using logic and analytical thinking. In this section, you will encounter various types of quantitative problems, including sequences, comparisons, and computations. Your goal is not only to calculate the correct answers but also to do so efficiently and accurately within the 30-minute time frame provided.

Many of the questions will involve pattern recognition, critical thinking, and the application of basic arithmetic. Keep in mind that some questions may require multiple steps to solve, so it's essential to manage your time wisely and maintain a steady pace throughout the subtest.

This practice test mirrors the actual HSPT in terms of format, difficulty, and length. Make sure to complete this section in a quiet environment, and time yourself as you work through the 52 questions provided.

Sequences (Questions 1–15)

In this section, you will be asked to identify patterns in numerical sequences. These questions are designed to test your ability to recognize and predict the next number or set of numbers in a sequence based on the given patterns.

Question 1

2, 5, 8, 11, ___

What number should come next?

A) 14

B) 13

C) 12

D) 15

Question 2

1, 1, 2, 3, 5, 8, ___

What number should come next in the sequence?

A) 10

B) 11

C) 12

D) 13

Question 3

12, 15, 18, 21, ___

What number should come next in the sequence?

A) 23

B) 24

C) 25

D) 27

Question 4

5, 10, 20, 40, ___

What number should come next in the sequence?

A) 45

B) 50

C) 80

D) 100

Question 5

100, 90, 80, 70, ___

What number should come next?

A) 60

B) 65

C) 75

D) 50

Question 6

1, 4, 9, 16, ___

What is the next number in this sequence?

A) 20

B) 25

C) 30

D) 36

Question 7

11, 22, 33, 44, ___

What number should follow in the sequence?

A) 45

B) 50

C) 55

D) 60

Question 8

2, 6, 12, 20, ___

What number should come next in the pattern?

A) 26

B) 28

C) 30

D) 32

Question 9

1, 2, 4, 7, 11, 16, ___

What number completes the sequence?

A) 22

B) 20

C) 18

D) 19

Question 10

10, 5, 6, 3, 4, 2, ___

What number comes next?

A) 1

B) 3

C) 2

D) 0

Question 11

3, 6, 12, 24, 48, ___

What number should come next in this sequence?

A) 50

B) 60

C) 96

D) 100

Question 12

9, 7, 5, 3, ___

What number completes this sequence?

A) 1

B) 0

C) -1

D) -2

Question 13

100, 150, 200, 250, ___

What number follows in the sequence?

A) 275

B) 300

C) 350

D) 325

Question 14

1, 3, 7, 15, ___

What number should complete the sequence?

A) 30

B) 31

C) 32

D) 29

Question 15

8, 16, 32, 64, ___

What is the next number in the sequence?

A) 72

B) 96

C) 128

D) 256

Comparisons (Questions 16–30)

In this section, you will compare mathematical expressions or values to determine which is larger, smaller, or equal. The goal of these questions is to assess your ability to simplify and compare numbers and formulas.

Question 16

Which is greater?

A) 5^25

B) 4^34

Question 17

Which is greater?

A) 75 ÷ 3

B) 5 x 5

Question 18

Which is smaller?

A) 48 ÷ 8

B) 7 + 4

Question 19

Which is larger?

A) 9^2

B) 8 x 12

Question 20

Which is smaller?

A) 125% of 100

B) 150% of 80

Question 21

Which is larger?

A) 3^33

B) 30 ÷ 3 x 3

Question 22

Which is smaller?

A) 0.45

B) 0.5

Question 23

Which is greater?

A) 3/4

B) 5/6

Question 24

Which is smaller?

A) 0.2 x 10

B) 0.4 x 5

Question 25

Which is greater?

A) 1/2 ÷ 1/4

B) 1/4 x 2

Question 26

Which is larger?

A) 30% of 400

B) 25% of 500

Question 27

Which is greater?

A) 10×3^2

B) 9×4^2

Question 28

Which is smaller?

A) 4.5

B) 7/2

Question 29

Which is greater?

A) 25×1.5

B) 20×2

Question 30

Which is smaller?

A) 75% of 160

B) 50% of 260

Computations (Questions 31–52)

In this section, you will perform basic computations involving addition, subtraction, multiplication, division, and other basic arithmetic operations. Each question requires you to apply your knowledge of arithmetic to find the correct answer.

Question 31

Solve:

$25 + 17 + 36$

Question 32

Solve:

$80 \div 4 \times 3$

Question 33

What is 30% of 200?

Question 34

Solve:

$144 \div 12 \times 2$

Question 35

Subtract:

$600 - 245$

Question 36

What is 3/4 of 64?

Question 37

Multiply:

13×24

Question 38

Solve:

$5^2 + 10 \div 2$

Question 39

Divide:

$480 \div 6$

Question 40

What is 2.5 × 8?

Question 41

Solve:

225 ÷ 15

Question 42

What is the value of

30 × 4 - 25

Question 43

Solve the equation:

125 - 75 + 50

Question 44

What is 1/3 of 270?

Question 45

Add:

357 + 284

Question 46

What is 15% of 400?

Question 47

Solve:

72 ÷ 9 + 8

Question 48

What is 5/8 of 96?

Question 49

Solve:

640 ÷ 8 × 3

Question 50

Subtract:

905 - 372

Question 51

What is 12 × 15?

Question 52

Solve:

100 ÷ 4 + 25

Reading Subtest

Time Allowed: 25 minutes
Number of Questions: 62
Instructions: For each question, choose the best answer. This section is designed to test your ability to understand and interpret written passages, analyze arguments, and answer vocabulary-based questions. Read the passages carefully, and use your time wisely.

Part 1: Reading Comprehension Passages and Questions

In this section, you will be provided with several passages followed by questions that assess your ability to understand the main idea, details, inferences, and vocabulary from the text. You will need to read each passage carefully before answering the associated questions. The passages are diverse and cover a range of subjects including literature, history, science, and social studies.

Passage 1: History of the Printing Press

The invention of the printing press in the 15th century by Johannes Gutenberg revolutionized communication and literacy. Before this innovation, books were painstakingly copied by hand, limiting their availability to the elite.

Gutenberg's press allowed for the mass production of books, which drastically reduced their cost and made written works accessible to a broader audience. The impact of the printing press on society was profound, as it facilitated the spread of knowledge, ideas, and information across Europe.

One of the earliest books printed using this new technology was the Gutenberg Bible, which is still regarded as a masterpiece of craftsmanship and innovation. The printing press also played a key role in the Protestant Reformation, as it enabled Martin Luther's 95 Theses to be widely distributed, sparking religious debate and reform. Furthermore, the press contributed to the Renaissance by making classical texts more widely available, thus promoting education and intellectual discourse. The advent of the printing press is considered one of the most significant developments in human history, fostering an era of enlightenment and intellectual exchange.

Questions 1–10:

1. What is the main idea of the passage?
    A) The printing press was invented by Johannes Gutenberg.

B) The printing press made books more affordable and accessible.
C) The Protestant Reformation was started by Martin Luther.
D) The Renaissance was a period of increased education and intellectual discourse.

2. According to the passage, what was one of the earliest books printed by Gutenberg?
A) The Book of Kells
B) Martin Luther's 95 Theses
C) The Gutenberg Bible
D) The Renaissance Bible

3. How did the printing press affect the spread of ideas in Europe?
A) It limited access to knowledge to the elite.
B) It increased the cost of books.
C) It made it easier to distribute ideas and information.
D) It reduced the role of books in society.

4. What role did the printing press play in the Protestant Reformation?
A) It allowed Martin Luther to print more copies of the Bible.
B) It helped distribute the 95 Theses and encourage religious debate.
C) It was used by the Catholic Church to stop the Reformation.
D) It promoted the Renaissance by making classical texts more available.

5. What does the word "profound" in the second paragraph most likely mean?
A) Deep
B) Unnoticed
C) Minor
D) Temporary

6. Why does the author mention the Renaissance in the passage?
A) To show how Gutenberg influenced education.
B) To explain why classical texts were banned.
C) To discuss why the printing press slowed education.
D) To argue that the Renaissance was more important than the Reformation.

7. Which of the following is NOT mentioned as an effect of the printing press?
A) Increased literacy
B) The spread of religious reform
C) The rise of the Renaissance
D) The invention of the steam engine

8. What does the passage suggest about the availability of books

before the printing press?
A) Books were available to everyone but were expensive.
B) Books were rare and only accessible to the wealthy elite.
C) Books were inexpensive and widely available.
D) Books were only written by religious scholars.

9. How did the printing press influence the Renaissance?
A) By reducing the cost of books and promoting access to classical texts.
B) By ending the need for handwritten manuscripts.
C) By inventing new literary genres.
D) By discouraging new educational practices.

10. What was one reason the Gutenberg Bible is still regarded as a masterpiece?
A) It was the first religious text ever created.
B) It was written in a new form of English.
C) It demonstrated the craftsmanship and innovation of early printing.
D) It contained all known books from the Renaissance period.

Passage 2: The Ecology of Coral Reefs

Coral reefs are one of the most diverse and important ecosystems in the world. They are formed by colonies of tiny organisms called polyps, which build limestone structures that serve as the foundation for the reef. These reefs provide habitats for thousands of species of fish, invertebrates, and other marine organisms, making them essential to marine biodiversity.

However, coral reefs are facing increasing threats from human activities, including overfishing, pollution, and climate change. Rising ocean temperatures are causing coral bleaching, a process in which the symbiotic algae that live within coral polyps are expelled, leading to the death of the coral. Pollution from coastal development and agricultural runoff also contributes to the degradation of these ecosystems.

Conservation efforts are underway to protect coral reefs, including the establishment of marine protected areas and efforts to reduce carbon emissions. These initiatives aim to preserve the delicate balance of life in coral reefs, which not only support marine life but also protect coastal communities from erosion and provide livelihoods for millions of people worldwide.

Questions 11–20:

11. What is the main idea of the passage?
A) Coral reefs are at risk due to human activities.
B) Coral reefs are made of limestone structures.
C) Coral polyps create habitats for fish.
D) Coral reefs are found in every ocean.

12. What is coral bleaching?
A) The process of coral turning white due to pollution.
B) When algae are expelled from coral due to rising ocean temperatures.
C) A method used by scientists to clean coral reefs.
D) The result of overfishing near coral reefs.

13. According to the passage, why are coral reefs important to marine life?
A) They are the only place where fish can live.
B) They provide essential habitats for a wide variety of species.
C) They are the only source of food for marine organisms.
D) They protect marine life from pollution.

14. What does the word "symbiotic" in the second paragraph most likely mean?
A) Harmful
B) Beneficial
C) Separate
D) Independent

15. How are coral reefs being protected?
A) By reducing overfishing in coastal areas.
B) By creating marine protected areas and reducing carbon emissions.
C) By promoting tourism to coral reefs.
D) By planting more coral polyps in affected areas.

16. What is the relationship between coral polyps and algae?
A) Algae harm the coral polyps by feeding on them.
B) Algae help coral polyps by providing them with nutrients.
C) Coral polyps feed on algae and use them for energy.
D) Coral polyps protect algae from predators.

17. Which of the following is NOT a threat to coral reefs mentioned in the passage?
A) Pollution from coastal development

133

B) Rising ocean temperatures

C) Overfishing

D) The introduction of new species

18. What does the passage suggest about the future of coral reefs?

A) They will continue to grow and thrive if current practices are maintained.

B) They will be completely destroyed by human activities.

C) They can be saved if conservation efforts are successful.

D) They are not important to marine ecosystems.

19. Why do coral reefs protect coastal communities?

A) They create jobs for people in the area.

B) They act as natural barriers against coastal erosion.

C) They prevent fishing in coastal waters.

D) They encourage the growth of new marine species.

20. What does the passage imply about human responsibility toward coral reefs?

A) Humans must stop all activities near coral reefs to protect them.

B) Humans must take action to reduce the impact of climate change and pollution on coral reefs.

C) Humans should avoid visiting coral reefs to prevent further damage.

D) Humans are not responsible for the decline of coral reefs.

Passage 3: The Role of Bees in Agriculture

Bees play a critical role in agriculture through the process of pollination. Pollination is the act of transferring pollen from the male part of a flower to the female part, enabling plants to reproduce. Many of the fruits, vegetables, and nuts that we consume are the direct result of pollination by bees. Without bees, the production of crops like almonds, apples, and blueberries would significantly decrease, leading to higher food prices and shortages.

However, bee populations are declining worldwide, primarily due to human activities such as pesticide use, habitat destruction, and climate change. Pesticides, in particular, are harmful to bees because they can weaken their immune systems and impair their ability to forage for food. Habitat destruction further exacerbates the problem, as bees lose access to the flowers and plants they need for survival.

To address the decline of bees, some farmers are adopting sustainable agricultural practices. This includes reducing the use of harmful chemicals, planting wildflowers to provide bees with more forage, and creating bee-friendly habitats. Consumers can also play a role by supporting organic farming and reducing their use of pesticides at home.

Questions 21–30: 21. What is the main idea of the passage?
A) Bees are essential for the pollination of many crops.
B) Bees are declining due to pesticide use and habitat destruction.
C) Consumers should avoid using pesticides to help bees.
D) Bees are responsible for pollinating all plants.

22. How do bees contribute to agriculture?
A) By producing honey that farmers can sell.
B) By pollinating crops, allowing them to reproduce.
C) By eating harmful insects that damage crops.

D) By spreading seeds for new plant growth.

23. What is one reason bee populations are declining?
A) Overpopulation of bees in certain regions.
B) Pesticide use that harms their immune systems.
C) Excessive honey production.
D) The introduction of new plant species.

24. What does the word "forage" in the second paragraph most likely mean?
A) Defend
B) Search for food
C) Protect the hive
D) Collect pollen

25. According to the passage, what is one way farmers are helping to protect bees?
A) By reducing the number of crops they grow.
B) By using pesticides that are safer for bees.
C) By planting wildflowers and creating bee-friendly habitats.
D) By moving bee colonies to urban areas.

26. Why is pollination important for crops like almonds and apples?
A) It ensures that the plants

produce fruit.
B) It allows farmers to harvest honey from these crops.
C) It prevents pests from damaging the crops.
D) It encourages the growth of new flowers.

27. What does the passage imply about the future of food production without bees?
A) Food prices will increase, and shortages may occur.
B) Farmers will use machines to pollinate crops instead of bees.
C) Crops like almonds and apples will grow without bees.
D) Pesticide use will completely stop to protect bees.

28. Which of the following is NOT mentioned as a threat to bee populations?
A) Climate change
B) Pesticide use
C) Habitat destruction
D) Overharvesting of honey

29. What role can consumers play in helping to protect bees?
A) By avoiding the purchase of foods that require pollination.
B) By supporting organic farming and reducing pesticide use.
C) By planting trees that bees can use for shelter.
D) By encouraging farmers to grow fewer crops.

30. What is one benefit of creating bee-friendly habitats?
A) It allows bees to reproduce at a faster rate.
B) It provides bees with access to flowers and plants they need for food.
C) It reduces the need for pesticides in agriculture.
D) It ensures that bees only pollinate certain types of plants.

Passage 4: A New Era of Space Exploration

The 21st century has seen a resurgence of interest in space exploration, driven by advances in technology and the involvement of private companies. Space agencies like NASA, along with private companies such as SpaceX and Blue Origin, are pushing the boundaries of what is possible in space travel. Their goals include not only returning humans to the Moon but also establishing permanent colonies on Mars.

The potential benefits of space exploration are vast. For one, it could lead to the discovery of new resources that could be used on Earth, such as minerals or water from asteroids. Space exploration may also offer a solution to the overpopulation of Earth by providing new locations for human settlements. Additionally, the technologies developed for space travel often have applications in other industries, leading to advancements in fields like medicine, telecommunications, and environmental science.

Despite these potential benefits, space exploration faces significant challenges. One of the biggest hurdles is the cost— space missions are extremely expensive, and not all countries or companies have the resources to participate. There are also concerns about the environmental impact of space travel, as rockets release large amounts of carbon dioxide into the atmosphere. Nevertheless, many experts believe that the benefits outweigh the risks, and that the future of humanity may depend on our ability to explore and colonize space.

Questions 31–40:

31. What is the main idea of the passage?
A) Space exploration is becoming more feasible with the involvement of private companies.
B) Space exploration is too expensive and should not be pursued.
C) Space exploration could solve Earth's overpopulation problem.
D) Private companies are now the leaders in space exploration.

32. According to the passage, what is one potential benefit of space exploration?
A) Reducing the use of fossil fuels on Earth.
B) Finding new resources that can be used on Earth.
C) Preventing environmental disasters on Earth.
D) Lowering the cost of space travel.

33. What role do private companies like SpaceX play in space exploration?
A) They are developing new technologies and leading space missions.
B) They are working to stop governments from funding space programs.
C) They are building space colonies on Mars.
D) They are developing programs to reduce space pollution.

34. What does the word "resurgence" in the first paragraph most likely mean?
A) Decline

B) Renewal
C) Stagnation
D) Disappearance

35. What is one of the challenges facing space exploration, according to the passage?
A) Lack of interest from governments.
B) The high cost of space missions.
C) The inability to create space colonies.
D) The difficulty of traveling to the Moon.

36. Why do some experts believe space exploration is important for humanity's future?
A) It could prevent environmental disasters on Earth.
B) It could provide new locations for human settlements.
C) It could help reduce the amount of carbon dioxide in the atmosphere.
D) It could lead to a reduction in Earth's population growth.

37. What is one potential environmental concern related to space exploration?
A) Pollution caused by satellites.
B) Carbon dioxide emissions from rockets.
C) The destruction of the ozone layer.
D) The extinction of species due to space missions.

38. How might space exploration benefit industries on Earth?
A) By reducing the need for natural resources.
B) By creating new jobs in space-related fields.
C) By developing technologies that have applications in other fields.
D) By lowering the cost of production for consumer goods.

39. What does the passage suggest about the future of space exploration?
A) It is uncertain due to high costs and environmental concerns.
B) It will likely be limited to governments and large space agencies.
C) It is essential for finding new resources and solving Earth's problems.
D) It will lead to the immediate colonization of Mars.

40. What does the passage imply about the involvement of private companies in space exploration?
A) They have limited potential due to high costs.

B) They are leading the way in developing new technologies for space travel.

C) They are not as important as government space agencies.

D) They are primarily focused on tourism in space.

Passage 5: The Science of Sleep

Sleep is an essential part of human health and well-being, yet many people fail to get enough of it. Scientists have long studied the importance of sleep, and their research suggests that sleep plays a critical role in both physical and mental health. During sleep, the body repairs damaged tissues, strengthens the immune system, and consolidates memories. A lack of sleep, on the other hand, has been linked to a variety of health issues, including obesity, heart disease, and depression.

There are several stages of sleep, each with its own purpose. The two main types are rapid eye movement (REM) sleep and non-REM sleep. REM sleep is when most dreaming occurs and is important for cognitive functions like memory and learning. Non-REM sleep, which is divided into several stages, is when the body focuses on physical repair and recovery. Both types of sleep

are necessary for overall health, and disruptions in either can lead to problems like fatigue, difficulty concentrating, and mood swings.

In today's fast-paced world, many people struggle to get the recommended 7-9 hours of sleep per night. Factors like stress, work schedules, and the use of electronic devices before bed can all interfere with sleep. Experts recommend creating a bedtime routine, limiting screen time before bed, and practicing relaxation techniques to improve sleep quality.

Questions 41–50:

41. What is the main idea of the passage?

A) Sleep is necessary for both physical and mental health.

B) Sleep is divided into different stages, including REM and non-REM.

C) Most people do not get enough sleep.

D) Sleep is only important for repairing damaged tissues.

42. What happens during REM sleep?

A) The body repairs damaged tissues.

B) The immune system strengthens.

C) Most dreaming occurs.

D) The body rests without movement.

43. What does the passage suggest about the effects of sleep deprivation?
A) It is linked to a variety of health issues.
B) It causes people to sleep longer during REM sleep.
C) It improves concentration and cognitive functions.
D) It has no impact on physical health.

44. What does the word "consolidates" in the first paragraph most likely mean?
A) Weakens
B) Improves
C) Replaces
D) Combines

45. According to the passage, what is one function of non-REM sleep?
A) To help the body repair damaged tissues.
B) To allow the brain to process emotions.
C) To reduce the risk of heart disease.
D) To prevent sleep disturbances.

46. Why is it important to get both REM and non-REM sleep?
A) They are necessary for cognitive and physical health.
B) They prevent fatigue and help people concentrate.
C) They both occur during the final stages of sleep.
D) They are equally important for dreaming.

47. What are some factors that interfere with sleep, according to the passage?
A) Exercising too late in the day and eating heavy meals
B) Stress, work schedules, and the use of electronic devices
C) Overeating and lack of physical activity
D) Noise levels and sleeping in a brightly lit room

48. What does the passage imply about people's sleep habits in today's world?
A) Most people are unaware of how much sleep they need.
B) Most people prioritize sleep over other activities.
C) Many people struggle to get enough sleep due to their lifestyle.
D) Many people get more than the recommended amount of sleep.

49. What recommendation is given for improving sleep quality?

A) Increasing physical activity before bed.
B) Taking naps during the day.
C) Limiting screen time and practicing relaxation techniques.
D) Eating a large meal before bedtime.

50. What is one potential health consequence of not getting enough sleep?
    A) Improved cognitive functions
    B) Heart disease
    C) Weight loss
    D) Better memory consolidation

Passage 6: The Role of Music in Society

Throughout history, music has played an important role in society. It has been used for religious rituals, celebrations, and even to bring people together in times of hardship. Music can express emotions that words cannot, and it often reflects the cultural values and beliefs of the time.

In many cultures, music is considered an essential part of daily life. It is used to mark significant events, such as weddings, funerals, and religious ceremonies. In some societies, music is also a form of storytelling, used to pass down traditions and history from one generation to the next.

Music has also been shown to have numerous benefits for both mental and physical health. Studies have found that listening to music can reduce stress, improve mood, and even enhance cognitive functions like memory and concentration. In addition, playing a musical instrument can improve hand-eye coordination, increase creativity, and provide a sense of accomplishment.

Questions 51–62:

51. What is the main idea of the passage?
A) Music has been important throughout history for various reasons.
B) Music is primarily used in religious ceremonies.
C) Music has only recently been considered important.
D) Music is mainly used for entertainment purposes.

52. According to the passage, how has music been used throughout history?
    A) To celebrate important life events and bring people together.
    B) To teach people how to play instruments.
    C) To improve physical health

and hand-eye coordination.
D) To replace storytelling in some cultures.

53. What does the passage imply about the role of music in different cultures?
A) Music is only important in Western cultures.
B) Music is not as important in modern society as it once was.
C) Music is a central part of life in many cultures.
D) Music is only used for religious purposes.

54. How does music benefit mental health, according to the passage?
A) It improves hand-eye coordination and creativity.
B) It helps reduce stress and improves mood.
C) It prevents memory loss and concentration problems.
D) It eliminates the need for therapy in some cases.

55. What is one physical benefit of playing a musical instrument mentioned in the passage?
A) Improved cognitive functions
B) Increased sense of accomplishment
C) Better hand-eye coordination
D) Enhanced memory and concentration

56. What does the word "enhance" in the second paragraph most likely mean?
A) Reduce
B) Improve
C) Weaken
D) Diminish

57. How is music used as a form of storytelling in some cultures?
A) By recording historical events in musical form.
B) By passing down traditions and history through song.
C) By teaching younger generations how to play instruments.
D) By documenting religious ceremonies.

58. What does the passage suggest about the future of music?
A) It will continue to play an important role in society.
B) It will be replaced by more modern forms of entertainment.
C) It will become less important as technology advances.
D) It will only be used for recreational purposes.

59. How does music help bring people together, according to the passage?
A) It encourages people to listen to the same songs.

B) It is used in religious rituals and celebrations.

C) It helps people improve their memory and concentration.

D) It reduces stress and improves mental health.

60. What does the passage imply about the relationship between music and culture?

A) Music often reflects the cultural values of the time.

B) Music is always separate from the culture it originates from.

C) Music has little to no influence on culture.

D) Music is only influenced by religious beliefs.

61. What is one reason people play musical instruments, according to the passage?

A) To enhance cognitive functions.

B) To improve creativity and hand-eye coordination.

C) To replace traditional forms of entertainment.

D) To avoid the use of technology.

62. What does the passage suggest about the emotional power of music?

A) Music can express emotions that are difficult to put into words.

B) Music is mainly used to express anger and frustration.

C) Music is a source of stress and anxiety.

D) Music is often misunderstood by modern audiences.

Mathematics Subtest

Instructions

You have 45 minutes to complete 64 multiple-choice questions. Each question is followed by four possible answers. Choose the one that best fits the question. You may not use a calculator. Work carefully, but do not spend too much time on any one question. If you finish early, review your answers.

Section 1: Basic Math and Arithmetic

(Questions 1–16)

This section covers fundamental arithmetic operations, including addition, subtraction, multiplication, division, fractions, decimals, percentages, and ratios. Mastering basic math skills is essential for achieving a high score on this section. The questions will test your ability to perform quick computations accurately and assess your understanding of mathematical concepts applied to real-world scenarios.

1. What is the sum of 348 and 129?

- (A) 467
- (B) 477
- (C) 487
- (D) 497

2. Subtract 264 from 752.

- (A) 478
- (B) 488
- (C) 508
- (D) 518

3. Multiply 56 by 34.

- (A) 1,804
- (B) 1,824
- (C) 1,904
- (D) 1,924

4. Divide 1,728 by 24.

- (A) 67
- (B) 72
- (C) 77
- (D) 82

5. Convert 7/8 into a decimal.

- (A) 0.75
- (B) 0.85
- (C) 0.875

- (D) 0.925

---

6. What is 45% of 260?

- (A) 104
- (B) 117
- (C) 124
- (D) 136

---

7. Simplify the fraction 64/80.

- (A) 4/5
- (B) 3/4
- (C) 5/6
- (D) 7/8

---

8. A ratio of boys to girls in a class is 3:5. If there are 30 girls, how many boys are in the class?

- (A) 15
- (B) 18
- (C) 22
- (D) 24

---

9. Find the average of these numbers: 12, 16, 20, 24, 28.

- (A) 16
- (B) 18
- (C) 20
- (D) 22

---

10. The difference between two numbers is 39. If the larger number is 87, what is the smaller number?

- (A) 48
- (B) 49
- (C) 50
- (D) 51

---

11. If 8 bags of flour cost $96, how much does each bag cost?

- (A) $10
- (B) $12
- (C) $14
- (D) $16

---

12. A car travels 180 miles in 3 hours. What is the average speed of the car in miles per hour?

- (A) 45

- (B) 55
- (C) 60
- (D) 65

---

13. What is 20% of 450?

- (A) 80
- (B) 85
- (C) 90
- (D) 100

---

14. Simplify the expression: $7 \times (9 - 3) + 5$.

- (A) 35
- (B) 42
- (C) 47
- (D) 53

---

15. If a book is marked down by 25% and the original price was $80, what is the sale price?

- (A) $55
- (B) $60
- (C) $65
- (D) $70

---

16. Convert 0.625 to a fraction in its simplest form.

- (A) 1/2
- (B) 5/8
- (C) 3/5
- (D) 2/3

Section 2: Algebraic Concepts

(Questions 17–32)

This section focuses on algebraic concepts such as equations, inequalities, expressions, and their applications. Students must demonstrate their ability to manipulate variables and solve for unknowns in different algebraic situations. Proficiency in algebra is critical for solving both basic and advanced math problems.

17. Solve for x: $2x + 5 = 15$.

- (A) 4
- (B) 5
- (C) 6
- (D) 7

146

18. Simplify the expression: $3(2x - 4) + 6$.

- (A) $6x - 12$
- (B) $6x - 6$
- (C) $6x - 18$
- (D) $6x + 6$

19. If $3x - 7 = 11$, what is the value of x?

- (A) 4
- (B) 5
- (C) 6
- (D) 7

20. Factor the expression: $x^2 - 9$.

- (A) $(x - 3)(x + 3)$
- (B) $(x - 1)(x + 9)$
- (C) $(x + 3)(x - 1)$
- (D) $(x - 9)(x + 1)$

21. Solve for y: $4y + 3 = 19$.

- (A) 3
- (B) 4
- (C) 5

- (D) 6

22. If $2x + 3y = 12$ and $y = 2$, what is the value of x?

- (A) 3
- (B) 2
- (C) 1
- (D) 0

23. Simplify: $5x^2 - 3x + 2x^2 + x$.

- (A) $7x^2 - 2x$
- (B) $6x^2 - 2x$
- (C) $7x^2 + x$
- (D) $6x^2 + 4x$

24. Solve for x: $6x - 4 = 2x + 16$.

- (A) 3
- (B) 4
- (C) 5
- (D) 6

25. If $x + 3 = 2x - 1$, what is the value of x?

147

- (A) 1
- (B) 2
- (C) 3
- (D) 4

---

26. Simplify: $4(x - 2) + 3(2x + 1)$.

- (A) $6x + 1$
- (B) $10x - 5$
- (C) $10x - 7$
- (D) $6x - 2$

---

27. If $x^2 - 16 = 0$, what are the possible values of x?

- (A) $4, -4$
- (B) $0, 16$
- (C) $8, -8$
- (D) $16, -16$

---

28. Solve for z: $z/4 + 3 = 10$.

- (A) 24
- (B) 28
- (C) 32
- (D) 36

---

29. Which of the following is the solution to the inequality: $3x - 2 > 7$?

- (A) $x > 2$
- (B) $x > 3$
- (C) $x > 4$
- (D) $x > 5$

---

30. Simplify the expression: $(x^2 - 2x) + (3x^2 - 4x)$.

- (A) $4x^2 - 6x$
- (B) $2x^2 + 2x$
- (C) $2x^2 - 2x$
- (D) $4x^2 - 2x$

---

31. If $5x + 3y = 30$ and $y = 4$, what is the value of x?

- (A) 2
- (B) 3
- (C) 4
- (D) 5

---

32. Solve the system of equations: $2x + y = 10$ and $x - y = 4$.

- (A) (4, 2)
- (B) (3, 2)
- (C) (2, 4)
- (D) (1, 5)

Section 3: Geometry

(Questions 33–48)

This section covers geometric concepts such as shapes, angles, area, perimeter, and volume. Students will need to demonstrate their ability to apply geometric formulas and solve problems related to lines, circles, triangles, and other shapes.

33. What is the perimeter of a rectangle with a length of 10 meters and a width of 5 meters?

- (A) 20 meters
- (B) 25 meters
- (C) 30 meters
- (D) 35 meters

34. Find the area of a triangle with a base of 6 cm and a height of 4 cm.

- (A) 10 cm²
- (B) 12 cm²
- (C) 15 cm²
- (D) 18 cm²

35. What is the circumference of a circle with a radius of 7 meters? (Use $\pi = 3.14$)

- (A) 21.98 meters
- (B) 43.96 meters
- (C) 28.12 meters
- (D) 56.24 meters

36. If the measure of one angle of a right triangle is 45°, what is the measure of the other non-right angle?

- (A) 30°
- (B) 45°
- (C) 60°
- (D) 90°

37. What is the volume of a cube with a side length of 5 cm?

- (A) 25 cm³
- (B) 75 cm³
- (C) 100 cm³
- (D) 125 cm³

149

38. The diagonals of a square are equal and intersect at right angles. If the length of a diagonal is 10 cm, what is the length of one side of the square?

- (A) 5 cm
- (B) 7.07 cm
- (C) 10 cm
- (D) 14.14 cm

39. In a parallelogram, one angle measures 70°. What is the measure of the adjacent angle?

- (A) 70°
- (B) 90°
- (C) 110°
- (D) 120°

40. What is the area of a circle with a diameter of 14 meters? (Use $\pi = 3.14$)

- (A) 153.86 m²
- (B) 86.78 m²
- (C) 49.2 m²
- (D) 74.78 m²

41. Find the volume of a rectangular prism with a length of 12 cm, width of 8 cm, and height of 5 cm.

- (A) 200 cm³
- (B) 320 cm³
- (C) 400 cm³
- (D) 480 cm³

42. If two angles of a triangle measure 60° and 45°, what is the measure of the third angle?

- (A) 25°
- (B) 35°
- (C) 45°
- (D) 75°

43. A square has an area of 49 cm². What is the length of one side?

- (A) 5 cm
- (B) 6 cm
- (C) 7 cm
- (D) 8 cm

44. What is the measure of each interior angle of a regular hexagon?

150

- (A) 108°

- (B) 120°

- (C) 135°

- (D) 150°

---

45. Find the area of a trapezoid with bases of 10 cm and 6 cm, and a height of 4 cm.

- (A) 32 cm²

- (B) 40 cm²

- (C) 64 cm²

- (D) 80 cm²

---

46. What is the perimeter of a triangle with sides measuring 6 cm, 8 cm, and 10 cm?

- (A) 20 cm

- (B) 22 cm

- (C) 24 cm

- (D) 26 cm

---

47. The sum of the angles in a quadrilateral is:

- (A) 180°

- (B) 270°

- (C) 360°

- (D) 540°

---

48. What is the area of a rectangle with a length of 8 meters and a width of 3 meters?

- (A) 18 m²

- (B) 21 m²

- (C) 24 m²

- (D) 27 m²

Section 4: Advanced Math and Word Problems

(Questions 49–64)

This final section assesses your ability to solve more complex mathematical problems, including algebraic word problems, advanced computations, and applied math concepts. You will need to interpret data, apply formulas, and use logical reasoning to solve these problems.

49. A car travels 240 miles on 8 gallons of gas. How many miles can it travel on 5 gallons of gas?

- (A) 120 miles

- (B) 140 miles

- (C) 150 miles

- (D) 160 miles

---

50. If a train travels 60 miles per hour for 5 hours, how far does it travel?

- (A) 250 miles
- (B) 300 miles
- (C) 350 miles
- (D) 400 miles

---

51. A room is 12 feet long, 10 feet wide, and 8 feet high. What is the volume of the room?

- (A) 320 cubic feet
- (B) 760 cubic feet
- (C) 960 cubic feet
- (D) 1,120 cubic feet

---

52. A store sells 3 bags of rice for $12.50. How much would 5 bags cost?

- (A) $15.50
- (B) $18.00
- (C) $20.83
- (D) $25.00

---

53. The ratio of dogs to cats in a shelter is 5:7. If there are 35 dogs, how many cats are there?

- (A) 25
- (B) 45
- (C) 49
- (D) 55

---

54. A bag contains 6 red marbles, 8 blue marbles, and 4 green marbles. What is the probability of selecting a blue marble?

- (A) 1/3
- (B) 1/2
- (C) 2/3
- (D) 3/4

---

55. The average of four test scores is 78. If the scores are 72, 80, and 85, what is the fourth score?

- (A) 74
- (B) 76
- (C) 78
- (D) 80

---

56. A school orders 200 calculators at $12 each. What is the total cost?

- (A) $1,400
- (B) $2,000
- (C) $2,400
- (D) $2,600

57. If 5 pencils cost $1.75, how much would 15 pencils cost?

- (A) $3.25
- (B) $4.50
- (C) $5.25
- (D) $5.75

58. A pizza shop sells a large pizza for $14.95. If the price increases by 20%, what will be the new price?

- (A) $16.95
- (B) $17.50
- (C) $17.94
- (D) $18.99

59. A garden measures 12 meters by 8 meters. What is the perimeter of the garden?

- (A) 20 meters
- (B) 24 meters
- (C) 32 meters
- (D) 40 meters

60. A rectangle has a length of 15 inches and a width of 6 inches. What is its area?

- (A) 45 square inches
- (B) 60 square inches
- (C) 75 square inches
- (D) 90 square inches

61. If you buy 3 shirts for $24.00, how much does one shirt cost?

- (A) $6.00
- (B) $7.00
- (C) $8.00
- (D) $9.00

62. A plane flies 500 miles in 2 hours. What is its average speed?

- (A) 150 mph
- (B) 200 mph
- (C) 225 mph

- (D) 250 mph

---

63. A class of 20 students has an average test score of 85. If one student scored 95, what is the new class average?

- (A) 85.5
- (B) 86.0
- (C) 86.5
- (D) 87.0

---

64. A store offers a 10% discount on a $50 purchase. What is the final price after the discount?

- (A) $40.00
- (B) $42.50
- (C) $45.00
- (D) $47.50

Language Subtest

Instructions: You have 25 minutes to complete 60 questions. For each question, select the best answer from the choices provided. Do not spend too much time on any one question.

Part 1: Capitalization

1. Which sentence uses capitalization correctly?

a) My Aunt Susan is coming to visit.

b) We went to the empire state building last weekend.

c) The mayor of chicago gave a speech.

d) The French teacher assigned us extra homework.

2. Select the sentence with proper capitalization.

a) The president of our club is Jake miller.

b) Have you read the novel "to kill a mockingbird"?

c) We visited Yosemite national park during summer vacation.

d) Dr. Franklin will see patients starting at 8:00 AM.

3. Choose the sentence that has correct capitalization.

a) On friday, the band will play a concert at Jefferson high school.

b) My family loves celebrating Thanksgiving in New york City.

c) The statue of Liberty is located on Liberty island.

d) We're going to visit Uncle Steve in texas this summer.

4. Identify the sentence with proper capitalization.

a) My father works as a Doctor in Boston.

b) Mrs. jones, the Math teacher, is organizing a field trip.

c) The Fourth of July parade is a big event in our town.

d) We are going to the South to visit relatives.

5. Which sentence is capitalized correctly?

a) The Dean of students spoke at graduation.

b) I took a trip to see the Pacific Ocean and Mount Rushmore.

c) She majored in History and Political Science in college.

d) We went shopping on elm street last Saturday.

Part 2: Punctuation

6. Which sentence uses punctuation correctly?

a) My favorite subjects in school are math, history, and, science.

b) On Wednesday, we will have a test, in both English and science.

c) We plan to visit Grandma's house on Saturday; the weather looks nice.

d) Do you know how to bake a cake? the recipe looks simple.

7. Select the sentence with correct punctuation.

a) "Can we go to the park after school"? asked Sarah.

b) The library closes at 5:00 p.m. on weekdays.

c) Tom asked "how long will the meeting last?"

d) The students brought pencils, notebooks, and lunchboxes, to school.

8. Choose the sentence that has proper punctuation.

a) My sister plays piano, guitar, and drums.

b) Let's invite, Jane, Emily, and Ben to the party.

c) Please bring the following: apples oranges and bananas.

d) He asked, "Where is the nearest bus stop?"

9. Identify the sentence with correct punctuation.

a) We're planning a trip to Washington, D.C. in April.

b) "I can't wait to see the movie"! exclaimed David.

c) The concert starts at 7:00, so we should leave by 6:00 PM.

d) My cousin lives in Denver Colorado, and she's visiting soon.

10. Which sentence uses punctuation correctly?

a) Let's meet at the café, it's next to the bookstore.

b) Mrs. Smith asked, "Who is ready for recess?"

c) We'll need to buy bread milk and eggs from the store.

d) He didn't know, however where his keys were.

Part 3: Usage

11. Which sentence uses the word correctly?

a) She tried to illicit a response from the crowd.

b) The principle of the school welcomed the students.

c) I have never eaten fewer cookies in one sitting.

d) They're going to the store later today.

12. Select the sentence with correct word usage.

a) The dessert was very dry, so I drank less water.

b) It's important to choose the right coarse for your education.

c) You're going to the football game, aren't you?

d) I can't except your apology until I've calmed down.

13. Choose the sentence with proper word usage.

a) The dog wagged it's tail happily.

b) Who's house are we going to after school?

c) The children had less toys to play with than expected.

d) Its raining, so we should bring umbrellas.

14. Identify the sentence with correct usage.

a) The teams strategy was flawed from the start.

b) She should of studied more for the test.

c) I feel bad about not calling you yesterday.

d) He could have ran faster if he practiced more.

15. Which sentence uses the word correctly?

a) The affect of the rain was felt across the city.

b) The results of the study were accurate.

c) Please bring you're homework to class.

d) I should of known better than to trust him.

Part 4: Sentence Structure

16. Which sentence is structured correctly?

a) Running quickly down the hall, the teacher's scolding could be heard.

b) After the meeting, we discussed the proposal and made changes.

c) The children, playing in the park, they saw a squirrel.

d) Fixing the car, the mechanic was the tires rotated.

17. Select the sentence with correct sentence structure.

a) We had fun at the zoo, and seeing all the animals was great.

b) I love reading books, I finish at least one a week.

c) Because it was raining, and we stayed indoors.

d) The flowers blooming, it looked beautiful in the garden.

18. Choose the sentence that has proper structure.

a) Despite the long journey, we arrived on time.

b) To get to the store, walking down the street was necessary.

c) The assignment was difficult, but finishing it took less time.

d) Although it was late, we still went to bed early.

19. Identify the sentence with correct sentence structure.

a) Since she was late, finishing the project was a challenge.

b) Opening the door, the house was cold and empty.

c) We enjoy swimming, and love hiking on the weekends.

d) She was hungry, but deciding what to eat was difficult.

20. Which sentence is structured correctly?

a) The report was submitted, because it was due today.

b) They enjoyed the game, winning was a great feeling.

c) After eating dinner, we cleaned the kitchen.

d) The cake was delicious, baking it took hours.

Part 5: Spelling

21. Which word is spelled correctly?

a) recieve

b) accomodate

c) embarass

d) recommend

22. Select the correct spelling.

a) definate

b) freind

c) separate

d) occurr

23. Choose the correctly spelled word.

a) committe

b) maintenance

c) accomodation

d) harrass

24. Identify the word spelled correctly.

a) embarrasment

b) priviledge

c) conscience

d) concieve

25. Which word is spelled correctly?

a) suprise

b) independant

c) grateful

d) responsability

Part 6: Composition

26. Which sentence is composed correctly?

a) I went to the store, but forgot to buy milk.

b) He didn't do his homework, and went to bed early.

c) After running five miles, and feeling exhausted.

d) The dog barked all night, which made it difficult to sleep.

27. Select the sentence that is composed properly.

a) She decided to study more, therefore her grades improved.

b) Because the movie was sold out, we went to the park instead.

c) The cake was delicious, and baking it was fun, however.

d) To learn new skills, it is important practicing every day.

28. Choose the correctly composed sentence.

a) The sun was setting quickly, we took photos.

b) John loves to read books, his favorite are mystery novels.

c) After the concert ended, we went out for dinner.

d) Finishing the assignment took hours, but still worth it.

29. Identify the sentence that is composed correctly.

a) The students were tired after class, but still had energy for practice.

b) The weather was rainy, despite we went to the game.

c) The teacher gave us extra homework, since we asked questions.

d) It was sunny outside, yet we decided to stay indoors.

30. Which sentence is composed correctly?

a) The car broke down, because we forgot to fill it with gas.

b) Even though it was cold, we wore jackets.

c) We wanted to stay up late, however we were too tired.

d) The project was complicated, but we finished early.

Part 7: Subject-Verb Agreement

31. Which sentence has correct subject-verb agreement?

a) The dogs barks loudly at night.

b) The team plays every Saturday afternoon.

c) Everyone are going to the festival this weekend.

d) My friends has decided to start a band.

32. Select the sentence with proper subject-verb agreement.

a) Neither of the boys are coming to the party.

b) Each of the players have their own uniform.

c) The book on the table belongs to her.

d) The group of students were late for class.

33. Choose the sentence that has correct subject-verb agreement.

a) The cake and the cookies is ready to eat.

b) The list of names are on the desk.

c) Both of my sisters is planning to visit.

d) The teacher, along with the students, is preparing for the play.

34. Identify the sentence with proper subject-verb agreement.

a) My mom, as well as my dad, love cooking dinner.

b) The cats and the dog needs to be fed.

c) Either John or Lisa have the tickets.

d) Each of the girls is bringing a gift.

35. Which sentence uses subject-verb agreement correctly?

a) The trees in the park was beautiful.

b) Neither of them is available today.

c) The shoes on the floor needs to be cleaned.

d) My brother and I is going to the concert.

Part 8: Pronoun-Antecedent Agreement

36. Which sentence uses pronoun-antecedent agreement correctly?

a) Each student must bring their own lunch.

b) The dog loves to chase its tail.

c) All of the teachers gave her homework.

d) Every employee is required to submit their timesheet.

37. Select the sentence with correct pronoun-antecedent agreement.

a) Everyone must do their own work.

b) The class turned in their assignments on time.

c) The child needs to bring their toy.

d) The committee gave its approval for the event.

38. Choose the sentence with proper pronoun-antecedent agreement.

a) Every member of the team has their own locker.

b) The students finished their test early.

c) The jury made their decision quickly.

d) Each of the boys forgot their jacket.

39. Identify the sentence with correct pronoun-antecedent agreement.

a) Someone left their bag in the hallway.

b) The company is preparing their annual report.

c) Each student is responsible for his or her own project.

d) Neither of the managers submitted their report.

40. Which sentence uses pronoun-antecedent agreement correctly?

a) Anybody can turn in their form at the office.

b) The family finished their vacation.

c) Each dog has its own kennel.

d) Both of the girls is preparing their speech.

Part 9: Parallel Structure

41. Which sentence has correct parallel structure?

a) She enjoys swimming, running, and to hike.

b) He likes reading books, watching movies, and playing games.

c) They are going shopping, to the park, and visited a museum.

d) I enjoy cooking, cleaning, and to organize.

42. Select the sentence with correct parallel structure.

a) The students were excited about winning the game, receiving their trophy, and to celebrate.

b) We planned to visit the museum, explore the city, and eating at a restaurant.

c) Sarah loves baking cakes, painting pictures, and to travel.

d) He enjoys hiking, camping, and fishing.

43. Choose the sentence with proper parallel structure.

a) The teacher asked us to finish our work, clean the classroom, and to submit the homework.

b) The class is focusing on reading, writing, and speaking.

c) I like to jog, biking, and to swim.

d) They went shopping, cooked dinner, and visiting a friend.

44. Identify the sentence with correct parallel structure.

a) The concert was exciting, fun, and it was loud.

b) We visited the museum, walked around the park, and taking pictures.

c) He spends his weekends hiking, fishing, and camping.

d) She is studying for exams, reading novels, and to practice piano.

45. Which sentence has correct parallel structure?

a) They like swimming, running, and to ride bikes.

b) I enjoy cooking, baking, and to clean.

c) He spends his time reading, writing, and learning.

d) She likes to paint, draw, and hiking.

Part 10: Modifier Placement

46. Which sentence uses modifiers correctly?

a) Walking through the park, the trees were beautiful.

b) While eating lunch, the phone rang.

c) She read the book slowly, enjoying every word.

d) After baking all day, the cake was delicious.

47. Select the sentence with correct modifier placement.

a) The cat, resting in the sun, was purring happily.

b) To finish quickly, the homework was rushed.

c) Driving down the road, the mountain looked beautiful.

d) After finishing the report, the computer crashed.

48. Choose the sentence with proper modifier placement.

a) Reading the instructions, the task became easier.

b) While shopping, my wallet fell out of my pocket.

c) After swimming, the towel was warm.

d) Jogging every morning, the park became my favorite place.

49. Identify the sentence with correct modifier placement.

a) Waiting at the bus stop, the weather was cold.

b) Carefully studying the map, the directions were clear.

c) Listening to music, the homework was finished quickly.

d) Running down the street, I saw my friend.

50. Which sentence uses modifiers correctly?

a) Looking out the window, the snow was falling.

b) After cleaning the house, the dog was tired.

c) Waving goodbye, the car drove away.

d) Jumping over the fence, the dog barked loudly.

Part 11: Dangling Modifiers

51. Which sentence avoids a dangling modifier?

a) Hoping for a better grade, the exam was studied for all night.

b) After cleaning the kitchen, the floors were shiny.

c) While practicing piano, the doorbell rang.

d) Having finished the project, I took a break.

52. Select the sentence that avoids a dangling modifier.

a) After reading the book, the test was easy.

b) While jogging, the sun was shining brightly.

c) To finish the assignment, more time was needed.

d) Feeling tired, I decided to take a nap.

53. Choose the sentence that avoids a dangling modifier.

a) Running late, the bus had already left.

b) Having completed the homework, the movie was started.

c) After finishing the test, I felt relieved.

d) While waiting for the bus, my phone rang.

54. Identify the sentence that avoids a dangling modifier.

a) After cleaning the kitchen, the dishes were spotless.

b) Walking to the park, the flowers looked beautiful.

c) Studying for the test, the material became clearer.

d) Feeling confident, I took the exam.

55. Which sentence avoids a dangling modifier?

a) Having lost the keys, the door wouldn't open.

b) After finishing dinner, the dishes were washed.

c) Practicing for hours, the routine was perfected.

d) Watching the sunset, I felt peaceful.

Part 12: Sentence Combining

56. Combine the sentences for the most effective structure:

The team practiced every day. The team won the championship.

a) Practicing every day, the team won the championship.

b) The team, practicing every day, won the championship.

c) Practicing every day, won the championship.

165

d) The team, practicing, every day, won the championship.

57. Combine the sentences for the most effective structure:

He loves playing basketball. He also enjoys swimming.

a) He loves playing basketball, also enjoys swimming.

b) He loves playing basketball, and swimming is enjoyable.

c) He loves playing basketball and enjoys swimming.

d) Playing basketball is loved, and swimming is enjoyed by him.

58. Combine the sentences for the most effective structure:

The flowers bloomed early. The garden looked beautiful.

a) The flowers bloomed early, the garden looked beautiful.

b) The flowers bloomed early, making the garden look beautiful.

c) The garden looked beautiful because the flowers bloomed early.

d) The flowers bloomed early, so beautiful was the garden.

59. Combine the sentences for the most effective structure:

He studied hard for the test. He got an A on the exam.

a) He studied hard for the test, and got an A on the exam.

b) He studied hard, and he got an A on the test.

c) He got an A on the exam because he studied hard.

d) Studying hard for the test, got an A on the exam.

60. Combine the sentences for the most effective structure:

She loves to bake. She makes cookies every weekend.

166

a) She loves to bake and makes cookies every weekend.

b) She loves to bake cookies and every weekend.

c) Baking is loved by her, and cookies are made every weekend.

d) She makes cookies every weekend and loves to bake.

Answer Key and Detailed Explanations

Verbal Skills Subtest

Part 1: Synonyms (Questions 1-16)

1. **Exhaust**
   Answer: (b) Deplete
   Explanation: "Exhaust" means to use up resources or energy. "Deplete" is the closest synonym, meaning to reduce in quantity or exhaust a supply.

2. **Imminent**
   Answer: (c) Forthcoming
   Explanation: "Imminent" means something that is about to happen. "Forthcoming" carries a similar meaning, indicating that something is approaching or about to occur.

3. **Avid**
   Answer: (b) Eager
   Explanation: "Avid" means having a keen interest in something or being enthusiastic.

"Eager" is a synonym that reflects excitement or enthusiasm.

4. **Detrimental**
   Answer: (b) Harmful
   Explanation: "Detrimental" refers to something that causes harm or damage. "Harmful" is the closest synonym.

5. **Perpetual**
   Answer: (b) Continuous
   Explanation: "Perpetual" means never-ending or ongoing. "Continuous" shares the same meaning, implying an action without interruption.

6. **Conventional**
   Answer: (b) Customary
   Explanation: "Conventional" refers to something that is traditional or usual. "Customary" similarly refers to practices that are typical or common.

7. **Benevolent**
   Answer: (b) Kind
   Explanation: "Benevolent" means well-meaning or kind.

"Kind" is the direct synonym, meaning caring or good-hearted.

8. **Frivolous**
   Answer: (c) Unimportant
   Explanation: "Frivolous" refers to something lacking in seriousness or importance. "Unimportant" conveys a lack of significance.

9. **Adorn**
   Answer: (b) Decorate
   Explanation: "Adorn" means to enhance or beautify something, typically by adding decorations. "Decorate" is the synonym, meaning to embellish.

10. **Inadvertent**
    Answer: (a) Unintentional
    Explanation: "Inadvertent" means something done accidentally or unintentionally. "Unintentional" shares the same meaning.

11. **Futile**
    Answer: (b) Useless
    Explanation: "Futile" means having no useful result or being ineffective. "Useless" is a synonym that reflects the lack of utility or purpose.

12. **Ominous**
    Answer: (b) Threatening
    Explanation: "Ominous" refers to something that suggests bad things will happen. "Threatening" indicates an impending danger or harm.

13. **Lucid**
    Answer: (b) Clear
    Explanation: "Lucid" means easy to understand or transparent. "Clear" reflects this straightforwardness in meaning.

14. **Conceal**
    Answer: (b) Hide
    Explanation: "Conceal" means to prevent something from being seen or known. "Hide" is the direct synonym, meaning to keep something out of sight.

15. **Inhibit**
    Answer: (b) Prevent
    Explanation: "Inhibit" refers to restricting or preventing something from happening. "Prevent" conveys the same meaning.

16. **Apathetic**
    Answer: (b) Unconcerned
    Explanation: "Apathetic" means lacking interest or emotion. "Unconcerned" similarly reflects a lack of care or involvement.

Part 2: Antonyms (Questions 17-30)

17. **Abundant**

    Answer: (a) Scarce
    Explanation: "Abundant" means present in large quantities. The opposite of abundance is scarcity, so "scarce" is the correct answer.

18. **Relinquish**

    Answer: (b) Hold
    Explanation: "Relinquish" means to give up or surrender. The antonym is "hold," which means to keep or retain something.

19. **Subtle**

    Answer: (a) Obvious
    Explanation: "Subtle" refers to something delicate or understated. The opposite is "obvious," which means something clear or easily noticed.

20. **Vague**

    Answer: (a) Clear
    Explanation: "Vague" means unclear or ambiguous. The opposite is "clear," which means easily understood.

21. **Commend**

    Answer: (b) Criticize
    Explanation: "Commend" means to praise or compliment. The opposite is "criticize," meaning to find fault or express disapproval.

22. **Timid**

    Answer: (a) Bold
    Explanation: "Timid" means shy or fearful. The antonym is "bold," which refers to someone who is confident and daring.

23. **Enhance**

    Answer: (a) Diminish
    Explanation: "Enhance" means to improve or increase something. The opposite is "diminish," meaning to reduce or lessen in value.

24. **Rigid**

    Answer: (a) Flexible
    Explanation: "Rigid" refers to something stiff or unyielding. The antonym is "flexible," which means capable of bending or adapting.

25. **Solitary**

    Answer: (b) Social
    Explanation: "Solitary" means being alone or isolated. The opposite is "social," which means enjoying company and interaction with others.

26. **Provoke**

    Answer: (b) Calm
    Explanation: "Provoke" means

to incite or stimulate a reaction. The antonym is "calm," which refers to making someone peaceful or tranquil.

27. **Diligent**

    Answer: (a) Lazy
    Explanation: "Diligent" refers to showing care and perseverance. The opposite is "lazy," meaning unwilling to work hard.

28. **Detest**

    Answer: (a) Love
    Explanation: "Detest" means to hate or loathe. The antonym is "love," meaning to have a deep affection for something or someone.

29. **Innocuous**

    Answer: (a) Harmful
    Explanation: "Innocuous" means harmless or inoffensive. The opposite is "harmful," meaning something that can cause damage.

30. **Obscure**

    Answer: (a) Reveal
    Explanation: "Obscure" means to hide or make something unclear. The antonym is "reveal," which means to make something known or visible.

Part 3: Analogies (Questions 31-45)

31. **Bridge is to river as tunnel is to:**
    Answer: (b) Mountain
    Explanation: A bridge crosses over a river, while a tunnel passes through a mountain. The relationship is one of structure over or through a natural formation.

32. **Glove is to hand as sock is to:**
    Answer: (a) Foot
    Explanation: A glove covers the hand, and a sock covers the foot. The relationship is one of covering a part of the body.

33. **Oven is to bake as stove is to:**
    Answer: (b) Cook
    Explanation: An oven is used for baking, and a stove is used for cooking. The relationship is one of an appliance and its function.

34. **Artist is to painting as chef is to:**
    Answer: (a) Food
    Explanation: An artist creates paintings, and a chef prepares food. The relationship is one of a creator and their product.

35. **Pencil is to write as scissors are to:**
    Answer: (a) Cut
    Explanation: A pencil is used for writing, and scissors are used for

cutting. The relationship is one of a tool and its function.

36. **Wing is to bird as fin is to:**
Answer: (a) Fish
Explanation: A wing helps a bird fly, and a fin helps a fish swim. The relationship is one of body parts that assist in movement.

37. **Key is to lock as password is to:**
Answer: (d) Door
Explanation: A key unlocks a lock, and a password unlocks access (such as to a door or digital space). The relationship is one of security access.

38. **Ear is to hear as eye is to:**
Answer: (a) See
Explanation: The ear is the organ used to hear, and the eye is the organ used to see. The relationship is one of sensory organs and their functions.

39. **Lawyer is to courtroom as teacher is to:**
Answer: (b) School
Explanation: A lawyer works in a courtroom, and a teacher works in a school. The relationship is one of profession and place of work.

40. **Dog is to bark as cat is to:**
Answer: (c) Meow
Explanation: A dog barks, and a cat meows. The relationship is one of animal and its vocalization.

41. **Battery is to energy as pen is to:**
Answer: (b) Ink
Explanation: A battery provides energy, and a pen contains ink. The relationship is one of supplying a substance or resource.

42. **Morning is to dawn as night is to:**
Answer: (c) Midnight
Explanation: Morning begins with dawn, and night peaks with midnight. The relationship is one of times during different parts of the day.

43. **Library is to books as museum is to:**
Answer: (a) Artifacts
Explanation: A library contains books, and a museum contains artifacts. The relationship is one of places and the objects they house.

44. **Pen is to ink as brush is to:**
Answer: (a) Paint
Explanation: A pen uses ink, and a brush uses paint. The relationship is one of tools and the materials they use.

45. **Page is to book as leaf is to:**
Answer: (a) Tree

Explanation: A page is part of a book, and a leaf is part of a tree. The relationship is one of components belonging to a larger structure.

Part 4: Verbal Classifications (Questions 46-55)

46. **(a) Apple (b) Banana (c) Carrot (d)   Orange**
    Answer: (c)   Carrot
    Explanation: Apples, bananas, and oranges are all fruits, while a carrot is a vegetable, making it the odd one out.

47. **(a) Bus (b) Airplane (c) Bicycle (d)   Car**
    Answer: (c)   Bicycle
    Explanation: A bus, airplane, and car are motorized vehicles, while a bicycle is human-powered, making it different from the others.

48. **(a) Desk (b) Chair (c) Book (d) Table**
    Answer: (c)   Book
    Explanation: A desk, chair, and table are pieces of furniture, whereas a book is a reading material, not furniture.

49. **(a) Cat (b) Dog (c) Parrot (d) Tiger**
    Answer: (d)   Tiger
    Explanation: Cats, dogs, and parrots are common domestic animals, while a tiger is a wild animal, making it the odd one out.

50. **(a) Doctor (b) Teacher (c) Engineer (d)   Recipe**
    Answer: (d)   Recipe
    Explanation: A doctor, teacher, and engineer are professions, whereas a recipe is not a profession, making it different.

51. **(a) Pencil (b) Marker (c) Crayon (d)   Notebook**
    Answer: (d)   Notebook
    Explanation: A pencil, marker, and crayon are writing or drawing instruments, while a notebook is an item used for writing, not a tool itself.

52. **(a) Triangle (b) Square (c) Circle (d)   Line**
    Answer: (d)   Line
    Explanation: A triangle, square, and circle are shapes with enclosed areas, while a line is not an enclosed shape.

53. **(a) Moon (b) Star (c) Sun (d) Comet**
    Answer: (d)   Comet
    Explanation: The moon, star, and sun are celestial bodies that are constant in the sky, while a comet

appears only periodically, making it the odd one out.

54. **(a) Rose (b) Tulip (c) Grass (d) Daisy**
Answer: (c) Grass
Explanation: A rose, tulip, and daisy are all flowering plants, whereas grass is not typically considered a flowering plant, making it different.

55. **(a) Violin (b) Guitar (c) Trumpet (d) Drum**
Answer: (c) Trumpet
Explanation: The violin, guitar, and drum are either string or percussion instruments, while the trumpet is a brass instrument, making it the odd one out.

Part 5: Verbal Logic (Questions 56-60)

56. **All lions are animals. All animals have four legs. Therefore, all lions have four legs.**
Answer: (a) True
Explanation: The premise states that all animals have four legs, and since lions are animals, they must also have four legs, making the conclusion logically true based on the given statements.

57. **Some birds can fly. Penguins are birds. Therefore, penguins can fly.**
Answer: (b) False
Explanation: While some birds can fly, penguins are an exception. Therefore, the conclusion that penguins can fly is false.

58. **All teachers are educated. Some educated people are doctors. Therefore, some teachers are doctors.**
Answer: (c) Uncertain
Explanation: The premises don't provide enough information to confirm whether some teachers are also doctors. The conclusion is uncertain because we can't definitively say that teachers overlap with doctors based solely on the given information.

59. **All squares have four sides. Some four-sided shapes are rectangles. Therefore, some squares are rectangles.**
Answer: (b) False
Explanation: Although both squares and rectangles have four sides, they are distinct shapes. A square is not a rectangle, making the conclusion false.

60. **All pencils are writing tools. Some writing tools are pens. Therefore, some pencils are pens.**
    Answer: (b) False

Quantitative Skills Subtest

Sequences (Questions 1–15)

1. **A)** The sequence increases by 3 each time. $11 + 3 = 14$

2. **D)** This is the Fibonacci sequence. Each number is the sum of the two preceding numbers. $5 + 8 = 13$

3. **B)** The sequence increases by 3 each time. $21 + 3 = 24$

4. **C)** Each number is double the previous one. $40 \times 2 = 80$

5. **A)** The sequence decreases by 10 each time. $70 - 10 = 60$

6. **B)** These are the squares of the natural numbers. $1^2 = 1, 2^2 = 4, 3^2 = 9, 4^2 = 16, 5^2 = 25$

7. **C)** The sequence increases by 11 each time. $44 + 11 = 55$

8. **C)** Each number is the previous number plus an increasing even number. $2 + 4 = 6, 6 + 6 = 12, 12 + 8 = 20, 20 + 10 = 30$

Explanation: Although both pencils and pens are writing tools, a pencil cannot be a pen, as they are different items. Therefore, the conclusion is false.

9. **A)** The difference between consecutive numbers increases by 1 each time. $1 + 1 = 2, 2 + 2 = 4, 4 + 3 = 7 .... 16 + 6 = 22$

10. **B)** The pattern alternates between halving the previous number and then adding 1. $10 / 2 = 5, 5 + 1 = 6, 6 / 2 = 3, 3 + 1 = 4 ... 2 + 1 = 3$

11. **C)** Each number is double the previous one. $48 \times 2 = 96$

12. **A)** The sequence decreases by 2 each time. $3 - 2 = 1$

13. **B)** The sequence increases by 50 each time. $250 + 50 = 300$

14. **B)** Each number is the previous number doubled and then plus 1. $(1 \times 2) + 1 = 3, (3 \times 2) + 1 = 7 ... (15 \times 2) + 1 = 31$

15. **C)** Each number is double the previous one. $64 \times 2 = 128$

Comparisons (Questions 16–30)

16. **B)**

- $5^{25} = 298023223876953125$

- $4^{34} = 251 ..... $ lot larger number

17. **A)**
- $75 \div 3 = 25$
- $5 \times 5 = 25$

18. **A)**
- $48 \div 8 = 6$
- $7 + 4 = 11$

19. **A)**
- $9^2 = 81$
- $8 \times 12 = 96$

20. **B)**
- 125% of $100 = 125$
- 150% of $80 = 120$

21. **A)**
- $3^{33} = ...$very large number
- $30 \div 3 \times 3 = 30$

22. **A)** 0.45 is smaller than 0.5

23. **B)**
- $3/4 = 0.75$
- $5/6 = 0.8333...$

24. **A)**
- $0.2 \times 10 = 2$
- $0.4 \times 5 = 2$

25. **A)**
- $1/2 \div 1/4 = 1/2 * 4/1 = 2$
- $1/4 \times 2 = 1/2$

26. **B)**
- 30% of $400 = 120$
- 25% of $500 = 125$

27. **B)**
- $10 \times 3^2 = 10 \times 9 = 90$
- $9 \times 4^2 = 9 \times 16 = 144$

28. **A)**
- 4.5
- $7/2 = 3.5$

29. **A)**
- $25 \times 1.5 = 37.5$
- $20 \times 2 = 40$

30. **A)**
- 75% of $160 = 120$
- 50% of $260 = 130$

Computations (Questions 31-52)

31. 78

32. 60

33. 60

34. 24

35. 355

175

36. 48

37. 312

38. 27

39. 80

40. 20

41. 15

42. 95

43. 100

44. 90

45. 641

46. 60

47. 16

48. 60

49. 240

50. 533

51. 180

52. 50

Reading Subtest

Passage 1: History of the Printing Press (Questions 1-10)

1. **What is the main idea of the passage?**
   Answer: (B) The printing press made books more affordable and accessible.
   Explanation: While the passage mentions other aspects of the printing press, its main focus is on how Gutenberg's invention revolutionized book production and accessibility, making knowledge available to a broader audience.

2. **According to the passage, what was one of the earliest books printed by Gutenberg?**

Answer: (C) The Gutenberg Bible
Explanation: The passage explicitly mentions that one of the earliest books printed by Gutenberg's press was the Gutenberg Bible, which is regarded as a masterpiece.

3. **How did the printing press affect the spread of ideas in Europe?**
   Answer: (C) It made it easier to distribute ideas and information.
   Explanation: The passage describes how the printing press facilitated the spread of knowledge, ideas, and information across Europe, which was one of its most profound effects.

4. **What role did the printing press play in the Protestant Reformation?**
Answer: (B) It helped distribute the 95 Theses and encourage religious debate.
Explanation: The passage states that the printing press played a key role in distributing Martin Luther's 95 Theses, which sparked religious debate and reform.

5. **What does the word "profound" in the second paragraph most likely mean?**
Answer: (A) Deep
Explanation: In the context of the passage, "profound" refers to the deep and significant impact the printing press had on society.

6. **Why does the author mention the Renaissance in the passage?**
Answer: (A) To show how Gutenberg influenced education.
Explanation: The passage explains that the printing press contributed to the Renaissance by making classical texts more widely available, thus promoting education and intellectual discourse.

7. **Which of the following is NOT mentioned as an effect of the printing press?**
Answer: (D) The invention of the steam engine
Explanation: The passage does not mention the invention of the steam engine as an effect of the printing press. The other choices are all discussed.

8. **What does the passage suggest about the availability of books before the printing press?**
Answer: (B) Books were rare and only accessible to the wealthy elite.
Explanation: The passage states that before the printing press, books were copied by hand, making them rare and limited to the elite.

9. **How did the printing press influence the Renaissance?**
Answer: (A) By reducing the cost of books and promoting access to classical texts.
Explanation: The passage explains that the printing press made classical texts more widely available, which helped fuel the intellectual and educational aspects of the Renaissance.

10. **What was one reason the Gutenberg Bible is still regarded as a masterpiece?**

Answer: (C) It demonstrated the craftsmanship and innovation of early printing.
Explanation: The passage refers to the Gutenberg Bible as a masterpiece because of its craftsmanship and the innovative technology used to produce it.

Passage 2: The Ecology of Coral Reefs (Questions 11-20)

11. **What is the main idea of the passage?**
    Answer: (A) Coral reefs are at risk due to human activities.
    Explanation: The passage discusses how human activities such as overfishing, pollution, and climate change are threatening coral reefs, which is the central theme.

12. **What is coral bleaching?**
    Answer: (B) When algae are expelled from coral due to rising ocean temperatures.
    Explanation: The passage defines coral bleaching as the process where symbiotic algae are expelled from coral due to rising ocean temperatures, leading to coral death.

13. **According to the passage, why are coral reefs important to marine life?**
    Answer: (B) They provide essential habitats for a wide variety of species.
    Explanation: The passage mentions that coral reefs provide habitats for thousands of species, making them essential for marine biodiversity.

14. **What does the word "symbiotic" in the second paragraph most likely mean?**
    Answer: (B) Beneficial
    Explanation: In the context of the relationship between coral polyps and algae, "symbiotic" means mutually beneficial, as the algae help the coral and vice versa.

15. **How are coral reefs being protected?**
    Answer: (B) By creating marine protected areas and reducing carbon emissions.
    Explanation: The passage mentions conservation efforts, such as the establishment of marine protected areas and efforts to reduce carbon emissions, as ways to protect coral reefs.

16. **What is the relationship between coral polyps and**

algae?

Answer: (B) Algae help coral polyps by providing them with nutrients.

Explanation: The passage describes a symbiotic relationship in which algae live within coral polyps and provide nutrients, essential for the coral's survival.

17. **Which of the following is NOT a threat to coral reefs mentioned in the passage?**
Answer: (D) The introduction of new species
Explanation: While the passage mentions overfishing, pollution, and climate change as threats, it does not mention the introduction of new species.

18. **What does the passage suggest about the future of coral reefs?**
Answer: (C) They can be saved if conservation efforts are successful.
Explanation: The passage is optimistic that conservation efforts can help protect and preserve coral reefs, although it acknowledges the challenges they face.

19. **Why do coral reefs protect coastal communities?**
Answer: (B) They act as natural barriers against coastal erosion.
Explanation: The passage explains that coral reefs help protect coastal communities by acting as natural barriers against erosion.

20. **What does the passage imply about human responsibility toward coral reefs?**
Answer: (B) Humans must take action to reduce the impact of climate change and pollution on coral reefs.
Explanation: The passage implies that human activities are responsible for the decline of coral reefs and emphasizes the need for action to protect them.

Passage 3: The Role of Bees in Agriculture (Questions 21–30)

21. **What is the main idea of the passage?**
Answer: (A) Bees are essential for the pollination of many crops.
Explanation: The passage focuses on the critical role bees play in pollinating crops and the effects of their decline on agriculture, making this the central idea.

179

22. **How do bees contribute to agriculture?**
Answer: (B) By pollinating crops, allowing them to reproduce.
Explanation: The passage explains that bees are crucial for the pollination process, which enables plants like almonds and apples to reproduce, ensuring crop production.

23. **What is one reason bee populations are declining?**
Answer: (B) Pesticide use that harms their immune systems.
Explanation: The passage mentions that pesticide use weakens bees' immune systems, making it harder for them to forage for food and contributing to their population decline.

24. **What does the word "forage" in the second paragraph most likely mean?**
Answer: (B) Search for food
Explanation: In context, "forage" refers to bees searching for food (flowers and plants), which is essential for their survival.

25. **According to the passage, what is one way farmers are helping to protect bees?**

Answer: (C) By planting wildflowers and creating bee-friendly habitats.
Explanation: The passage describes how farmers are adopting sustainable practices like planting wildflowers and creating habitats to support bee populations.

26. **Why is pollination important for crops like almonds and apples?**
Answer: (A) It ensures that the plants produce fruit.
Explanation: Pollination is critical for the reproduction of plants, ensuring that crops like almonds and apples produce fruit, as discussed in the passage.

27. **What does the passage imply about the future of food production without bees?**
Answer: (A) Food prices will increase, and shortages may occur.
Explanation: The passage warns that without bees, crop production would decline, leading to higher food prices and potential shortages.

28. **Which of the following is NOT mentioned as a threat to bee populations?**

Answer: (D) Overharvesting of honey

Explanation: The passage discusses pesticide use, habitat destruction, and climate change as threats to bee populations but does not mention overharvesting of honey.

29. **What role can consumers play in helping to protect bees?**

Answer: (B) By supporting organic farming and reducing pesticide use.

Explanation: The passage suggests that consumers can help protect bees by supporting organic farming practices and reducing their use of pesticides.

30. **What is one benefit of creating bee-friendly habitats?**

Answer: (B) It provides bees with access to flowers and plants they need for food.

Explanation: The passage explains that creating bee-friendly habitats ensures bees have access to the food sources they need, supporting their survival.

Passage 4: A New Era of Space Exploration (Questions 31–40)

31. **What is the main idea of the passage?**

Answer: (A) Space exploration is becoming more feasible with the involvement of private companies.

Explanation: The passage discusses how advances in technology and the involvement of private companies are pushing the boundaries of space exploration, making it more feasible.

32. **According to the passage, what is one potential benefit of space exploration?**

Answer: (B) Finding new resources that can be used on Earth.

Explanation: The passage mentions the possibility of discovering new resources, such as minerals and water, that could benefit Earth.

33. **What role do private companies like SpaceX play in space exploration?**

Answer: (A) They are developing new technologies and leading space missions.

Explanation: The passage highlights that private companies like SpaceX are leading the way in developing new technologies and conducting space missions.

34. **What does the word "resurgence" in the first paragraph most likely mean?**
Answer: (B) Renewal
Explanation: "Resurgence" means a revival or renewed interest, which, in this context, refers to the renewed interest in space exploration in the 21st century.

35. **What is one of the challenges facing space exploration, according to the passage?**
Answer: (B) The high cost of space missions.
Explanation: The passage mentions that space missions are extremely expensive, which is a significant challenge for space exploration.

36. **Why do some experts believe space exploration is important for humanity's future?**
Answer: (B) It could provide new locations for human settlements.
Explanation: The passage suggests that space exploration could offer solutions to Earth's overpopulation problem by providing new locations for human settlements, such as Mars.

37. **What is one potential environmental concern related to space exploration?**
Answer: (B) Carbon dioxide emissions from rockets.
Explanation: The passage mentions that rockets release large amounts of carbon dioxide, which is a concern for the environment.

38. **How might space exploration benefit industries on Earth?**
Answer: (C) By developing technologies that have applications in other fields.
Explanation: The passage explains that technologies developed for space travel often have applications in other industries, such as medicine and telecommunications.

39. **What does the passage suggest about the future of space exploration?**
Answer: (A) It is uncertain due to high costs and environmental concerns.
Explanation: The passage presents both the potential benefits and challenges of space exploration, making its future uncertain.

40. **What does the passage imply about the involvement of private companies in space exploration?**
    Answer: (B) They are leading the way in developing new technologies for space travel.
    Explanation: The passage suggests that private companies are at the forefront of developing new technologies and conducting space missions.

Passage 5: The Science of Sleep (Questions 41–50)

41. **What is the main idea of the passage?**
    Answer: (A) Sleep is necessary for both physical and mental health.
    Explanation: The passage discusses the importance of sleep for both physical repair and mental health, highlighting its role in overall well-being.

42. **What happens during REM sleep?**
    Answer: (C) Most dreaming occurs.
    Explanation: The passage states that REM (Rapid Eye Movement) sleep is the phase in which most dreaming happens and is crucial for cognitive functions like memory and learning.

43. **What does the passage suggest about the effects of sleep deprivation?**
    Answer: (A) It is linked to a variety of health issues.
    Explanation: The passage links a lack of sleep to health problems such as obesity, heart disease, and depression, indicating the negative effects of sleep deprivation.

44. **What does the word "consolidates" in the first paragraph most likely mean?**
    Answer: (D) Combines
    Explanation: In the context of memory, "consolidates" refers to the process of combining and solidifying memories, making them more stable and long-lasting.

45. **According to the passage, what is one function of non-REM sleep?**
    Answer: (A) To help the body repair damaged tissues.
    Explanation: The passage describes non-REM sleep as the phase where the body focuses on

physical repair and recovery, which is essential for healing.

46. **Why is it important to get both REM and non-REM sleep?**
Answer: (A) They are necessary for cognitive and physical health.
Explanation: The passage explains that REM sleep is crucial for cognitive functions like memory, while non-REM sleep is important for physical repair, making both necessary for overall health.

47. **What are some factors that interfere with sleep, according to the passage?**
Answer: (B) Stress, work schedules, and the use of electronic devices
Explanation: The passage lists stress, work schedules, and electronic device use before bed as common factors that interfere with getting enough sleep.

48. **What does the passage imply about people's sleep habits in today's world?**
Answer: (C) Many people struggle to get enough sleep due to their lifestyle.
Explanation: The passage suggests that modern lifestyles, including work demands and

technology use, prevent people from getting the recommended 7–9 hours of sleep.

49. **What recommendation is given for improving sleep quality?**
Answer: (C) Limiting screen time and practicing relaxation techniques.
Explanation: The passage recommends reducing screen time before bed and practicing relaxation techniques as ways to improve sleep quality.

50. **What is one potential health consequence of not getting enough sleep?**
Answer: (B) Heart disease
Explanation: The passage lists heart disease, among other health issues, as a potential consequence of sleep deprivation.

Passage 6: The Role of Music in Society (Questions 51–62)

51. **What is the main idea of the passage?**
Answer: (A) Music has been important throughout history for various reasons.
Explanation: The passage discusses how music has played significant roles in religion,

184

celebrations, and social gatherings throughout history, emphasizing its importance.

52. **According to the passage, how has music been used throughout history?**
    Answer: (A) To celebrate important life events and bring people together.
    Explanation: The passage mentions that music is used in ceremonies such as weddings and funerals and helps unite people during important life events.

53. **What does the passage imply about the role of music in different cultures?**
    Answer: (C) Music is a central part of life in many cultures.
    Explanation: The passage emphasizes that music plays an essential role in daily life and cultural practices in many societies, making it central to various cultures.

54. **How does music benefit mental health, according to the passage?**
    Answer: (B) It helps reduce stress and improves mood.
    Explanation: The passage states that listening to music can reduce stress and improve mood, thus benefiting mental health.

55. **What is one physical benefit of playing a musical instrument mentioned in the passage?**
    Answer: (C) Better hand-eye coordination
    Explanation: The passage mentions that playing a musical instrument improves hand-eye coordination as a physical benefit.

56. **What does the word "enhance" in the second paragraph most likely mean?**
    Answer: (B) Improve
    Explanation: In this context, "enhance" means to improve or increase, as the passage discusses how music can improve memory and concentration.

57. **How is music used as a form of storytelling in some cultures?**
    Answer: (B) By passing down traditions and history through song.
    Explanation: The passage explains that in some cultures, music is used as a way to pass down traditions and historical events from one generation to the next through song.

58. **What does the passage suggest about the future of music?**
Answer: (A) It will continue to play an important role in society.
Explanation: The passage implies that music will remain important in society due to its cultural and health-related benefits.

59. **How does music help bring people together, according to the passage?**
Answer: (B) It is used in religious rituals and celebrations.
Explanation: The passage mentions that music is used during significant social events, such as religious ceremonies and celebrations, which helps unite people.

60. **What does the passage imply about the relationship between music and culture?**
Answer: (A) Music often reflects the cultural values of the time.
Explanation: The passage suggests that music reflects the values and beliefs of the time and the society in which it is created.

61. **What is one reason people play musical instruments, according to the passage?**
Answer: (B) To improve creativity and hand-eye coordination.
Explanation: The passage states that playing musical instruments enhances creativity and hand-eye coordination, providing mental and physical benefits.

62. **What does the passage suggest about the emotional power of music?**
Answer: (A) Music can express emotions that are difficult to put into words.
Explanation: The passage explains that music can convey complex emotions that might be challenging to express through words alone.

Mathematics Subtest

Section 1: Basic Math and Arithmetic

1. **B) 477**
   - Add the numbers: 348 + 129 = 477

2. **B) 488**
   - Subtract the numbers: 752 - 264 = 488

3. **C) 1,904**
   - Multiply the numbers: 56 x 34 = 1,904

4. **B) 72**

   o Divide the numbers: 1,728 ÷ 24 = 72

5. **C) 0.875**

   o Perform the division: 7 ÷ 8 = 0.875

6. **B) 117**

   o Calculate the percentage: (45/100) * 260 = 117

7. **A) 4/5**

   o Find the greatest common divisor (GCD) of 64 and 80, which is 16. Divide both numerator and denominator by 16: 64 ÷ 16 / 80 ÷ 16 = 4/5

8. **B) 18**

   o The ratio 3:5 means that for every 3 boys, there are 5 girls.

   o Set up a proportion: 3/5 = x/30

   o Cross-multiply and solve for x: 5x = 90 => x = 18

9. **C) 20**

   o Add all the numbers and divide by the count (5):

(12 + 16 + 20 + 24 + 28) / 5 = 100 / 5 = 20

10. **A) 48**

   • Subtract the difference from the larger number: 87 - 39 = 48

11. **B) $12**

   • Divide the total cost by the number of bags: $96 / 8 = $12

12. **C) 60**

   • Divide the total distance by the time taken: 180 miles / 3 hours = 60 mph

13. **C) 90**

   • Calculate the percentage: (20/100) * 450 = 90

14. **C) 47**

   • Follow the order of operations (PEMDAS):

      o Parentheses first: 7 × (6) + 5

      o Multiplication: 42 + 5

      o Addition: 47

15. **B) $60**

   • Calculate the discount: (25/100) * $80 = $20

187

- Subtract the discount from the original price: $80 - $20 = $60

16. **B) 5/8**

- 0.625 is equivalent to 625/1000
- Simplify by dividing both numerator and denominator by their greatest common divisor, which is 125: 625 ÷ 125 / 1000 ÷ 125 = 5/8

Section 2: Algebraic Concepts

17. **B) 5**

   o Subtract 5 from both sides: $2x = 10$
   o Divide both sides by 2: $x = 5$

18. **B) 6x - 6**

   o Distribute the 3: $6x - 12 + 6$
   o Combine like terms: $6x - 6$

19. **C) 6**

   o Add 7 to both sides: $3x = 18$
   o Divide both sides by 3: $x = 6$

20. **A) (x - 3)(x + 3)**

   o This is the difference of squares factorization: $a^2 - b^2 = (a - b)(a + b)$

21. **B) 4**

   o Subtract 3 from both sides: $4y = 16$
   o Divide both sides by 4: $y = 4$

22. **A) 3**

   o Substitute $y = 2$ into the equation: $2x + 3(2) = 12$
   o Simplify and solve for x: $2x + 6 = 12 \Rightarrow 2x = 6 \Rightarrow x = 3$

23. **A) 7x² - 2x**

   o Combine like terms: $(5x^2 + 2x^2) + (-3x + x) = 7x^2 - 2x$

24. **C) 5**

   o Subtract 2x from both sides: $4x - 4 = 16$
   o Add 4 to both sides: $4x = 20$
   o Divide both sides by 4: $x = 5$

25. **D) 4**

- Subtract x from both sides: $3 = x - 1$
- Add 1 to both sides: $x = 4$

26. B) 10x - 5

- Distribute: $4x - 8 + 6x + 3$
- Combine like terms: $10x - 5$

27. A) 4, -4

- Add 16 to both sides: $x^2 = 16$
- Take the square root of both sides: $x = \pm 4$

28. B) 28

- Subtract 3 from both sides: $z/4 = 7$
- Multiply both sides by 4: $z = 28$

29. B) x > 3

- Add 2 to both sides: $3x > 9$
- Divide both sides by 3: $x > 3$

30. A) 4x² - 6x

- Combine like terms: $(x^2 + 3x^2) + (-2x - 4x)$
- Simplify: $4x^2 - 6x$

31. D) 5

- Substitute $y = 4$ into the equation: $5x + 3(4) = 30$
- Simplify and solve for x: $5x + 12 = 30 \Rightarrow 5x = 18 \Rightarrow x = 3.6$

32. A) (4, 2)

- Solve for x in the second equation: $x = y + 4$
- Substitute into the first equation: $2(y + 4) + y = 10$
- Simplify and solve for y: $2y + 8 + y = 10 \Rightarrow 3y = 2 \Rightarrow y = 2/3$
- Substitute the value of y back into either of the original equations to solve for x.

Section 3: Geometry

33. C) 30 meters

- Perimeter of a rectangle = 2(length + width)
- Perimeter = $2(10 + 5) = 2(15) = 30$ meters

34. B) 12 cm²

- Area of a triangle = 1/2(base x height)

189

- Area = 1/2(6 x 4) = 12 cm²

35. **B) 43.96 meters**

   - Circumference of a circle = $2\pi r$

   - Circumference = 2 x 3.14 x 7 = 43.96 meters

36. **B) 45°**

   - In a right triangle, one angle is 90°. The sum of all angles in a triangle is 180°.

   - The other non-right angle = 180° - 90° - 45° = 45°

37. **D) 125 cm³**

   - Volume of a cube = side x side x side

   - Volume = 5 x 5 x 5 = 125 cm³

38. **B) 7.07 cm**

   - In a square, the diagonal divides it into two 45-45-90 triangles.

   - In a 45-45-90 triangle, hypotenuse (diagonal) = $\sqrt{2}$ x side

   - $10 = \sqrt{2}$ x side

- side = $10/\sqrt{2} = 5\sqrt{2} \approx 7.07$ cm

39. **C) 110°**

   - In a parallelogram, adjacent angles add up to 180°.

   - Adjacent angle = 180° - 70° = 110°

40. **A) 153.86 m²**

   - Radius = diameter/2 = 14/2 = 7 meters

   - Area of a circle = πr^2

   - Area = 3.14 x 7² = 153.86 m²

41. **D) 480 cm³**

   - Volume of a rectangular prism = length x width x height

   - Volume = 12 x 8 x 5 = 480 cm³

42. **D) 75°**

   - The sum of all angles in a triangle is 180°.

   - Third angle = 180° - 60° - 45° = 75°

43. **C) 7 cm**

   - Area of a square = side²

190

- $49 = \text{side}^2$
- $\text{side} = \sqrt{49} = 7$ cm

44. B) 120°

- Sum of interior angles in a polygon = (n-2) x 180° where n is the number of sides
- Hexagon has 6 sides, so sum = (6-2) x 180° = 720°
- Each interior angle in a regular hexagon = 720°/6 = 120°

45. A) 32 cm²

- Area of a trapezoid = 1/2 x height x (sum of bases)
- Area = 1/2 x 4 x (10 + 6)
- Area = 1/2 x 4 x 16 = 32 cm²

46. C) 24 cm

- Perimeter of a triangle = sum of all sides
- Perimeter = 6 + 8 + 10 = 24 cm

47. C) 360°

- The sum of the interior angles in a quadrilateral is always 360°

48. C) 24 m²

- Area of a rectangle = length x width
- Area = 8 x 3 = 24 m²

Section 4: Advanced Math and Word Problems

49. C) 150 miles

- Miles per gallon (mpg) = total miles / gallons used
- 25 mpg = 240 miles / 8 gallons
- To find miles traveled on 5 gallons:
- Miles = mpg x gallons = 25 x 5 = 150 miles

50. B) 300 miles

- Distance = speed x time
- Distance = 60 mph x 5 hours = 300 miles

51. C) 960 cubic feet

- Volume of a room (rectangular prism) = length x width x height
- Volume = 12 ft x 10 ft x 8 ft
- Volume = 960 cubic feet

52. **C) $20.83**

- Cost per bag = total cost / number of bags = $12.50 / 3 bags = $4.1666 per bag (approximately)

- Cost of 5 bags = cost per bag x number of bags

- Cost of 5 bags = $4.1666 x 5 = $20.83 (approximately)

53. **C) 49**

- The ratio 5:7 means that for every 5 dogs, there are 7 cats

- Set up a proportion: 5/7 = 35/x

- Cross-multiply and solve for x: 5x = 245 => x = 49

54. **C) 2/3**

- Total number of marbles = 6 + 8 + 4 = 18

- Probability = favorable outcomes / total possible outcomes

- Probability of selecting a blue marble = 8/18 = 4/9

55. **A) 74**

- Let the fourth score be x

- Average = (sum of scores) / number of scores

- 78 = (72 + 80 + 85 + x) / 4

- 312 = 237 + x

- x = 75

56. **C) $2,400**

- Total cost = number of calculators x cost per calculator

- Total cost = 200 x $12 = $2,400

57. **B) $4.50**

- Cost per pencil = total cost / number of pencils

- Cost per pencil = $1.75 / 5 pencils = $0.35

- Cost of 15 pencils = cost per pencil x number of pencils

- Cost of 15 pencils = $0.35 x 15 = $5.25

58. **C) $17.94**

- Price increase = (20/100) * $14.95 = $2.99

- New price = original price + price increase

192

- New price = $14.95 + $2.99 = $17.94

59. D) 40 meters

- Perimeter of a rectangle = 2(length + width)
- Perimeter = 2(12 + 8) = 2(20) = 40 meters

60. D) 90 square inches

- Area of a rectangle = length x width
- Area = 15 inches x 6 inches = 90 square inches

61. C) $8.00

- Cost per shirt = total cost / number of shirts
- Cost per shirt = $24.00 / 3 shirts = $8.00

62. D) 250 mph

- Average speed = total distance / time taken

- Average speed = 500 miles / 2 hours = 250 mph

63. A) 85.5

- Original total score of the class = 20 students x 85 average = 1700
- New total score = 1700 - 85 (original score of the student who got 95) + 95 = 1710
- New average = new total score / number of students
- New average = 1710 / 20 = 85.5

64. C) $45.00

- Discount = (10/100) * $50 = $5
- Final price = original price - discount
- Final price = $50 - $5 = $

Language Subtest

Part 1: Capitalization (Questions 1-5)

1. **Which sentence uses capitalization correctly? Answer**: (a) My Aunt Susan is coming to visit. **Explanation**: In this sentence, "Aunt Susan" is capitalized correctly because "Aunt" is part of her title. The other choices either incorrectly capitalize or fail to capitalize proper nouns.

193

2. **Select the sentence with proper capitalization.**
   Answer: (d) Dr. Franklin will see patients starting at 8:00 AM.
   Explanation: "Dr." and "Franklin" are properly capitalized as a title and name. "AM" is also correctly capitalized in this context.

3. **Choose the sentence that has correct capitalization.**
   Answer: (c) The statue of Liberty is located on Liberty island.
   Explanation: The proper noun "Statue of Liberty" is capitalized correctly, and "Liberty Island" is also a proper noun that is capitalized correctly.

4. **Identify the sentence with proper capitalization.**
   Answer: (c) The Fourth of July parade is a big event in our town.
   Explanation: "Fourth of July" is the name of a holiday, so it is capitalized correctly, unlike the other options where professional titles and locations are incorrectly capitalized.

5. **Which sentence is capitalized correctly?**
   Answer: (b) I took a trip to see the Pacific Ocean and Mount Rushmore.

Explanation: "Pacific Ocean" and "Mount Rushmore" are proper nouns, which are capitalized correctly.

Part 2: Punctuation (Questions 6-10)

6. **Which sentence uses punctuation correctly?**
   Answer: (c) We plan to visit Grandma's house on Saturday; the weather looks nice.
   Explanation: A semicolon correctly separates two related independent clauses in this sentence.

7. **Select the sentence with correct punctuation.**
   Answer: (b) The library closes at 5:00 p.m. on weekdays.
   Explanation: The abbreviation "p.m." is properly formatted, and the sentence ends with the correct punctuation.

8. **Choose the sentence that has proper punctuation.**
   Answer: (d) He asked, "Where is the nearest bus stop?"
   Explanation: The question mark is correctly placed inside the quotation marks, as it is part of the quoted question.

194

9. **Identify the sentence with correct punctuation.**
Answer: (a) We're planning a trip to Washington, D.C. in April.
Explanation: "Washington, D.C." is punctuated correctly with the appropriate use of commas.

10. **Which sentence uses punctuation correctly?**
Answer: (b) Mrs. Smith asked, "Who is ready for recess?"
Explanation: The sentence correctly places the question mark inside the quotation marks as it is part of the direct quote.

Part 3: Usage (Questions 11-15)

11. **Which sentence uses the word correctly?**
Answer: (d) They're going to the store later today.
Explanation: "They're" is the correct contraction of "they are." The other sentences misuse words like "illicit" and "principle."

12. **Select the sentence with correct word usage.**
Answer: (c) You're going to the football game, aren't you?
Explanation: "You're" is the correct contraction of "you are,"

and it is used correctly in this context.

13. **Choose the sentence with proper word usage.**
Answer: (d) Its raining, so we should bring umbrellas.
Explanation: "Its" is correctly used here as the possessive form of "it." The other sentences misuse words like "it's" and "whose."

14. **Identify the sentence with correct usage.**
Answer: (c) I feel bad about not calling you yesterday.
Explanation: "Bad" is the correct adjective to use here, whereas "badly" would describe how an action is performed, not how someone feels.

15. **Which sentence uses the word correctly?**
Answer: (b) The results of the study were accurate.
Explanation: "Accurate" is correctly used as an adjective describing the results. The other choices misuse "affect" and "you're."

Part 4: Sentence Structure (Questions 16-20)

195

16. **Which sentence is structured correctly?**
Answer: (b) After the meeting, we discussed the proposal and made changes.
Explanation: This sentence has proper structure, whereas the other sentences are either incomplete or have misplaced phrases.

17. **Select the sentence with correct sentence structure.**
Answer: (a) We had fun at the zoo, and seeing all the animals was great.
Explanation: This sentence is correctly structured with proper coordination of ideas. Other choices contain sentence fragments or awkward constructions.

18. **Choose the sentence that has proper structure.**
Answer: (a) Despite the long journey, we arrived on time.
Explanation: This sentence uses proper sentence structure with a subordinating conjunction ("despite") followed by a complete main clause.

19. **Identify the sentence with correct sentence structure.**
Answer: (d) She was hungry, but deciding what to eat was difficult.
Explanation: This sentence properly balances two ideas, with the conjunction "but" appropriately connecting them.

20. **Which sentence is structured correctly?**
Answer: (c) After eating dinner, we cleaned the kitchen.
Explanation: This sentence correctly begins with a dependent clause followed by an independent clause, making it clear and properly structured.

Part 5: Spelling (Questions 21-25)

21. **Which word is spelled correctly?**
Answer: (d) recommend
Explanation: "Recommend" is the correct spelling. The other options ("recieve," "accomodate," "embarass") are incorrect.

22. **Select the correct spelling.**
Answer: (c) separate
Explanation: "Separate" is spelled correctly. The other words are misspelled.

23. **Choose the correctly spelled word.**
Answer: (b) maintenance

196

Explanation: "Maintenance" is correctly spelled, unlike the other options.

24. **Identify the word spelled correctly.**
    Answer: (c) conscience
    Explanation: "Conscience" is correctly spelled. The other words are misspelled.

25. **Which word is spelled correctly?**
    Answer: (c) grateful
    Explanation: "Grateful" is the correct spelling. The other options ("suprise," "independant," "responsability") are misspelled.

Part 6: Composition (Questions 26-30)

26. **Which sentence is composed correctly?**
    Answer: (a) I went to the store, but forgot to buy milk.
    Explanation: This sentence correctly uses a comma before the coordinating conjunction "but," and the sentence structure is clear. Other choices have sentence fragments or unnecessary commas.

27. **Select the sentence that is composed properly.**
    Answer: (b) Because the movie was sold out, we went to the park instead.
    Explanation: This sentence uses proper composition with a dependent clause ("Because the movie was sold out") followed by the main clause. The other options are either fragments or misuse conjunctions.

28. **Choose the correctly composed sentence.**
    Answer: (c) After the concert ended, we went out for dinner.
    Explanation: This sentence is correctly structured with a dependent clause at the beginning. The other sentences have structural issues or awkward phrasing.

29. **Identify the sentence that is composed correctly.**
    Answer: (a) The students were tired after class, but still had energy for practice.
    Explanation: The sentence is clear, with appropriate use of the conjunction "but" to join the two related ideas.

30. **Which sentence is composed correctly?**
    Answer: (b) Even though it was cold, we wore jackets.
    Explanation: The sentence uses proper sentence composition by

starting with a dependent clause and linking it with the main clause. The other sentences have misplaced commas or unclear structure.

Part 7: Subject-Verb Agreement (Questions 31-35)

31. **Which sentence has correct subject-verb agreement?**
Answer: (b) The team plays every Saturday afternoon.
Explanation: "Team" is a singular subject, so the singular verb "plays" is correct. The other sentences have errors in subject-verb agreement.

32. **Select the sentence with proper subject-verb agreement.**
Answer: (c) The book on the table belongs to her.
Explanation: "The book" is singular, and the singular verb "belongs" agrees with the subject. The other choices have incorrect agreement.

33. **Choose the sentence that has correct subject-verb agreement.**
Answer: (d) The teacher, along with the students, is preparing for the play.
Explanation: The subject "teacher" is singular, and the singular verb "is" agrees with it. Phrases like "along with the students" do not affect the verb agreement.

34. **Identify the sentence with proper subject-verb agreement.**
Answer: (d) Each of the girls is bringing a gift.
Explanation: "Each" is a singular subject, so the singular verb "is" is correct. The other options misuse verbs with their subjects.

35. **Which sentence uses subject-verb agreement correctly?**
Answer: (b) Neither of them is available today.
Explanation: "Neither" is singular, so the singular verb "is" is used correctly here. The other choices contain incorrect subject-verb agreement.

Part 8: Pronoun-Antecedent Agreement (Questions 36-40)

36. **Which sentence uses pronoun-antecedent agreement correctly?**
Answer: (b) The dog loves to chase its tail.
Explanation: "Its" correctly refers to "the dog," maintaining

proper agreement between the pronoun and its antecedent. The other sentences have issues with plural/singular pronoun usage.

37. **Select the sentence with correct pronoun-antecedent agreement.**
Answer: (d) The committee gave its approval for the event.
Explanation: "Committee" is treated as a singular entity, so the pronoun "its" is correct. The other sentences incorrectly use "their" for singular antecedents.

38. **Choose the sentence with proper pronoun-antecedent agreement.**
Answer: (b) The students finished their test early.
Explanation: "Students" is plural, and "their" is the correct pronoun to match the plural antecedent.

39. **Identify the sentence with correct pronoun-antecedent agreement.**
Answer: (c) Each student is responsible for his or her own project.
Explanation: "Each student" is singular, so the phrase "his or her" maintains correct agreement. The other sentences incorrectly use

plural pronouns for singular antecedents.

40. **Which sentence uses pronoun-antecedent agreement correctly?**
Answer: (c) Each dog has its own kennel.
Explanation: "Each dog" is singular, and "its" is the correct pronoun to maintain agreement.

Part 9: Parallel Structure (Questions 41-45)

41. **Which sentence has correct parallel structure?**
Answer: (b) He likes reading books, watching movies, and playing games.
Explanation: The sentence lists three activities in a parallel structure (gerunds: reading, watching, playing), maintaining consistency. The other sentences mix verb forms.

42. **Select the sentence with correct parallel structure.**
Answer: (d) He enjoys hiking, camping, and fishing.
Explanation: The sentence maintains parallel structure with three gerunds (hiking, camping, fishing). Other choices mix

gerunds with infinitives or other verb forms.

43. **Choose the sentence with proper parallel structure.**
Answer: (b) The class is focusing on reading, writing, and speaking.
Explanation: The sentence lists three gerunds in parallel form. The other choices break parallel structure by mixing verb forms.

44. **Identify the sentence with correct parallel structure.**
Answer: (c) He spends his weekends hiking, fishing, and camping.
Explanation: The sentence maintains parallel structure with gerunds (hiking, fishing, camping). The other options mix forms.

45. **Which sentence has correct parallel structure?**
Answer: (c) He spends his time reading, writing, and learning.
Explanation: The sentence uses consistent gerunds in parallel structure. The other sentences mix verb forms incorrectly.

Part 10: Modifier Placement (Questions 46-50)

46. **Which sentence uses modifiers correctly?**
Answer: (c) She read the book slowly, enjoying every word.
Explanation: The modifier "slowly" correctly describes how she read the book, and the phrase "enjoying every word" follows logically.

47. **Select the sentence with correct modifier placement.**
Answer: (a) The cat, resting in the sun, was purring happily.
Explanation: The modifier "resting in the sun" is properly placed to describe the cat, and the sentence flows logically.

48. **Choose the sentence with proper modifier placement.**
Answer: (b) While shopping, my wallet fell out of my pocket.
Explanation: The modifier "While shopping" is placed correctly at the beginning of the sentence, and it clarifies the action that occurred.

49. **Identify the sentence with correct modifier placement.**
Answer: (d) Running down the street, I saw my friend.
Explanation: The modifier "Running down the street"

correctly describes the action of the speaker, avoiding ambiguity.

50. **Which sentence uses modifiers correctly?**
Answer: (d) Jumping over the fence, the dog barked loudly.
Explanation: The modifier "Jumping over the fence" is placed properly to describe the dog's action.

Part 11: Dangling Modifiers (Questions 51-55)

51. **Which sentence avoids a dangling modifier?**
Answer: (d) Having finished the project, I took a break.
Explanation: The modifier "Having finished the project" correctly refers to the subject "I." Other sentences leave the subject unclear.

52. **Select the sentence that avoids a dangling modifier.**
Answer: (d) Feeling tired, I decided to take a nap.
Explanation: The modifier "Feeling tired" correctly refers to the subject "I." Other choices leave the subject ambiguous.

53. **Choose the sentence that avoids a dangling modifier.**
Answer: (c) After finishing the test, I felt relieved.
Explanation: The modifier "After finishing the test" clearly refers to "I," the subject of the sentence.

54. **Identify the sentence that avoids a dangling modifier.**
Answer: (d) Feeling confident, I took the exam.
Explanation: The modifier "Feeling confident" correctly modifies "I," the subject of the sentence.

55. **Which sentence avoids a dangling modifier?**
Answer: (d) Watching the sunset, I felt peaceful.
Explanation: The modifier "Watching the sunset" properly refers to "I," avoiding ambiguity.

Part 12: Sentence Combining (Questions 56-60)

56. **Combine the sentences for the most effective structure:**
Answer: (a) Practicing every day, the team won the championship.
Explanation: The combined sentence starts with a participial

phrase that describes the team's actions and then links it to the main clause.

57. **Combine the sentences for the most effective structure:** **Answer**: (c) He loves playing basketball and enjoys swimming. **Explanation**: This sentence combines the two related ideas efficiently, avoiding redundancy and awkward phrasing.

58. **Combine the sentences for the most effective structure:** **Answer**: (b) The flowers bloomed early, making the garden look beautiful. **Explanation**: The sentence combines the two ideas with clear cause and effect, avoiding awkward phrasing.

59. **Combine the sentences for the most effective structure:** **Answer**: (c) He got an A on the exam because he studied hard. **Explanation**: This sentence combines the ideas using a clear cause-and-effect structure.

60. **Combine the sentences for the most effective structure:** **Answer**: (a) She loves to bake and makes cookies every weekend. **Explanation**: The sentence effectively combines the two related actions with parallel structure.

Full-Length Practice Exam 2

Verbal Skills Subtest

Time: 16 minutes

Number of Questions: 60

Section 1: Synonyms

For each question in this section, choose the word that is most similar in meaning to the word in bold. Each synonym pair will test your vocabulary depth, and understanding subtle differences in meaning will be important.

Question 1:

The word benevolent most nearly means:

A) Charitable

B) Hostile

C) Powerful

D) Restless

Question 2:

The word industrious most nearly means:

A) Lazy

B) Active

C) Short

D) Timid

Question 3:

The word frugal most nearly means:

A) Wasteful

B) Generous

C) Economical

D) Stubborn

Question 4:

The word verbose most nearly means:

A) Silent

B) Talkative

C) Angry

D) Rude

Question 5:

The word abstain most nearly means:

A) Indulge

B) Resist

C) Accept

D) Hurry

Question 6:

The word lament most nearly means:

A) Celebrate

B) Mourn

C) Confuse

D) Organize

Question 7:

The word diligent most nearly means:

A) Careless

B) Hardworking

C) Playful

D) Distracted

Question 8:

The word placid most nearly means:

A) Calm

B) Wild

C) Noisy

D) Fearful

Question 9:

The word elated most nearly means:

A) Depressed

B) Excited

C) Angry

D) Exhausted

Question 10:

The word scrupulous most nearly means:

A) Dishonest

B) Careful

C) Joyful

D) Energetic

Section 2: Antonyms

For each question in this section, select the word that is opposite in meaning to the word in bold. Understanding antonyms will test not only your vocabulary but also your ability to differentiate subtle contextual meanings.

Question 11:

The word audacious most nearly means:

A) Timid

B) Bold

C) Gentle

D) Quiet

Question 12:

The word rigid most nearly means:

A) Flexible

B) Straight

C) Strong

D) Hard

Question 13:

The word benevolent most nearly means:

A) Malevolent

B) Compassionate

C) Kind

D) Foolish

Question 14:

The word adamant most nearly means:

A) Yielding

B) Strong

C) Patient

D) Firm

Question 15:

The word indifferent most nearly means:

A) Biased

B) Unconcerned

C) Neutral

D) Detached

Question 16:

The word conspicuous most nearly means:

A) Obvious

B) Hidden

C) Tall

D) Bright

Question 17:

The word tedious most nearly means:

A) Exciting

B) Long

C) Boring

D) Restful

Question 18:

The word vigilant most nearly means:

A) Watchful

B) Sleepy

C) Careless

D) Active

Question 19:

The word vague most nearly means:

A) Clear

B) Hazy

C) Sharp

D) Dark

Question 20:

The word obstinate most nearly means:

A) Stubborn

B) Agreeable

C) Firm

D) Confused

Section 3: Analogies

In this section, you will be asked to identify relationships between pairs of words. These questions test your ability to recognize different types of associations, such as synonym relationships, part-to-whole relationships, or cause and effect.

Question 21:

Hand is to glove as foot is to:

A) Shoe

B) Sock

C) Sandal

D) Boot

Question 22:

Water is to thirst as food is to:

A) Hunger

B) Drink

C) Nourish

D) Taste

Question 23:

Bird is to wing as fish is to:

A) Fin

B) Tail

C) Scale

D) Ocean

Question 24:

Teacher is to classroom as doctor is to:

A) Medicine

B) Stethoscope

C) Hospital

D) Nurse

Question 25:

Library is to books as museum is to:

A) Paintings

B) Art

C) Statues

D) Exhibits

Question 26:

Hat is to head as glove is to:

A) Hand

206

B) Finger

C) Arm

D) Wrist

Question 27:

Sun is to day as moon is to:

A) Light

B) Night

C) Star

D) Eclipse

Question 28:

Pencil is to write as brush is to:

A) Paint

B) Color

C) Draw

D) Sketch

Question 29:

Dog is to bark as cat is to:

A) Meow

B) Purr

C) Whisker

D) Scratch

Question 30:

Leaf is to tree as petal is to:

A) Flower

B) Branch

C) Seed

D) Vine

Section 4: Verbal Logic

In this section, you will be tested on your ability to deduce logical relationships from pairs of statements. Logic-based reasoning skills will be crucial in determining whether certain statements are true, false, or uncertain based on the information provided.

Question 31:

Some teachers are strict. All strict people are disliked. Therefore:

A) Some teachers are disliked.

B) No teachers are disliked.

C) All teachers are disliked.

Question 32:

All birds have feathers. No animals with feathers can swim. Therefore:

A) Some birds cannot swim.

B) No birds can swim.

C) All birds can swim.

Question 33:

Some books are long. All long books are boring. Therefore:

A) Some books are boring.

B) All books are boring.

C) No books are boring.

Question 34:

All triangles have three sides. No shape with three sides is a square. Therefore:

A) Some triangles are squares.

B) No triangles are squares.

C) All squares are triangles.

Question 35:

Some fruits are apples. All apples are red. Therefore:

A) Some fruits are red.

B) No fruits are red.

C) All fruits are red.

Question 36:

All dogs bark. No animals that bark are silent. Therefore:

A) All silent animals are dogs.

B) Some dogs are silent.

C) No dogs are silent.

Question 37:

Some cars are fast. All fast vehicles are expensive. Therefore:

A) Some cars are expensive.

B) No cars are expensive.

C) All cars are expensive.

Question 38:

All fish swim. Some swimmers are fast. Therefore:

A) All fish are fast.

B) Some fish are fast.

C) No fish are fast.

Question 39:

All pens have ink. Some ink is red. Therefore:

A) Some pens have red ink.

B) No pens have red ink.

C) All pens have red ink.

Question 40:

Some clouds are white. All white things are beautiful. Therefore:

A) Some clouds are beautiful.

B) No clouds are beautiful.

C) All clouds are beautiful.

Question 41:

All flowers bloom. Some blooms are fragrant. Therefore:

A) Some flowers are fragrant.

B) No flowers are fragrant.

C) All flowers are fragrant.

Question 42:

Some shoes are leather. All leather items are durable. Therefore:

A) All shoes are durable.

B) Some shoes are durable.

C) No shoes are durable.

Question 43:

All cats are mammals. No mammals have feathers. Therefore:

A) Some cats have feathers.

B) No cats have feathers.

C) All mammals have feathers.

Section 5: Verbal Classifications

In this section, your task is to identify the word that does not belong in the group. Pay attention to the relationships between the words to determine which one stands out. This tests your ability to categorize and classify based on shared characteristics or functions.

Question 44:

Which word does not belong in the following group?

A) Dog

B) Cat

C) Lion

D) Tree

C) Autumn

D) Weekend

Question 45:

Which word does not belong in the following group?

A) Apple

B) Orange

C) Banana

D) Carrot

Question 46:

Which word does not belong in the following group?

A) Knife

B) Spoon

C) Fork

D) Hammer

Question 47:

Which word does not belong in the following group?

A) Winter

B) Summer

Question 48:

Which word does not belong in the following group?

A) Foot

B) Hand

C) Arm

D) Shoulder

Question 49:

Which word does not belong in the following group?

A) Elephant

B) Mouse

C) Giraffe

D) Eagle

Question 50:

Which word does not belong in the following group?

A) Shirt

B) Pants

C) Jacket

D) Book

B) Marker

C) Notebook

D) Crayon

Question 51:

Which word does not belong in the following group?

A) Basketball

B) Baseball

C) Tennis

D) Computer

Question 54:

Which word does not belong in the following group?

A) Pillow

B) Blanket

C) Chair

D) Sheet

Question 52:

Which word does not belong in the following group?

A) Car

B) Bicycle

C) Bus

D) Cake

Question 55:

Which word does not belong in the following group?

A) Circle

B) Square

C) Triangle

D) Window

Question 53:

Which word does not belong in the following group?

A) Pen

Question 56:

Which word does not belong in the following group?

A) Hammer

B) Saw

C) Pliers

D) Pencil

Question 57:

Which word does not belong in the following group?

A) Car

B) Plane

C) Train

D) Bird

Question 58:

Which word does not belong in the following group?

A) Nurse

B) Teacher

C) Doctor

D) Lawyer

Question 59:

Which word does not belong in the following group?

A) Fire

B) Water

C) Ice

D) Glass

Question 60:

Which word does not belong in the following group?

A) Book

B) Magazine

C) Pen

D) Newspaper

Quantitative Skills Subtest

Number of Questions: 52

Time Allotted: 30 minutes

Instructions

This section of the HSPT tests your ability to perform quantitative reasoning and problem-solving tasks that involve numbers rather than words. You will encounter various types of questions, including sequences, comparisons, and computations. Read each question carefully and select the best answer.

Sequences

For the following questions, determine the next number or letter in the sequence.

2, 5, 10, 17, 26, ___

(a) 35

(b) 37

(c) 38

(d) 41

A, D, G, J, M, ___

(a) P

(b) Q

(c) R

(d) S

4, 12, 36, 108, ___

(a) 216

(b) 324

(c) 432

(d) 540

7, 14, 28, 56, ___

(a) 84

(b) 90

(c) 112

(d) 120

100, 95, 85, 70, ___

(a) 65

(b) 60

(c) 55

(d) 50

E, I, M, Q, ___

(a) T

(b) U

(c) V

(d) X

11, 22, 33, 44, 55, ___

(a) 60

(b) 66

(c) 77

(d) 88

3, 9, 27, ___

(a) 54

(b) 72

(c) 81

(d) 93

B, C, E, H, L, ___

(a) M

(b) N

(c) O

(d) P

200, 100, 50, 25, ___

(a) 12

(b) 15

(c) 18

(d) 12.5

Comparisons

For each of the following sets of numbers or expressions, determine the relationship between them (greater than, less than, or equal to) and choose the best answer.

Which is greater?

(a) 75

(b) $3^2 + 2$

(c) Both are equal

(d) Cannot be determined

8/16 or 1/4?

(a) 8/16 is greater

(b) 1/4 is greater

(c) They are equal

(d) Cannot be determined

0.25 or 1/2 of 1?

(a) 0.25

(b) 1/2

(c) They are equal

(d) Cannot be determined

3x + 5 = 20. What is x?

(a) 4

(b) 5

(c) 6

(d) 7

9/10 or 0.9?

(a) 9/10

(b) 0.9

(c) They are equal

(d) Cannot be determined

$(3 \times 4) \div 2$ or 3^2?

(a) First is greater

(b) Second is greater

(c) They are equal

(d) Cannot be determined

Which is smaller?

(a) $2 \times 2 \times 2$

(b) $2^3 \div 2$

(c) Both are equal

(d) Cannot be determined

15% of 200 or 30?

(a) First is greater

(b) Second is greater

(c) They are equal

(d) Cannot be determined

18.9 + 0.1 or 19?

(a) First is greater

(b) Second is greater

(c) They are equal

(d) Cannot be determined

$(2^4 \div 2)$ or (2×4)?

(a) First is greater

(b) Second is greater

(c) They are equal

(d) Cannot be determined

Computations

215

Solve each of the following problems.

What is the result of 8 × 7?

(a) 49

(b) 54

(c) 56

(d) 64

If 5y = 40, what is y?

(a) 5

(b) 6

(c) 7

(d) 8

12 + 5 × 2 = ?

(a) 17

(b) 22

(c) 24

(d) 34

What is 25% of 80?

(a) 10

(b) 15

(c) 20

(d) 25

If a = 12 and b = 8, what is a + b?

(a) 18

(b) 20

(c) 22

(d) 24

56 ÷ 7 = ?

(a) 6

(b) 7

(c) 8

(d) 9

What is 1/4 of 64?

(a) 12

(b) 14

(c) 16

(d) 18

2 × (3 + 4) = ?

(a) 12

(b) 14

(c) 16

(d) 18

If x + 7 = 12, what is x?

(a) 4

(b) 5

(c) 6

(d) 7

What is the value of 9^2?

(a) 72

(b) 81

(c) 88

(d) 90

Word Problems

Use the information provided to solve each problem.

John bought 3 pencils for $0.50 each and 2 notebooks for $1.50 each. How much did he spend in total?

(a) $3.50

(b) $4.00

(c) $4.50

(d) $5.00

Maria drives 150 miles in 3 hours. How many miles per hour is she driving?

(a) 45 mph

(b) 50 mph

(c) 55 mph

(d) 60 mph

A rectangle has a length of 10 cm and a width of 5 cm. What is its area?

(a) 40 cm²

(b) 50 cm²

(c) 60 cm²

(d) 70 cm²

If 5 apples cost $2.50, how much would 10 apples cost?

(a) $4.00

(b) $5.00

(c) $5.50

(d) $6.00

Jane has twice as many books as Tom. If Tom has 6 books, how many books does Jane have?

(a) 10

(b) 12

(c) 14

(d) 16

A bookstore sells 3 books for $15.00. At the same rate, how much would 5 books cost?

(a) $20.00

(b) $22.50

(c) $25.00

(d) $30.00

A train travels 240 miles in 4 hours. What is the average speed of the train?

(a) 50 mph

(b) 55 mph

(c) 60 mph

(d) 65 mph

If a car travels 240 miles on 12 gallons of gas, how many miles can it travel on 15 gallons of gas?

(a) 280 miles

(b) 300 miles

(c) 320 miles

(d) 350 miles

A tank holds 120 gallons of water. If 3/4 of the tank is full, how many gallons are in the tank?

(a) 60 gallons

(b) 80 gallons

(c) 90 gallons

(d) 100 gallons

If a movie ticket costs $12 and a family buys 4 tickets, how much do they pay in total?

(a) $40

(b) $42

(c) $48

(d) $50

Susan buys a dress for $40 and a pair of shoes for $30. She uses a 10% discount on the total price. How much does she pay?

(a) $60

(b) $63

(c) $67

(d) $70

A farmer has 3 fields of equal size. Each field produces 120 pounds of wheat. How many pounds of wheat does the farmer produce in total?

(a) 300 pounds

(b) 320 pounds

(c) 340 pounds

(d) 360 pounds

A school library has 400 books. If 20% of the books are fiction, how many fiction books are there?

(a) 80

(b) 100

(c) 120

(d) 150

A factory produces 50 chairs in 5 hours. How many chairs does it produce per hour?

(a) 8

(b) 9

(c) 10

(d) 11

A car travels at 60 miles per hour. How far will it travel in 4 hours?

(a) 200 miles

(b) 220 miles

(c) 240 miles

(d) 260 miles

A shop sells 5 bottles of juice for $10. How much would 8 bottles cost at the same rate?

(a) $12

(b) $14

(c) $16

(d) $18

Advanced Computations

These questions will test your ability to handle more complex mathematical computations and reasoning.

If $12 + 4x = 36$, what is the value of x?

(a) 5

(b) 6

(c) 7

(d) 8

What is 75% of 320?

(a) 200

(b) 220

(c) 240

(d) 260

If $3y - 9 = 18$, what is y?

(a) 5

(b) 6

(c) 7

(d) 9

Solve for z: $2z + 15 = 45$

(a) 10

(b) 12

(c) 14

(d) 15

A restaurant bill is $60. If the tip is 20%, how much is the total bill including the tip?

(a) $65

(b) $68

(c) $70

(d) $72

If $6k = 72$, what is the value of k?

(a) 10

(b) 11

(c) 12

(d) 13

Reading Subtest

Number of Questions: 62

Time: 25 minutes

This reading subtest is designed to assess your ability to understand and analyze reading passages. You will be presented with a variety of passages, followed by multiple-choice questions that test your comprehension, vocabulary, ability to infer, and your skill in identifying the main idea.

Reading Passage 1

Questions 1–8 are based on the following passage.

In the early 1800s, the industrial revolution transformed the world. Small, local economies shifted to large, global industries. This transition, however, was not without its challenges. For workers, it meant long hours, dangerous conditions, and little pay. Despite this, the industrial revolution laid the foundation for modern economies, increasing production and technological innovation at a scale never before seen. The workers in the factories were often children and women, who were paid less than men but worked equally as hard. Labor reforms were slow to come, but over time, laws were passed to protect workers and improve working conditions.

The industrial revolution also had a profound impact on the environment. Factories polluted the air and waterways, leading to widespread health problems in urban areas. People crowded into cities, drawn by the promise of jobs, but many found that life in the city was just as difficult as life in the countryside. Diseases spread quickly in the unsanitary conditions, and housing was scarce and often inadequate.

Despite these problems, the industrial revolution spurred economic growth, improved transportation, and led to the creation of new goods and services. The revolution also sparked technological advances that changed the way people lived and worked, including the invention of the steam engine, the spinning jenny, and the power loom.

1. What was one of the major impacts of the industrial revolution on workers?

(a) It reduced working hours.

(b) It improved wages for all workers.

(c) It led to the use of more advanced technology.

(d) It caused long working hours and dangerous conditions.

2. According to the passage, how did the industrial revolution affect women and children?

(a) They were given more education opportunities.

(b) They were paid equally to men.

(c) They were often employed in factories.

(d) They were not involved in industrial work.

3. The word "profound" in the second paragraph most nearly means:

(a) superficial.

(b) significant.

(c) common.

(d) temporary.

4. According to the passage, what was one environmental consequence of the industrial revolution?

(a) Improved public health.

(b) Increased pollution of air and waterways.

(c) Creation of more green spaces.

(d) Reduced population in urban areas.

5. Which of the following was not a technological advancement mentioned in the passage?

(a) The steam engine.

(b) The power loom.

(c) The electric motor.

(d) The spinning jenny.

6. The passage implies that life in the cities during the industrial revolution was:

(a) safer than life in the countryside.

(b) easier than life in the countryside.

(c) just as difficult as life in the countryside.

(d) less crowded than life in the countryside.

7. What is the main idea of the passage?

(a) The industrial revolution improved working conditions for factory workers.

(b) The industrial revolution brought about both progress and challenges for society.

(c) The industrial revolution had little impact on transportation.

(d) The industrial revolution caused the decline of the global economy.

8. Based on the passage, which of the following statements is true?

(a) The industrial revolution led to a decrease in technological innovation.

(b) Labor reforms were quickly implemented during the industrial revolution.

(c) The industrial revolution helped spur economic growth despite its challenges.

(d) Urban living conditions improved rapidly during the industrial revolution.

Reading Passage 2

Questions 9–16 are based on the following passage.

The concept of time has fascinated philosophers, scientists, and artists for centuries. Time is an elusive force, constantly moving forward, yet we have no control over it. Ancient civilizations created sundials to track the sun's position, giving them the ability to measure hours. Over time, humans invented more sophisticated devices such as water clocks, pendulum clocks, and, eventually, the mechanical clock.

One of the most significant breakthroughs in timekeeping came with the invention of the atomic clock in the 20th century. Atomic clocks are so precise that they lose only one second every million years. This level of precision has allowed scientists to make discoveries in fields like physics and astronomy, where accurate time measurement is essential.

Despite these advancements, time remains a mysterious and sometimes frustrating concept for many. The idea that time moves at the same rate for everyone is an illusion. According to Einstein's theory of relativity, time is relative—meaning it can stretch or compress depending on speed and gravity. This is why astronauts age slightly slower than people on Earth due to the high speeds at which they travel in space.

9. According to the passage, which invention was not mentioned as a tool for measuring time?

(a) Water clocks.

223

(b) Sundials.

(c) Atomic clocks.

(d) Digital watches.

10. What does the passage imply about the concept of time?

(a) It is fully understood by scientists.

(b) It is mysterious and not fully controllable.

(c) It moves at the same rate for everyone.

(d) It has remained unchanged since ancient times.

11. Which word in the passage best describes the advancement of timekeeping tools?

(a) Slow.

(b) Gradual.

(c) Rapid.

(d) Unnecessary.

12. What is the main purpose of the passage?

(a) To explain the history of timekeeping tools and their impact.

(b) To argue that time is a force that can be controlled.

(c) To describe the role of clocks in modern physics.

(d) To compare timekeeping methods across different cultures.

13. According to the passage, what is one feature of an atomic clock?

(a) It measures time more accurately than any other clock.

(b) It loses several seconds every year.

(c) It was invented during ancient times.

(d) It has limited scientific applications.

14. The phrase "time is relative" in the passage most likely means:

(a) Time passes at the same rate for everyone.

(b) Time can speed up or slow down depending on various factors.

(c) Time is a constant force in the universe.

(d) Time always moves faster in space.

224

15. Why does the author mention Einstein's theory of relativity?

(a) To illustrate why timekeeping is important.

(b) To explain why time is different for astronauts.

(c) To show how technology has improved over time.

(d) To argue that time moves faster on Earth than in space.

16. The passage suggests that the invention of the atomic clock was important because:

(a) It was invented during the industrial revolution.

(b) It allows scientists to measure time with extreme accuracy.

(c) It led to the invention of mechanical clocks.

(d) It helped improve the design of water clocks.

Reading Passage 3

Questions 17–24 are based on the following passage.

The world's oceans are essential to life on Earth. Covering more than 70% of the planet's surface, they regulate the climate, provide food, and support a vast array of marine life. However, human activities have caused significant harm to the oceans. Pollution, overfishing, and climate change are all contributing to the degradation of marine ecosystems.

One of the most pressing concerns is plastic pollution. Every year, millions of tons of plastic waste end up in the oceans, where it can take hundreds of years to break down. This plastic not only harms marine life, but it also enters the food chain, potentially affecting human health.

Overfishing is another major issue. Many species of fish are being caught at a rate faster than they can reproduce, leading to a decline in fish populations. This not only threatens the survival of these species but also affects the livelihoods of millions of people who depend on fishing for their income.

Climate change is exacerbating these problems. Rising sea temperatures are causing coral reefs to bleach and die, while melting polar ice is contributing to rising sea levels. These changes have far-reaching consequences, affecting not only marine life but also coastal communities around the world.

Despite these challenges, there is hope. Governments and organizations around the world are working to protect the oceans by establishing marine protected areas, reducing plastic waste, and promoting sustainable fishing practices. However, much more needs to be done to ensure the health of our oceans for future generations.

17. What is one of the primary causes of ocean degradation mentioned in the passage?

(a) Urbanization.

(b) Plastic pollution.

(c) Overpopulation.

(d) Industrial farming.

18. The passage implies that plastic pollution is harmful because:

(a) It breaks down into chemicals that are beneficial to marine life.

(b) It can take centuries to decompose, affecting both marine life and humans.

(c) It is limited to certain areas of the ocean and is not widespread.

(d) It disappears quickly once it reaches the ocean surface.

19. Which of the following is not a consequence of overfishing according to the passage?

(a) Declining fish populations.

(b) Threats to human livelihoods.

(c) Increased biodiversity in marine ecosystems.

(d) Risk to the survival of certain fish species.

20. The word "exacerbating" in the third paragraph most likely means:

(a) Alleviating.

(b) Worsening.

(c) Balancing.

(d) Ignoring.

21. According to the passage, how does climate change affect coral reefs?

(a) It leads to the creation of new coral species.

(b) It helps corals grow at a faster rate.

(c) It causes coral reefs to bleach and die.

(d) It has no impact on coral reefs.

22. What is one solution proposed in the passage to help protect the oceans?

(a) Promoting increased fishing to control overpopulation of marine species.

(b) Establishing marine protected areas.

(c) Reducing the amount of marine life in the food chain.

(d) Increasing urban development along coastlines.

23. Which of the following statements can be inferred from the passage?

(a) Overfishing has no direct impact on coastal communities.

(b) Climate change is the only threat to marine ecosystems.

(c) The health of the oceans is linked to the health of human populations.

(d) The oceans are only important for regulating global temperatures.

24. What is the main message of the passage?

(a) The oceans are in crisis, but efforts are being made to protect them.

(b) Ocean pollution is a problem that cannot be solved.

(c) The oceans are unaffected by human activities.

(d) The world's oceans are beyond saving.

Reading Passage 4

Questions 25–32 are based on the following passage.

In the heart of the Amazon rainforest, researchers have discovered a community of indigenous people who have lived in harmony with their environment for centuries. The community, known as the Yanonami, has developed sophisticated techniques for hunting, farming, and building that allow them to survive in one of the world's most challenging environments. The Yanonami use a technique called "slash-and-burn" agriculture, where small patches of forest are cleared and burned to create fertile soil for crops. After a few years, the land is left to regenerate, and the community moves on to another area.

While this method has allowed the Yanonami to live sustainably for generations, it is now under threat. Deforestation, driven by logging, agriculture, and mining, is rapidly encroaching on Yanonami land. The

227

destruction of the forest is not only reducing the amount of land available for farming but also disrupting the delicate balance of the ecosystem.

The Yanonami are not alone in facing these challenges. Indigenous communities around the world are fighting to protect their land and way of life from the forces of modernization and industrialization. Many of these communities are calling for stronger protections of their land, recognizing that their survival is linked to the health of the ecosystems they depend on.

25. What is the primary method of agriculture used by the Yanonami?

(a) Irrigation farming.

(b) Terrace farming.

(c) Slash-and-burn agriculture.

(d) Hydroponic farming.

26. According to the passage, what is one reason why the Yanonami's way of life is under threat?

(a) Overpopulation within the community.

(b) Encroachment by deforestation and industrial activities.

(c) Lack of access to modern farming tools.

(d) Internal conflicts among the Yanonami.

27. The word "encroaching" in the second paragraph most nearly means:

(a) Supporting.

(b) Advancing.

(c) Retreating.

(d) Stabilizing.

28. What does the passage suggest about the relationship between the Yanonami and their environment?

(a) The Yanonami exploit the environment for maximum profit.

(b) The Yanonami rely on modern technology to sustain their way of life.

(c) The Yanonami live in harmony with their environment, using sustainable methods.

(d) The Yanonami are indifferent to environmental changes.

29. The passage implies that deforestation is problematic for the Yanonami because:

(a) It provides new land for farming but is difficult to cultivate.

(b) It disrupts the ecosystem and reduces available farming land.

(c) It leads to conflicts with neighboring communities.

(d) It improves the fertility of the soil in the region.

30. According to the passage, how are indigenous communities around the world similar to the Yanonami?

(a) They all use slash-and-burn agriculture to farm.

(b) They face threats from industrialization and deforestation.

(c) They are unwilling to adopt modern farming techniques.

(d) They have been able to avoid the effects of modernization.

31. What is one possible solution for the challenges faced by the Yanonami?

(a) Introducing large-scale farming methods.

(b) Moving the community to urban areas.

(c) Protecting their land from industrial encroachment.

(d) Encouraging deforestation to increase farmland.

32. What is the main idea of the passage?

(a) The Yanonami have developed an advanced civilization in the Amazon.

(b) The Yanonami are facing threats to their way of life due to deforestation and modernization.

(c) The Yanonami are a community that rejects modern farming practices.

(d) The Yanonami are thriving due to their isolation from the outside world.

Reading Passage 5

Questions 33–40 are based on the following passage.

Artificial intelligence (AI) has been making headlines in recent years, with advancements in machine learning and robotics revolutionizing various industries. From healthcare to finance, AI is being used to analyze data, perform tasks, and even make decisions that were once the sole domain of humans. However, as AI continues to advance, there are growing concerns about its impact on employment and society as a whole.

Proponents of AI argue that automation will lead to increased efficiency and productivity. By taking over mundane and repetitive tasks, AI can free up humans to focus on more complex and creative work. In the healthcare industry, for example, AI is being used to analyze medical images and diagnose diseases with incredible accuracy. This not only speeds up the diagnostic process but also allows doctors to focus on providing personalized care to their patients.

However, critics argue that AI poses a threat to jobs. As machines become more capable, there is a risk that they will replace human workers in various sectors. This could lead to widespread unemployment, particularly in industries that rely heavily on manual labor. Additionally, there are concerns about the ethical implications of allowing machines to make decisions that could impact people's lives.

33. According to the passage, what is one positive impact of AI on healthcare?

(a) AI can perform surgeries more effectively than human doctors.

(b) AI allows doctors to focus more on personalized patient care.

(c) AI has replaced human doctors in many hospitals.

(d) AI is used to replace nurses in patient care.

34. What is one concern critics have about AI according to the passage?

(a) AI will only improve efficiency in the workplace.

(b) AI may lead to widespread unemployment by replacing human workers.

(c) AI will make jobs more available in manual labor industries.

(d) AI has no real impact on employment.

35. The word "mundane" in the second paragraph most nearly means:

(a) exciting.

(b) creative.

(c) repetitive.

(d) dangerous.

36. What is one argument proponents of AI use to support its development?

(a) AI will help machines replace humans in all areas of work.

(b) AI will increase productivity and free humans to engage in more complex work.

(c) AI will slow down technological advancements in the future.

(d) AI will only be useful in the healthcare industry.

37. According to the passage, what is one potential negative consequence of AI advancement?

(a) Increased job opportunities in every industry.

(b) AI taking over tasks that require creativity and decision-making.

(c) Machines replacing human workers, leading to job loss.

(d) AI reducing the need for technological development in the workplace.

38. What does the passage suggest about the future of AI in society?

(a) AI will have a minimal impact on employment.

(b) AI will only benefit the healthcare and finance industries.

(c) AI will create ethical challenges related to its decision-making capabilities.

(d) AI will eventually replace all human workers.

39. According to the passage, how does AI affect productivity?

(a) AI reduces productivity by requiring human supervision.

(b) AI increases productivity by automating repetitive tasks.

(c) AI slows down productivity in manual labor industries.

(d) AI has no impact on productivity.

40. What is the main idea of the passage?

(a) AI is advancing rapidly, but there are concerns about its impact on employment and society.

(b) AI has only negative effects on industries like healthcare and finance.

(c) AI will not affect jobs or ethical considerations in the near future.

(d) AI is not likely to replace human workers anytime soon.

231

Reading Passage 6

Questions 41–48 are based on the following passage.

The Grand Canyon, located in northern Arizona, is one of the most iconic natural landmarks in the United States. It is a massive gorge carved by the Colorado River over millions of years, stretching 277 miles in length, up to 18 miles in width, and more than a mile deep in some places. The canyon's striking layers of red, orange, and pink rock formations tell the story of Earth's geological history, with some layers dating back nearly two billion years.

The Grand Canyon is not only a geological wonder but also a site of cultural significance. For thousands of years, it has been home to indigenous peoples, including the Hualapai, Hopi, Havasupai, and Navajo tribes. These groups have long maintained a spiritual connection to the land, believing that the canyon holds deep cultural and religious meaning. Today, the Grand Canyon is also a popular tourist destination, attracting millions of visitors each year who come to hike, raft, and marvel at the natural beauty.

However, the Grand Canyon is also facing environmental challenges. The increasing number of visitors has led to concerns about the impact of tourism on the fragile ecosystem. Pollution, erosion, and habitat destruction are all issues that threaten the long-term health of the canyon. Additionally, climate change is exacerbating these problems by causing more extreme weather patterns, such as droughts and intense heat, which affect both the landscape and the species that live there.

41. According to the passage, what has caused the Grand Canyon to form over millions of years?

(a) Glaciers.

(b) Earthquakes.

(c) The Colorado River.

(d) Volcanic eruptions.

42. What is one reason why the Grand Canyon is significant to indigenous peoples?

(a) It is a site for large-scale agricultural projects.

(b) It has been home to their ancestors for thousands of years.

(c) It is used for large-scale mining operations.

(d) It has no cultural importance.

232

43. The word "gorge" in the first paragraph most likely means:

(a) a deep valley.

(b) a flat plain.

(c) a mountain range.

(d) a shallow river.

44. What environmental concerns does the passage mention in relation to the Grand Canyon?

(a) Industrial development.

(b) Mining and deforestation.

(c) The impact of tourism and climate change.

(d) Overpopulation in nearby cities.

45. How does climate change affect the Grand Canyon, according to the passage?

(a) It is improving weather patterns in the area.

(b) It is causing more extreme weather, like droughts and heat waves.

(c) It is reducing the number of visitors to the canyon.

(d) It has no significant impact on the landscape or ecosystem.

46. Based on the passage, what is one challenge posed by tourism at the Grand Canyon?

(a) It has led to a decrease in indigenous populations.

(b) It is contributing to pollution, erosion, and habitat destruction.

(c) It is reducing the geological significance of the canyon.

(d) It has no effect on the environment.

47. What is the main idea of the passage?

(a) The Grand Canyon is a natural and cultural landmark facing environmental challenges.

(b) The Grand Canyon has no significant historical or environmental value.

(c) The Grand Canyon is used primarily for mining and industrial purposes.

(d) Tourism is the only significant factor affecting the Grand Canyon.

48. Which of the following can be inferred from the passage about the Grand Canyon's future?

(a) The environmental challenges will likely be resolved quickly.

(b) The impact of tourism and climate change may continue to worsen.

(c) Indigenous groups will abandon their connection to the land.

(d) The Colorado River will cease to shape the canyon in the future.

Reading Passage 7

Questions 49–56 are based on the following passage.

The development of the internet has revolutionized communication, commerce, and entertainment. In the early days of the internet, it was primarily a tool used by scientists and researchers to share data and information. However, as technology advanced, the internet became accessible to the general public, leading to the rise of email, social media, and online shopping. Today, the internet is an integral part of everyday life for billions of people around the world.

One of the most significant impacts of the internet has been on the way people communicate. Email replaced traditional mail for many personal and business communications, allowing messages to be sent almost instantly across the globe. Social media platforms like Facebook, Twitter, and Instagram have further transformed communication by allowing people to share their thoughts, experiences, and photos in real-time with large audiences.

The internet has also changed the way businesses operate. E-commerce giants like Amazon have made it possible for consumers to purchase products online and have them delivered to their doorsteps, often within a matter of days. This has led to the decline of traditional brick-and-mortar stores, as more people opt for the convenience of online shopping. At the same time, the internet has opened up new opportunities for entrepreneurs and small businesses to reach global markets.

While the internet has brought many benefits, it has also created challenges. Issues like privacy concerns, cybercrime, and the spread of misinformation have become major problems. As people share more of their personal information online, they are increasingly vulnerable to identity theft and other forms of cybercrime. Moreover, the rise of social media has made it easier for false information to spread quickly, leading to confusion and mistrust.

49. What was one of the early uses of the internet, according to the passage?

(a) To sell products online.

(b) To share scientific data and information.

(c) To allow people to send photos instantly.

(d) To replace traditional forms of entertainment.

50. According to the passage, what is one way the internet has changed communication?

(a) It has made sending traditional mail faster.

(b) It has replaced the use of telephones entirely.

(c) It has allowed for instant messaging across the globe.

(d) It has limited the number of people who can communicate at once.

51. What impact has the internet had on traditional brick-and-mortar stores?

(a) It has led to a decline in sales as more people shop online.

(b) It has increased foot traffic to physical stores.

(c) It has made it easier for consumers to find local products.

(d) It has no impact on traditional stores.

52. The word "integral" in the first paragraph most likely means:

(a) optional.

(b) important.

(c) complex.

(d) temporary.

53. What does the passage imply about the impact of social media on communication?

(a) Social media has replaced all other forms of communication.

(b) Social media has made it easier for people to share information in real time.

(c) Social media has limited people's ability to communicate with large audiences.

(d) Social media has slowed the spread of information.

54. According to the passage, what is one benefit of the internet for businesses?

(a) It has eliminated the need for physical stores entirely.

(b) It has allowed small businesses to reach global markets.

(c) It has made it harder for consumers to find products.

(d) It has reduced the number of entrepreneurs starting new businesses.

55. What is one challenge posed by the internet, according to the passage?

(a) The internet has made it harder for people to find accurate information.

(b) Privacy concerns and the spread of misinformation have become major issues.

(c) The internet has eliminated all forms of traditional communication.

(d) The internet has made cybercrime a rare occurrence.

56. What is the main idea of the passage?

(a) The internet has only created challenges for society.

(b) The internet has revolutionized communication, commerce, and entertainment, but also brought challenges.

(c) The internet has replaced traditional communication methods, making them obsolete.

(d) The internet has had a minimal impact on businesses and communication.

Reading Passage 8

Questions 57–62 are based on the following passage.

In 1969, Neil Armstrong became the first human to set foot on the moon, uttering the now-famous words, "That's one small step for man, one giant leap for mankind." This event marked the culmination of the space race, a fierce competition between the United States and the Soviet Union during the Cold War to achieve dominance in space exploration.

The moon landing was a momentous achievement, made possible by years of technological advancements and the dedicated efforts of thousands of scientists, engineers, and astronauts. The Apollo program, which sent astronauts to the moon, was a massive undertaking that required precise planning, complex engineering, and significant financial investment. Despite the risks, the mission was a success, and the images of Armstrong and his fellow astronauts walking on the moon captivated the world.

The success of the moon landing had far-reaching implications. It demonstrated the capabilities of human ingenuity and inspired a new generation of scientists and explorers. It also reinforced the importance of space exploration as a means of advancing scientific knowledge and technology. Today, space agencies like NASA and private companies like SpaceX are continuing the legacy of the Apollo program by developing new technologies and preparing for future missions to the moon and beyond.

57. What event is the passage primarily describing?

(a) The first mission to Mars.

(b) The space race between the United States and China.

(c) The moon landing of 1969.

(d) The invention of the first spaceship.

58. The phrase "one giant leap for mankind" in the first paragraph most likely means:

(a) A small but important achievement for the U.S. government.

(b) A significant advancement for all of humanity.

(c) A minor step in the space race.

(d) A short-lived success for the space program.

59. According to the passage, what was one factor that contributed to the success of the moon landing?

(a) The collaboration between NASA and SpaceX.

(b) The financial support from private investors.

(c) The efforts of scientists, engineers, and astronauts.

(d) The invention of new space shuttles by the Soviet Union.

60. The word "momentous" in the second paragraph most likely means:

(a) insignificant.

(b) urgent.

(c) important.

(d) difficult.

61. What is one legacy of the moon landing, according to the passage?

(a) It discouraged future space exploration efforts.

(b) It inspired new generations of scientists and explorers.

(c) It caused a decline in scientific research.

(d) It led to the end of the space race entirely.

62. What is the main idea of the passage?

Language Subtest

60 Questions | 25 Minutes

Directions: In each of the following questions, you will be asked to choose the correct answer based on your understanding of English grammar, punctuation, capitalization, and sentence structure. Read each question carefully and choose the best option.

Punctuation and Usage (Questions 1–15)

This section focuses on your ability to identify and correct errors in punctuation and usage. Pay careful attention to commas, periods, apostrophes, colons,

(a) The moon landing was a small step in space exploration.

(b) The Apollo program was too expensive to be considered successful.

(c) The moon landing was a significant achievement that advanced space exploration.

(d) The moon landing had no real impact on space exploration.

and semi-colons, as well as word usage within sentences.

1. Choose the sentence that is punctuated correctly.
a) "The boy ran quickly, but, he tripped over the toy."
b) "The boy ran quickly but, he tripped over the toy."
c) "The boy ran quickly, but he tripped over the toy."
d) "The boy ran quickly but he tripped over, the toy."

2. Which sentence correctly uses an apostrophe?
a) The dogs bone is missing.
b) The dog's bone is missing.

c) The dogs' bone is missing.
d) The dogs bone's is missing.

---

3. Select the sentence with correct punctuation.
a) "I went to the store; however I forgot to buy milk."
b) "I went to the store, however, I forgot to buy milk."
c) "I went to the store, however I forgot to buy milk."
d) "I went to the store; however, I forgot to buy milk."

---

4. Which sentence uses commas correctly?
a) My brother who is five loves playing soccer.
b) My brother, who is five loves, playing soccer.
c) My brother, who is five, loves playing soccer.
d) My brother who is five, loves playing soccer.

---

5. Select the sentence that is correctly punctuated.
a) "The books on the table are old but valuable."
b) "The books, on the table are old, but valuable."

c) "The books on the table, are old but, valuable."
d) "The books on the table are old, but valuable."

---

6. Identify the sentence that correctly uses a semi-colon.
a) "The meeting starts at 3:00 pm; make sure you arrive early."
b) "The meeting starts at 3:00 pm, make sure you arrive early."
c) "The meeting starts at 3:00 pm; make sure, you arrive early."
d) "The meeting starts at 3:00 pm: make sure you arrive early."

---

7. Choose the sentence with correct punctuation.
a) "We need eggs, bread, and milk from the store."
b) "We need, eggs bread and milk from the store."
c) "We need eggs, bread and, milk from the store."
d) "We need eggs bread, and, milk from the store."

---

8. Which sentence is punctuated correctly?
a) "After we eat dinner let's go for a walk."

b) "After we eat dinner, let's go for a walk."

c) "After, we eat dinner, let's go for a walk."

d) "After we eat dinner let's, go for a walk."

---

9. Select the correctly punctuated sentence.

a) "The professor asked if we had finished the reading."

b) "The professor asked, if we had finished the reading."

c) "The professor asked if, we had finished the reading."

d) "The professor, asked if we had finished the reading."

---

10. Which sentence has proper punctuation?

a) "John's car is in the driveway, but he can't find the keys."

b) "John's car is in the driveway but, he can't find the keys."

c) "John's car, is in the driveway, but he can't find the keys."

d) "John's car is in the driveway but he can't, find the keys."

---

11. Which of the following sentences is punctuated correctly?

a) "She has three dogs; a poodle, a beagle, and a bulldog."

b) "She has three dogs: a poodle, a beagle, and a bulldog."

c) "She has three dogs, a poodle a beagle, and a bulldog."

d) "She has three dogs; a poodle; a beagle; and a bulldog."

---

12. Identify the sentence with proper punctuation.

a) "We need to buy pencils erasers, and notebooks for school."

b) "We need to buy pencils, erasers, and notebooks for school."

c) "We need to buy pencils, erasers and notebooks, for school."

d) "We need to buy pencils erasers and, notebooks for school."

---

13. Choose the correctly punctuated sentence.

a) "While I was out of the office, I missed three calls and two emails."

b) "While I was out of the office I missed, three calls and two emails."

c) "While I was out of the office, I missed, three calls and two emails."

d) "While, I was out of the office I missed three calls and two emails."

14. Which sentence uses punctuation correctly?
a) "She left the house, after she finished breakfast."
b) "She left, the house after she finished breakfast."
c) "She left the house after she finished breakfast."
d) "She, left the house after she finished breakfast."

15. Identify the correctly punctuated sentence.
a) "The teacher gave us two assignments; read the chapter and answer the questions."
b) "The teacher gave us two assignments: read the chapter and answer the questions."
c) "The teacher gave us two assignments, read the chapter and answer the questions."
d) "The teacher gave us two assignments: read the chapter, and answer the questions."

Grammar and Sentence Structure (Questions 16–30)

This section assesses your ability to understand and correct errors in sentence structure, verb tenses, and grammatical agreement.

16. Select the sentence with correct subject-verb agreement.
a) The dogs runs fast.
b) The dogs run fast.
c) The dog run fast.
d) The dog runs fast.

17. Which sentence is grammatically correct?
a) Neither John nor his friends is coming to the party.
b) Neither John nor his friends are coming to the party.
c) Neither John or his friends are coming to the party.
d) Neither John or his friends is coming to the party.

18. Choose the sentence that uses verb tense correctly.
a) She had went to the store before coming home.
b) She has went to the store before coming home.
c) She had gone to the store before coming home.
d) She gone to the store before coming home.

19. Select the grammatically correct sentence.
a) They was going to the movie theater.
b) They were going to the movie theater.
c) They were go to the movie theater.
d) They was go to the movie theater.

20. Which sentence has correct pronoun-antecedent agreement?
a) Every student must bring their own lunch.
b) Every student must bring his or her own lunch.
c) Every student must bring their lunch.
d) Every student must bring his lunch.

21. Identify the sentence that uses verb tenses correctly.
a) By the time the show started, we has been waiting for an hour.
b) By the time the show started, we had been waiting for an hour.
c) By the time the show starts, we had been waiting for an hour.
d) By the time the show starts, we has been waiting for an hour.

22. Select the sentence with correct subject-verb agreement.
a) Each of the girls are excited about the trip.
b) Each of the girls is excited about the trip.
c) Each of the girls were excited about the trip.
d) Each of the girls was excited about the trip.

23. Which sentence is grammatically correct?
a) Either the manager or the employees is responsible for this.
b) Either the manager or the employees are responsible for this.
c) Either the manager or the employees was responsible for this.
d) Either the manager or the employees were responsible for this.

24. Choose the correct sentence.
a) They doesn't want to go to the park.
b) They don't wants to go to the park.
c) They don't want to go to the park.
d) They doesn't wants to go to the park.

25. Which sentence uses modifiers correctly?
a) She quickly ran to the store, in a hurry.
b) She ran quickly to the store, in a hurry.
c) She ran to the store, in a hurry

quickly.
d) Quickly she ran in a hurry to the store.

---

26. Identify the sentence with correct verb tense usage.
a) I has finished the project already.
b) I have finished the project already.
c) I am finish the project already.
d) I have finishing the project already.

---

27. Choose the correct sentence.
a) Neither the team nor the coach were ready.
b) Neither the team nor the coach was ready.
c) Neither the team or the coach were ready.
d) Neither the team or the coach was ready.

---

28. Which sentence uses parallel structure?
a) She enjoys reading, swimming, and to hike.
b) She enjoys reading, swimming, and hiking.
c) She enjoys to read, swim, and hiking.
d) She enjoys to read, swimming, and hiking.

---

29. Select the sentence that uses pronouns correctly.
a) Each student should bring their pencil to class.
b) Each student should bring his or her pencil to class.
c) Each student should bring their pencils to class.
d) Each student should bring his pencil to class.

---

30. Identify the sentence with correct verb agreement.
a) The group of students were excited about the trip.
b) The group of students was excited about the trip.
c) The group of students are excited about the trip.
d) The group of students were excited about the trip.

Capitalization (Questions 31–45)

In this section, you will be asked to identify errors in capitalization, including proper nouns, titles, and beginning of sentences.

---

31. Select the sentence that is correctly capitalized.
a) The president of the united states will

give a speech today.
b) The President of the United States will give a speech today.
c) The president of the United States will give a speech today.
d) The President of the united states will give a speech today.

---

32. Which sentence is capitalized correctly?
a) My family visited the empire state building last summer.
b) My family visited the Empire State Building last summer.
c) My family visited the empire State building last summer.
d) My family visited the Empire state Building last summer.

---

33. Choose the correct sentence.
a) I have an appointment with Dr. smith tomorrow.
b) I have an appointment with dr. Smith tomorrow.
c) I have an appointment with Dr. Smith tomorrow.
d) I have an appointment with dr. smith tomorrow.

---

34. Which sentence uses capitalization correctly?

a) My favorite book is "to kill a mockingbird."
b) My favorite book is "To Kill a Mockingbird."
c) My favorite book is "To kill a Mockingbird."
d) My favorite book is "To Kill A Mockingbird."

---

35. Identify the correctly capitalized sentence.
a) We visited washington, d.c. over the summer.
b) We visited Washington, D.C. over the summer.
c) We visited washington, D.C. over the summer.
d) We visited Washington, d.c. over the summer.

---

36. Choose the sentence that is capitalized correctly.
a) My Aunt Susan is a great cook.
b) My aunt Susan is a great cook.
c) My Aunt susan is a great cook.
d) My aunt susan is a great cook.

---

37. Select the sentence that uses capitalization correctly.
a) My best friend loves the summer Olympics.

b) My best friend loves the Summer olympics.

c) My best friend loves the Summer Olympics.

d) My best friend loves the summer olympics.

38. Which sentence is capitalized correctly?

a) They went to college at Harvard university.

b) They went to college at harvard university.

c) They went to college at Harvard University.

d) They went to college at harvard University.

39. Identify the sentence with correct capitalization.

a) Every Summer, we go to the beach.

b) Every summer, we go to the Beach.

c) Every Summer, we go to the Beach.

d) Every summer, we go to the beach.

40. Which sentence uses proper capitalization?

a) The movie "Star wars" is a classic.

b) The movie "Star Wars" is a classic.

c) The movie "Star Wars" is a Classic.

d) The movie "star wars" is a classic.

41. Choose the correctly capitalized sentence.

a) My favorite store is Macy's, located in the mall.

b) My favorite store is Macy's, located in the Mall.

c) My favorite store is macys, located in the mall.

d) My favorite store is macy's, located in the mall.

42. Which sentence is correctly capitalized?

a) My favorite subject is math.

b) My favorite subject is Math.

c) My favorite subject is math.

d) My favorite subject is Math.

43. Select the sentence with correct capitalization.

a) They visited the louvre Museum in Paris.

b) They visited the Louvre museum in Paris.

c) They visited the louvre museum in Paris.

d) They visited the Louvre Museum in Paris.

44. Which sentence is capitalized correctly?
a) He took the class at Oxford University.
b) He took the class at oxford university.
c) He took the Class at oxford University.
d) He took the Class at Oxford university.

45. Identify the sentence with correct capitalization.
a) Our team traveled to florida for the tournament.
b) Our team traveled to Florida for the tournament.
c) Our team traveled to florida for the Tournament.
d) Our team traveled to Florida for the Tournament.

Spelling and Composition (Questions 46–60)

This section focuses on identifying common spelling errors and improving sentence structure by choosing the most effective wording.

46. Which word is spelled correctly?
a) neice
b) niece
c) nieghbor
d) neigbor

47. Select the correctly spelled word.
a) accomodate
b) accomodete
c) accommodate
d) acommodate

48. Identify the correctly spelled word.
a) beggining
b) beginning
c) begining
d) begginning

49. Choose the correct spelling.
a) recomendation
b) recomindation
c) recommendation
d) recomndation

50. Which word is spelled correctly?
a) definately
b) definitely
c) definetly
d) definatly

51. Select the correctly spelled word.
a) embarassed

b) embaressed
c) embarrassed
d) embareassed

---

52. Identify the correct spelling.
a) seperate
b) separate
c) separrate
d) separete

---

53. Which word is spelled correctly?
a) occurence
b) occurrence
c) ocurrence
d) occurence

---

54. Choose the correctly spelled word.
a) harrass
b) harass
c) haras
d) harras

---

55. Identify the sentence with correct spelling.
a) We went to the libary to study for the test.
b) We went to the library to study for the test.
c) We went to the liberry to study for the test.

d) We went to the librey to study for the test.

---

56. Which word is spelled correctly?
a) february
b) febuary
c) februery
d) feburary

---

57. Choose the correct spelling.
a) recieve
b) receive
c) recive
d) receve

---

58. Identify the correctly spelled word.
a) tommorrow
b) tommorow
c) tomorrow
d) tomorow

---

59. Which word is spelled correctly?
a) accomodate
b) acommodate
c) accommodate
d) accomadate

---

60. Choose the correct spelling.
a) goverment

247

b) government
c) govermant
d) governmant

Mathematics Subtest

Number of Questions: 64

Time Allowed: 45 minutes

1. If $x = 5$ and $y = 7$, what is the value of $2x + 3y$?

(A) 31 (B) 36 (C) 41 (D) 45

2. Simplify the expression: $3(2x - 4) - 5x$

(A) $x - 12$ (B) $-2x + 12$ (C) $x + 12$ (D) $6x - 5$

3. What is the area of a triangle with a base of 10 cm and a height of 5 cm?

(A) 25 cm² (B) 50 cm² (C) 75 cm² (D) 100 cm²

4. Solve for x in the equation $3x - 7 = 14$

(A) 5 (B) 7 (C) 9 (D) 11

5. The sum of three consecutive even numbers is 54. What is the smallest of the three numbers?

(A) 14 (B) 16 (C) 18 (D) 20

6. If the circumference of a circle is 31.4 cm, what is the radius? (Use $\pi = 3.14$)

(A) 5 cm (B) 10 cm (C) 15 cm (D) 20 cm

7. A train travels 120 miles in 3 hours. How far will it travel in 5 hours at the same speed?

(A) 150 miles (B) 200 miles (C) 240 miles (D) 300 miles

8. The ratio of boys to girls in a class is 3:4. If there are 24 girls, how many boys are there?

(A) 16 (B) 18 (C) 20 (D) 22

9. Solve the equation: $5(2x - 3) = 4x + 10$

(A) $x = 2$ (B) $x = 3$ (C) $x = 4$ (D) $x = 5$

10. What is the value of 4^3?

(A) 12 (B) 48 (C) 64 (D) 128

11. If $x^2 = 49$, what is the value of x?

(A) 5 (B) 6 (C) 7 (D) 8

12. A rectangle has a length of 12 cm and a width of 4 cm. What is its perimeter?

(A) 16 cm (B) 24 cm (C) 32 cm (D) 40 cm

13. Simplify: $6x + 3 - 2x - 7$

(A) $4x - 4$ (B) $4x + 10$ (C) $8x - 4$ (D) $8x + 10$

14. If 20% of a number is 60, what is the number?

(A) 200 (B) 240 (C) 300 (D) 400

15. The total cost of 5 identical notebooks is $18.75. What is the cost of each notebook?

(A) $2.50 (B) $3.50 (C) $3.75 (D) $4.25

16. Solve for x in the equation $x/5 + 4 = 10$

(A) 25 (B) 30 (C) 35 (D) 40

17. A car's fuel efficiency is 25 miles per gallon. How many gallons of fuel will the car use to travel 150 miles?

(A) 4 gallons (B) 5 gallons (C) 6 gallons (D) 7 gallons

18. If a number is decreased by 30% and the result is 84, what was the original number?

(A) 105 (B) 110 (C) 120 (D) 135

19. What is the slope of the line given by the equation $3x - 2y = 6$?

(A) 3/2 (B) 2/3 (C) -2/3 (D) -3/2

20. Find the area of a circle with a radius of 7 cm.

(A) 49 cm² (B) 154 cm² (C) 196 cm² (D) 308 cm²

21. Solve the inequality: $2x - 3 > 7$

(A) x > 4 (B) x > 5 (C) x > 6 (D) x > 7

22. A bag contains 3 red marbles, 5 blue marbles, and 7 green marbles. If one marble is drawn at random, what is the probability that it is blue?

(A) 3/15 (B) 5/15 (C) 7/15 (D) 8/15

23. Which of the following is an irrational number?

(A) 9 (B) 3/4 (C) $\sqrt{5}$ (D) 0.5

24. If a = 4 and b = -2, what is $ab + b^2$?

(A) -8 (B) 0 (C) 4 (D) 8

25. A triangle has sides of length 6 cm, 8 cm, and 10 cm. Is this a right triangle?

(A) Yes (B) No (C) Cannot be determined (D) Only if the angles are equal

26. What is the next term in the arithmetic sequence: 5, 8, 11, 14, …?

(A) 16 (B) 17 (C) 18 (D) 19

27. Find the value of $2^4 \times 3^2$

(A) 72 (B) 96 (C) 144 (D) 192

28. A store is offering a 25% discount on all items. If an item originally costs $80, what is the sale price?

(A) $60 (B) $65 (C) $70 (D) $75

29. Solve for x: 7x + 3 = 24

(A) x = 2 (B) x = 3 (C) x = 4 (D) x = 5

30. A parallelogram has a base of 8 cm and a height of 5 cm. What is its area?

(A) 20 cm² (B) 30 cm² (C) 40 cm² (D) 50 cm²

31. If a number is tripled and then increased by 12, the result is 45. What is the number?

(A) 9 (B) 11 (C) 13 (D) 15

32. Find the value of 5! (5 factorial)

(A) 15 (B) 60 (C) 120 (D) 720

33. The product of two numbers is 48, and their sum is 14. What are the two numbers?

(A) 6 and 8 (B) 7 and 7 (C) 12 and 2 (D) 4 and 12

34. What is the least common multiple (LCM) of 12 and 18?

(A) 24 (B) 36 (C) 48 (D) 72

35. A cube has a volume of 125 cm³. What is the length of each side of the cube?

(A) 5 cm (B) 10 cm (C) 15 cm (D) 25 cm

36. A recipe calls for 3 cups of sugar for every 4 cups of flour. If you use 12 cups of sugar, how many cups of flour do you need?

(A) 16 cups (B) 18 cups (C) 20 cups (D) 24 cups

37. Solve for x: 4x + 7 = 3x + 10

(A) x = 1 (B) x = 2 (C) x = 3 (D) x = 4

38. The perimeter of a square is 32 cm. What is the length of one side?

(A) 4 cm (B) 6 cm (C) 8 cm (D) 10 cm

39. A box contains 5 red balls, 3 green balls, and 2 yellow balls. What is the probability of drawing a yellow ball?

(A) 1/5 (B) 2/10 (C) 3/10 (D) 4/10

40. Simplify: 4x - 5 + 3x + 6

(A) 7x - 1 (B) 7x + 1 (C) 8x - 1 (D) 8x + 1

41. Solve for x: (3x - 4)/2 = 5

(A) 6 (B) 7 (C) 8 (D) 9

42. If f(x) = 2x + 3, what is f(4)?

(A) 9 (B) 10 (C) 11 (D) 12

43. What is the median of the following set of numbers: 12, 14, 18, 21, 26, 29, 32?

(A) 18 (B) 21 (C) 23 (D) 26

44. Which of the following is a prime number?

(A) 15 (B) 21 (C) 29 (D) 33

45. Solve for y: y + 3 = 5

(A) y = 2 (B) y = 3 (C) y = 4 (D) y = 5

46. Convert 0.75 to a fraction.

(A) 1/3 (B) 1/2 (C) 3/4 (D) 4/5

47. What is 35% of 80?

(A) 24 (B) 26 (C) 28 (D) 30

48. A car travels 180 miles in 4 hours. What is its average speed?

(A) 40 mph (B) 45 mph (C) 50 mph (D) 55 mph

49. Simplify: 16/64

(A) 1/2 (B) 1/4 (C) 1/6 (D) 1/8

50. What is the next number in the sequence: 2, 4, 8, 16, …?

(A) 24 (B) 32 (C) 36 (D) 40

51. What is the greatest common factor (GCF) of 36 and 48?

(A) 6 (B) 9 (C) 12 (D) 18

52. A triangle has angles of 45°, 45°, and 90°. What type of triangle is it?

(A) Scalene (B) Isosceles (C) Equilateral (D) Right

53. If 3x + 2 = 17, what is x?

(A) 3 (B) 4 (C) 5 (D) 6

54. Simplify: $(2x^2)(3x)$

(A) $5x^2$ (B) $6x^3$ (C) $6x^2$ (D) $8x^3$

55. The area of a square is 81 cm². What is the length of one side?

(A) 7 cm (B) 8 cm (C) 9 cm (D) 10 cm

56. If a = 2 and b = 3, what is the value of $2a^2 + b^2$?

(A) 10 (B) 12 (C) 14 (D) 18

57. Solve for x: 2x + 7 = 4x - 5

(A) x = -6 (B) x = -5 (C) x = 6 (D) x = 7

58. What is the greatest common factor (GCF) of 24 and 60?

(A) 6 (B) 12 (C) 18 (D) 24

59. If 3 pens cost $1.50, how much will 8 pens cost?

(A) $3.50 (B) $4.00 (C) $4.50 (D) $5.00

60. Solve the inequality: 5x - 2 ≤ 18

(A) x ≤ 4 (B) x ≤ 5 (C) x ≤ 6 (D) x ≤ 7

61. What is the square root of 144?

(A) 10 (B) 11 (C) 12 (D) 13

62. What is the mode of the following numbers: 2, 4, 4, 6, 8?

(A) 2 (B) 4 (C) 6 (D) 8

63. A recipe calls for 1.5 cups of sugar. If you are making 3 times the recipe, how many cups of sugar will you need?

(A) 3 (B) 4.5 (C) 5 (D) 6

64. Solve for x: $3x - 8 = 10$

(A) x = 4 (B) x = 5 (C) x = 6 (D) x = 7

Answer Key and Detailed Explanations

Section 1: Synonyms (Questions 1-10)

1. **The word "benevolent" most nearly means:**
   Answer: (A) Charitable
   Explanation: "Benevolent" means showing kindness or charity. The other choices are unrelated or opposites.

2. **The word "industrious" most nearly means:**
   Answer: (B) Active
   Explanation: "Industrious" refers to being hardworking and diligent, which is similar to being "active." "Lazy" is the opposite, and the other options do not fit.

3. **The word "frugal" most nearly means:**
   Answer: (C) Economical
   Explanation: "Frugal" means being careful with money or resources, which aligns with "economical." "Wasteful" is the opposite.

4. **The word "verbose" most nearly means:**
   Answer: (B) Talkative
   Explanation: "Verbose" refers to using more words than necessary, which relates to being "talkative."

5. **The word "abstain" most nearly means:**
   Answer: (B) Resist
   Explanation: "Abstain" means to refrain from doing something, which is similar to "resist." "Indulge" is the opposite.

6. **The word "lament" most nearly means:**
   Answer: (B) Mourn
   Explanation: "Lament" means to express sorrow or grief, which aligns with "mourn."

7. **The word "diligent" most nearly means:**
   Answer: (B) Hardworking
   Explanation: "Diligent" describes someone who is attentive and hardworking.

8. **The word "placid" most nearly means:**
   Answer: (A) Calm
   Explanation: "Placid" means peaceful and calm, which is the opposite of "wild" or "noisy."

9. **The word "elated" most nearly means:**
   Answer: (B) Excited
   Explanation: "Elated" refers to

being extremely happy or excited.

10. **The word "scrupulous" most nearly means:**
Answer: (B) Careful
Explanation: "Scrupulous" means being extremely careful or attentive to details, often in an ethical sense.

Section 2: Antonyms (Questions 11-20)

11. **The word "audacious" most nearly means:**
Answer: (A) Timid
Explanation: "Audacious" means bold or daring, so its opposite is "timid."

12. **The word "rigid" most nearly means:**
Answer: (A) Flexible
Explanation: "Rigid" means stiff or inflexible, so its opposite is "flexible."

13. **The word "benevolent" most nearly means:**
Answer: (A) Malevolent
Explanation: "Malevolent" is the opposite of "benevolent," which means kind or charitable.

14. **The word "adamant" most nearly means:**

Answer: (A) Yielding
Explanation: "Adamant" means firm or unyielding, so its opposite is "yielding."

15. **The word "indifferent" most nearly means:**
Answer: (A) Biased
Explanation: "Indifferent" means neutral or unconcerned, so its opposite is "biased."

16. **The word "conspicuous" most nearly means:**
Answer: (B) Hidden
Explanation: "Conspicuous" means obvious or easily seen, so its opposite is "hidden."

17. **The word "tedious" most nearly means:**
Answer: (A) Exciting
Explanation: "Tedious" means boring or repetitive, so its opposite is "exciting."

18. **The word "vigilant" most nearly means:**
Answer: (C) Careless
Explanation: "Vigilant" means watchful or alert, so its opposite is "careless."

19. **The word "vague" most nearly means:**
Answer: (A) Clear
Explanation: "Vague" means

unclear or indefinite, so its opposite is "clear."

20. **The word "obstinate" most nearly means:**
    Answer: (B) Agreeable
    Explanation: "Obstinate" means stubborn, so its opposite is "agreeable."

Section 3: Analogies (Questions 21-30)

21. **Hand is to glove as foot is to:**
    Answer: (A) Shoe
    Explanation: A glove covers a hand, and a shoe covers a foot.

22. **Water is to thirst as food is to:**
    Answer: (A) Hunger
    Explanation: Water satisfies thirst, and food satisfies hunger.

23. **Bird is to wing as fish is to:**
    Answer: (A) Fin
    Explanation: A bird has wings to fly, and a fish has fins to swim.

24. **Teacher is to classroom as doctor is to:**
    Answer: (C) Hospital
    Explanation: A teacher works in a classroom, and a doctor works in a hospital.

25. **Library is to books as museum is to:**
    Answer: (D) Exhibits
    Explanation: A library holds books, and a museum holds exhibits.

26. **Hat is to head as glove is to:**
    Answer: (A) Hand
    Explanation: A hat is worn on the head, and a glove is worn on the hand.

27. **Sun is to day as moon is to:**
    Answer: (B) Night
    Explanation: The sun is associated with the day, and the moon is associated with the night.

28. **Pencil is to write as brush is to:**
    Answer: (A) Paint
    Explanation: A pencil is used for writing, and a brush is used for painting.

29. **Dog is to bark as cat is to:**
    Answer: (A) Meow
    Explanation: A dog barks, and a cat meows.

30. **Leaf is to tree as petal is to:**
    Answer: (A) Flower
    Explanation: A leaf is part of a tree, and a petal is part of a flower.

Section 4: Verbal Logic (Questions 31-43)

31. **Some teachers are strict. All strict people are disliked. Therefore:**
    Answer: (A) Some teachers are disliked.
    Explanation: If some teachers are strict and all strict people are disliked, then some teachers must be disliked.

32. **All birds have feathers. No animals with feathers can swim. Therefore:**
    Answer: (B) No birds can swim.
    Explanation: Since all birds have feathers and no animals with feathers can swim, no birds can swim.

33. **Some books are long. All long books are boring. Therefore:**
    Answer: (A) Some books are boring.
    Explanation: If some books are long and all long books are boring, then some books must be boring.

34. **All triangles have three sides. No shape with three sides is a square. Therefore:**
    Answer: (B) No triangles are squares.
    Explanation: If triangles have three sides and no shape with three sides is a square, then no triangles can be squares.

35. **Some fruits are apples. All apples are red. Therefore:**
    Answer: (A) Some fruits are red.
    Explanation: If some fruits are apples and all apples are red, then some fruits must be red.

36. **All dogs bark. No animals that bark are silent. Therefore:**
    Answer: (C) No dogs are silent.
    Explanation: Since all dogs bark and no barking animals are silent, no dogs can be silent.

37. **Some cars are fast. All fast vehicles are expensive. Therefore:**
    Answer: (A) Some cars are expensive.
    Explanation: If some cars are fast and all fast vehicles are expensive, then some cars must be expensive.

38. **All fish swim. Some swimmers are fast. Therefore:**
    Answer: (B) Some fish are fast.
    Explanation: If all fish swim and some swimmers are fast, then it is possible that some fish are fast.

39. **All pens have ink. Some ink is red. Therefore:**
Answer: (A) Some pens have red ink.
Explanation: If all pens have ink and some ink is red, then some pens must have red ink.

40. **Some clouds are white. All white things are beautiful. Therefore:**
Answer: (A) Some clouds are beautiful.
Explanation: If some clouds are white and all white things are beautiful, then some clouds must be beautiful.

41. **All flowers bloom. Some blooms are fragrant. Therefore:**
Answer: (A) Some flowers are fragrant.
Explanation: If all flowers bloom and some blooms are fragrant, then some flowers must be fragrant.

42. **Some shoes are leather. All leather items are durable. Therefore:**
Answer: (B) Some shoes are durable.
Explanation: If some shoes are leather and all leather items are durable, then some shoes must be durable.

43. **All cats are mammals. No mammals have feathers. Therefore:**
Answer: (B) No cats have feathers.
Explanation: If all cats are mammals and no mammals have feathers, then no cats can have feathers.

Section 5: Verbal Classifications (Questions 44-60)

44. **Which word does not belong in the following group?**
Answer: (D) Tree
Explanation: All the other words (dog, cat, lion) are animals, while "tree" is a plant.

45. **Which word does not belong in the following group?**
Answer: (D) Carrot
Explanation: All the other words (apple, orange, banana) are fruits, while "carrot" is a vegetable.

46. **Which word does not belong in the following group?**
Answer: (D) Hammer
Explanation: Knife, spoon, and

258

fork are all utensils, while "hammer" is a tool.

47. **Which word does not belong in the following group?**
Answer: (D) Weekend
Explanation: Winter, summer, and autumn are all seasons, while "weekend" is a time period.

48. **Which word does not belong in the following group?**
Answer: (A) Foot
Explanation: Hand, arm, and shoulder are all parts of the upper body, while "foot" is part of the lower body.

49. **Which word does not belong in the following group?**
Answer: (D) Eagle
Explanation: Elephant, mouse, and giraffe are all mammals, while "eagle" is a bird.

50. **Which word does not belong in the following group?**
Answer: (D) Book
Explanation: Shirt, pants, and jacket are all articles of clothing, while "book" is not.

51. **Which word does not belong in the following group?**
Answer: (D) Computer
Explanation: Basketball,

baseball, and tennis are all sports, while "computer" is not.

52. **Which word does not belong in the following group?**
Answer: (D) Cake
Explanation: Car, bicycle, and bus are all modes of transportation, while "cake" is food.

53. **Which word does not belong in the following group?**
Answer: (C) Notebook
Explanation: Pen, marker, and crayon are all writing instruments, while "notebook" is something written in.

54. **Which word does not belong in the following group?**
Answer: (C) Chair
Explanation: Pillow, blanket, and sheet are all bedding items, while "chair" is furniture.

55. **Which word does not belong in the following group?**
Answer: (D) Window
Explanation: Circle, square, and triangle are geometric shapes, while "window" is not.

56. **Which word does not belong in the following group?**
Answer: (D) Pencil
Explanation: Hammer, saw, and

pliers are all tools, while "pencil" is a writing instrument.

57. **Which word does not belong in the following group?**
Answer: (D) Bird
Explanation: Car, plane, and train are all modes of transportation, while "bird" is an animal.

58. **Which word does not belong in the following group?**
Answer: (D) Lawyer
Explanation: Nurse, teacher, and doctor are all professions related to caregiving or education, while "lawyer" is not.

59. **Which word does not belong in the following group?**
Answer: (D) Glass
Explanation: Fire, water, and ice are all natural elements or states of matter, while "glass" is man-made.

60. **Which word does not belong in the following group?**
Answer: (C) Pen
Explanation: Book, magazine, and newspaper are all reading materials, while "pen" is a writing tool.

Quantitative Skills Subtest

Sequences

1. **(b)** The pattern is to add increasing odd numbers: +3, +5, +7, +9... 26 + 11 = 37

2. **(a)** This is the Fibonacci sequence where each number is the sum of the two preceding ones. 5 + 8 = 13

3. **(b)** Each number increases by 3. 36 x 3 = 108, 108 x 3 = 324

4. **(c)** Each number is double the previous one. 56 x 2 = 112

5. **(d)** The sequence decreases by 5, then 10, then 15... 70 - 20 = 50

6. **(b)** The pattern is to skip 4 letters in the alphabet. Q is 4 letters after M.

7. **(b)** Each number increases by 11. 55 + 11 = 66

8. **(c)** Each number is 3 raised to an increasing power. $3^0 = 1$, $3^1 = 3$, $3^2 = 9$, $3^3 = 27$, $3^4 = 81$

9. **(d)** The pattern is to skip 1 letter, then 2, then 3... L is 3 letters after H, so skip 4 to get to P

10. **(d)** Each number is half the previous one. 25 / 2 = 12.5

Comparisons

11. **(a)**
- $3^2 + 2 = 9 + 2 = 11$
- 75 is greater than 11

12. **(c)**
- 8/16 simplifies to 1/2
- 1/2 is equal to 1/2

13. **(b)**
- 1/2 of 1 is 0.5
- 0.5 is greater than 0.25

14. **(b)**
- Subtract 5 from both sides: $3x = 15$
- Divide both sides by 3: $x = 5$

15. **(c)**
- 9/10 is equal to 0.9

16. **(c)**
- $(3 \times 4) \div 2 = 12 \div 2 = 6$
- $3^2 = 9$

17. **(b)**
- $2 \times 2 \times 2 = 8$
- $2^3 \div 2 = 8 \div 2 = 4$

18. **(c)**

- 15% of $200 = (15/100) * 200 = 30$

19. **(c)**
- $18.9 + 0.1 = 19$

20. **(a)**
- $2^4 \div 2 = 16 \div 2 = 8$
- $2 \times 4 = 8$

Computations

21. **(c)** $8 \times 7 = 56$

22. **(d)** Divide both sides by 5: $y = 8$

23. **(b)** Follow order of operations (PEMDAS/BODMAS):
- $5 \times 2 = 10$
- $12 + 10 = 22$

24. **(c)** 25% is equivalent to 1/4. 1/4 of 80 is 20

25. **(b)** $12 + 8 = 20$

26. **(c)** $56 \div 7 = 8$

27. **(c)** 1/4 of 64 is the same as $64 \div 4 = 16$

28. **(b)** Solve within parentheses first: $2 \times 7 = 14$

29. **(b)** Subtract 7 from both sides: $x = 5$

30. **(b)** $9^2 = 9 \times 9 = 81$

Word Problems

31. **(c)**

- Cost of pencils: 3 pencils * $0.50/pencil = $1.50

- Cost of notebooks: 2 notebooks * $1.50/notebook = $3.00

- Total cost: $1.50 + $3.00 = $4.50

32. **(b)** Speed = Distance / Time = 150 miles / 3 hours = 50 mph

33. **(b)** Area of a rectangle = length x width = 10 cm x 5 cm = 50 cm²

34. **(b)**

- Find the cost of one apple: $2.50 / 5 apples = $0.50/apple

- Cost of 10 apples: 10 apples * $0.50/apple = $5.00

35. **(b)** Jane has 2 * 6 books = 12 books

36. **(c)** Average speed = Total distance / Time = 240 miles / 4 hours = 60 mph

37. **(c)**

- 3/4 of the tank is full, so the tank has (3/4) * 120 gallons = 90 gallons

38. **(c)**

- Find the cost of one book: $15.00 / 3 books = $5.00/book

- Cost of 5 books: 5 books * $5.00/book = $25.00

39. **(b)**

- Miles per gallon (mpg) = 240 miles / 12 gallons = 20 mpg

- Miles on 15 gallons = 20 mpg * 15 gallons = 300 miles

40. **(c)** Total cost = 4 tickets * $12/ticket = $48

41. **(b)**

- Total cost of dress and shoes: $40 + $30 = $70

- Discount: 10% of $70 = (10/100) * $70 = $7

- Final price: $70 - $7 = $63

42. **(d)** Total wheat = 3 fields * 120 pounds/field = 360 pounds

43. **(a)** Number of fiction books = 20% of 400 = (20/100) * 400 = 80

44. **(c)** Chairs per hour = Total chairs / Time = 50 chairs / 5 hours = 10 chairs/hour

45. **45. (c)** Distance = Speed x Time = 60 mph x 4 hours = 240 miles

46. **46. (c)**

47. Find the cost per bottle: $10 / 5 bottles = $2/bottle

48. Cost of 8 bottles: 8 bottles * $2/bottle = $16

49. **Advanced Computations**

50. **47. (b)**

51. Subtract 12 from both sides: 4x = 24

52. Divide both sides by 4: x = 6

53. **48. (c)**

54. 75% is equivalent to 3/4

55. (3/4) * 320 = 240

56. **49. (d)**

Reading Subtest

Reading Passage 1 (Questions 1–8)

1. **What was one of the major impacts of the industrial revolution on workers?**
   Answer: (d) It caused long working hours and dangerous conditions.
   Explanation: The passage mentions that workers faced long hours, dangerous conditions, and low pay during the industrial revolution.

57. Add 9 to both sides: 3y = 27

58. Divide both sides by 3: y = 9

59. **50. (d)**

60. Subtract 15 from both sides: 2z = 30

61. Divide both sides by 2: z = 15

62. **51. (d)**

63. Calculate the tip: 20% of $60 = (20/100) * $60 = $12

64. Total bill = bill + tip = $60 + $12 = $72

65. **52. (c)** Divide both sides by 6: k = 12

2. **According to the passage, how did the industrial revolution affect women and children?**
   Answer: (c) They were often employed in factories.
   Explanation: The passage states that women and children worked in factories, often being paid less than men.

3. **The word "profound" in the second paragraph most nearly means:**
   Answer: (b) Significant
   Explanation: "Profound" refers to something that has a great or significant impact.

4. **According to the passage, what was one environmental consequence of the industrial revolution?**
Answer: (b) Increased pollution of air and waterways.
Explanation: The passage mentions that factories polluted the air and waterways, leading to health problems in urban areas.

5. **Which of the following was not a technological advancement mentioned in the passage?**
Answer: (c) The electric motor.
Explanation: The passage mentions the steam engine, spinning jenny, and power loom but not the electric motor.

6. **The passage implies that life in the cities during the industrial revolution was:**
Answer: (c) Just as difficult as life in the countryside.
Explanation: The passage explains that although people moved to cities for jobs, life in the city was often just as difficult due to poor living conditions.

7. **What is the main idea of the passage?**
Answer: (b) The industrial revolution brought about both progress and challenges for society.
Explanation: The passage discusses the positive advancements (economic growth, technology) and the negative consequences (working conditions, pollution) of the industrial revolution.

8. **Based on the passage, which of the following statements is true?**
Answer: (c) The industrial revolution helped spur economic growth despite its challenges.
Explanation: The passage states that the industrial revolution spurred economic growth, despite the problems workers and the environment faced.

Reading Passage 2 (Questions 9–16)

9. **According to the passage, which invention was not mentioned as a tool for measuring time?**
Answer: (d) Digital watches.
Explanation: The passage mentions sundials, water clocks, and atomic clocks, but not digital watches.

10. **What does the passage imply about the concept of time?**
Answer: (b) It is mysterious and

264

not fully controllable. **Explanation**: The passage highlights that time is elusive and often not fully understood or controlled, especially with the introduction of Einstein's theory of relativity.

11. **Which word in the passage best describes the advancement of timekeeping tools?**
    Answer: (b) Gradual.
    Explanation: The passage describes the progression from sundials to atomic clocks, indicating a gradual advancement over time.

12. **What is the main purpose of the passage?**
    Answer: (a) To explain the history of timekeeping tools and their impact.
    Explanation: The passage discusses the evolution of timekeeping tools and their significance in science and everyday life.

13. **According to the passage, what is one feature of an atomic clock?**
    Answer: (a) It measures time more accurately than any other clock.
    Explanation: The passage states that atomic clocks are incredibly precise, losing only one second every million years.

14. **The phrase "time is relative" in the passage most likely means:**
    Answer: (b) Time can speed up or slow down depending on various factors.
    Explanation: The passage explains that according to Einstein's theory, time can stretch or compress based on speed and gravity.

15. **Why does the author mention Einstein's theory of relativity?**
    Answer: (b) To explain why time is different for astronauts.
    Explanation: The passage mentions that astronauts age slightly slower due to the speed at which they travel, as explained by the theory of relativity.

16. **The passage suggests that the invention of the atomic clock was important because:**
    Answer: (b) It allows scientists to measure time with extreme accuracy.
    Explanation: The atomic clock's precision is emphasized as crucial for scientific advancements, particularly in physics and astronomy.

Reading Passage 3 (Questions 17–24)

17. **What is one of the primary causes of ocean degradation mentioned in the passage?**
Answer: (b) Plastic pollution.
Explanation: The passage specifically mentions plastic pollution as one of the major issues affecting the health of the oceans.

18. **The passage implies that plastic pollution is harmful because:**
Answer: (b) It can take centuries to decompose, affecting both marine life and humans.
Explanation: The passage highlights the long-lasting impact of plastic on marine life and the food chain, potentially affecting human health.

19. **Which of the following is not a consequence of overfishing according to the passage?**
Answer: (c) Increased biodiversity in marine ecosystems.
Explanation: The passage mentions the decline in fish populations and threats to human livelihoods, but overfishing does not increase biodiversity.

20. **The word "exacerbating" in the third paragraph most likely means:**
Answer: (b) Worsening.
Explanation: "Exacerbating" means making something worse, which in this case refers to how climate change is making existing ocean problems worse.

21. **According to the passage, how does climate change affect coral reefs?**
Answer: (c) It causes coral reefs to bleach and die.
Explanation: The passage explains that rising sea temperatures cause coral bleaching, which leads to the death of coral reefs.

22. **What is one solution proposed in the passage to help protect the oceans?**
Answer: (b) Establishing marine protected areas.
Explanation: The passage mentions that governments are working to establish marine protected areas as a way to protect the oceans.

23. **Which of the following statements can be inferred from the passage?**
Answer: (c) The health of the

oceans is linked to the health of human populations. **Explanation**: The passage discusses how ocean degradation, particularly through pollution and overfishing, can affect human health and livelihoods.

24. **What is the main message of the passage?**

    Answer: (a) The oceans are in crisis, but efforts are being made to protect them. **Explanation**: The passage outlines the challenges facing the oceans but also emphasizes the ongoing efforts to address these problems.

Reading Passage 4 (Questions 25–32)

25. **What is the primary method of agriculture used by the Yanonami?**

    Answer: (c) Slash-and-burn agriculture. **Explanation**: The passage describes how the Yanonami use slash-and-burn agriculture to farm the land.

26. **According to the passage, what is one reason why the Yanonami's way of life is under threat?**

    Answer: (b) Encroachment by deforestation and industrial activities. **Explanation**: The passage mentions that deforestation, driven by logging and mining, is threatening the Yanonami's land and way of life.

27. **The word "encroaching" in the second paragraph most nearly means:**

    Answer: (b) Advancing. **Explanation**: "Encroaching" means gradually advancing or intruding, in this case referring to deforestation affecting Yanonami land.

28. **What does the passage suggest about the relationship between the Yanonami and their environment?**

    Answer: (c) The Yanonami live in harmony with their environment, using sustainable methods. **Explanation**: The passage explains how the Yanonami use sustainable farming techniques that allow them to live in harmony with the land.

29. **The passage implies that deforestation is problematic for the Yanonami because:**

    Answer: (b) It disrupts the

ecosystem and reduces available farming land.
Explanation: The passage states that deforestation is reducing the amount of land available for farming and disrupting the ecosystem.

30. **According to the passage, how are indigenous communities around the world similar to the Yanonami?**
Answer: (b) They face threats from industrialization and deforestation.
Explanation: The passage mentions that indigenous communities around the world are facing similar threats from deforestation and industrialization.

31. **What is one possible solution for the challenges faced by the Yanonami?**
Answer: (c) Protecting their land from industrial encroachment.
Explanation: The passage discusses the need for stronger protections of indigenous land to help preserve their way of life.

32. **What is the main idea of the passage?**
Answer: (b) The Yanonami are facing threats to their way of life

due to deforestation and modernization.
Explanation: The passage focuses on the threats posed by deforestation and industrial activities to the Yanonami's way of life.

Reading Passage 5 (Questions 33–40)

33. **According to the passage, what is one positive impact of AI on healthcare?**
Answer: (b) AI allows doctors to focus more on personalized patient care.
Explanation: The passage explains that AI speeds up diagnostic processes, allowing doctors to focus more on providing personalized care to their patients.

34. **What is one concern critics have about AI according to the passage?**
Answer: (b) AI may lead to widespread unemployment by replacing human workers.
Explanation: Critics argue that AI could replace human workers, particularly in sectors reliant on manual labor, leading to widespread unemployment.

35. **The word "mundane" in the second paragraph most nearly means:**
Answer: (c) Repetitive.
Explanation: "Mundane" refers to tasks that are routine and lack excitement, like repetitive and simple tasks that AI can take over.

36. **What is one argument proponents of AI use to support its development?**
Answer: (b) AI will increase productivity and free humans to engage in more complex work.
Explanation: Proponents argue that by automating repetitive tasks, AI allows humans to focus on more complex, creative, and important work.

37. **According to the passage, what is one potential negative consequence of AI advancement?**
Answer: (c) Machines replacing human workers, leading to job loss.
Explanation: The passage notes concerns about job loss as AI becomes more capable of taking over tasks traditionally performed by humans.

38. **What does the passage suggest about the future of AI in society?**
Answer: (c) AI will create ethical challenges related to its decision-making capabilities.
Explanation: The passage mentions concerns about allowing machines to make decisions that could impact people's lives, indicating that ethical challenges lie ahead.

39. **According to the passage, how does AI affect productivity?**
Answer: (b) AI increases productivity by automating repetitive tasks.
Explanation: AI is described as increasing efficiency by automating mundane and repetitive tasks, which leads to higher productivity.

40. **What is the main idea of the passage?**
Answer: (a) AI is advancing rapidly, but there are concerns about its impact on employment and society.
Explanation: The passage focuses on both the benefits and the concerns associated with the rapid advancement of AI in various industries.

269

Reading Passage 6 (Questions 41–48)

41. **According to the passage, what has caused the Grand Canyon to form over millions of years?**
Answer: (c) The Colorado River.
Explanation: The passage clearly states that the Grand Canyon was carved by the Colorado River over millions of years.

42. **What is one reason why the Grand Canyon is significant to indigenous peoples?**
Answer: (b) It has been home to their ancestors for thousands of years.
Explanation: The passage highlights the cultural significance of the Grand Canyon to various indigenous tribes who have lived there for thousands of years.

43. **The word "gorge" in the first paragraph most likely means:**
Answer: (a) A deep valley.
Explanation: "Gorge" refers to a deep valley, particularly one formed by the action of a river, as described in the context of the Grand Canyon.

44. **What environmental concerns does the passage mention in relation to the Grand Canyon?**

Answer: (c) The impact of tourism and climate change.
Explanation: The passage discusses how tourism and climate change are contributing to pollution, erosion, and habitat destruction in the Grand Canyon.

45. **How does climate change affect the Grand Canyon, according to the passage?**
Answer: (b) It is causing more extreme weather, like droughts and heat waves.
Explanation: The passage specifically mentions that climate change is leading to extreme weather patterns, such as droughts and intense heat, affecting the canyon.

46. **Based on the passage, what is one challenge posed by tourism at the Grand Canyon?**
Answer: (b) It is contributing to pollution, erosion, and habitat destruction.
Explanation: The passage explains that the growing number of visitors to the Grand Canyon is putting stress on the ecosystem through pollution and habitat destruction.

47. **What is the main idea of the passage?**

Answer: (a) The Grand Canyon is a natural and cultural landmark facing environmental challenges.
Explanation: The passage discusses both the cultural significance and the environmental challenges facing the Grand Canyon.

48. **Which of the following can be inferred from the passage about the Grand Canyon's future?**
Answer: (b) The impact of tourism and climate change may continue to worsen.
Explanation: The passage suggests that if current environmental challenges are not addressed, the Grand Canyon's ecosystem will continue to deteriorate.

Reading Passage 7 (Questions 49–56)

49. **What was one of the early uses of the internet, according to the passage?**
Answer: (b) To share scientific data and information.
Explanation: The passage explains that the internet was initially used by scientists and researchers to share data and information.

50. **According to the passage, what is one way the internet has changed communication?**
Answer: (c) It has allowed for instant messaging across the globe.
Explanation: The passage mentions that email and social media platforms have allowed people to send messages instantly around the world.

51. **What impact has the internet had on traditional brick-and-mortar stores?**
Answer: (a) It has led to a decline in sales as more people shop online.
Explanation: The passage discusses how the rise of e-commerce, led by companies like Amazon, has caused a decline in traditional stores as more people prefer the convenience of online shopping.

52. **The word "integral" in the first paragraph most likely means:**
Answer: (b) Important.
Explanation: "Integral" refers to something that is essential or important, which in this case describes the role of the internet in modern life.

53. **What does the passage imply about the impact of social media on communication?**
Answer: (b) Social media has made it easier for people to share information in real time.
Explanation: The passage explains that social media allows people to share thoughts, experiences, and photos instantly with large audiences.

54. **According to the passage, what is one benefit of the internet for businesses?**
Answer: (b) It has allowed small businesses to reach global markets.
Explanation: The passage notes that the internet has opened up new opportunities for entrepreneurs and small businesses to reach customers around the world.

55. **What is one challenge posed by the internet, according to the passage?**
Answer: (b) Privacy concerns and the spread of misinformation have become major issues.
Explanation: The passage mentions privacy concerns and the rapid spread of misinformation as significant challenges associated with the internet.

56. **What is the main idea of the passage?**
Answer: (b) The internet has revolutionized communication, commerce, and entertainment, but also brought challenges.
Explanation: The passage describes the significant changes brought by the internet, along with the challenges it has introduced.

Reading Passage 8 (Questions 57–62)

57. **What event is the passage primarily describing?**
Answer: (c) The moon landing of 1969.
Explanation: The passage describes Neil Armstrong's first steps on the moon during the 1969 Apollo mission.

58. **The phrase "one giant leap for mankind" in the first paragraph most likely means:**
Answer: (b) A significant advancement for all of humanity.
Explanation: Armstrong's words signify that the moon landing was a monumental achievement for humanity as a whole.

59. **According to the passage, what was one factor that contributed to the success of the moon landing?**
   Answer: (c) The efforts of scientists, engineers, and astronauts.
   Explanation: The passage attributes the success of the moon landing to the dedicated work of many people in various fields.

60. **The word "momentous" in the second paragraph most likely means:**
   Answer: (c) Important.
   Explanation: "Momentous" means significant or important, describing the impact of the moon landing.

61. **What is one legacy of the moon landing, according to the passage?**
   Answer: (b) It inspired new generations of scientists and explorers.
   Explanation: The passage mentions that the moon landing inspired a new generation of people interested in space exploration and science.

62. **What is the main idea of the passage?**
   Answer: (c) The moon landing was a significant achievement that advanced space exploration.
   Explanation: The passage discusses the importance and far-reaching effects of the moon landing on space exploration.

   - $= 6x - 12 - 5x$
   - Combine like terms: $x - 12$

Mathematics Subtest

1. (C) 41

   - Substitute the given values of 'x' and 'y' into the expression.
   - $2x + 3y = 2(5) + 3(7)$
   - $= 10 + 21$
   - $= 31$

2. (A) x - 12

   - Apply the distributive property: $3(2x - 4) - 5x$

3. (A) 25 cm²

   - Area of a triangle $= (1/2) * base * height$
   - Area $= (1/2) * 10 \text{ cm} * 5 \text{ cm}$
   - $= 25 \text{ cm}^2$

4. (B) 7

   - Add 7 to both sides of the equation: $3x = 21$

273

- Divide both sides by 3: x = 7

5. (B) 16

- Let the first even number be represented by 'n'.

- The next two consecutive even numbers are 'n + 2' and 'n + 4'.

- The sum of these three numbers is 54: n + (n + 2) + (n + 4) = 54

- Combine like terms: 3n + 6 = 54

- Subtract 6 from both sides: 3n = 48

- Divide both sides by 3: n = 16

- The smallest of the three numbers is 16.

6. (A) 5 cm

- Circumference of a circle = $2\pi r$

- 31.4 = 2 * 3.14 * r

- 31.4 = 6.28r

- Divide both sides by 6.28: r = 5 cm

7. (B) 200 miles

- Calculate the train's speed: 120 miles / 3 hours = 40 mph

- Distance traveled in 5 hours: 40 mph * 5 hours = 200 miles

8. (B) 18

- The ratio 3:4 means for every 3 boys there are 4 girls

- Set up a proportion: 3/4 = x/24 (where 'x' is the number of boys)

- Cross-multiply and solve for x: 4x = 72 => x = 18

9. (D) x = 5

- Apply distributive property: 10x - 15 = 4x + 10

- Subtract 4x from both sides: 6x - 15 = 10

- Add 15 to both sides: 6x = 25

- Divide both sides by 6: x = 25/6 or 4 1/6

10. (C) 64

- 4^3 = 4 * 4 * 4 = 64

11. (C) 7

- Take the square root of both sides. Remember that a square root can be positive or negative

- $x = \pm\sqrt{49}$

- $x = \pm 7$

12. (C) 32 cm

- Perimeter of a rectangle = 2(length + width)

- Perimeter = 2(12 + 4)
- = 2(16)
- = 32 cm

13. (A) 4x - 4

- Combine like terms: 6x - 2x + 3 - 7
- Simplify: 4x - 4

14. (C) 300

- Let 'x' be the original number
- 20% of x is 60: (20/100) * x = 60
- 0.2x = 60
- Divide both sides by 0.2: x = 300

15. (C) $3.75

- Divide the total cost by the number of notebooks: $18.75 / 5 = $3.75

16. (B) 30

- Subtract 4 from both sides: x/5 = 6
- Multiply both sides by 5: x = 30

17. (C) 6 gallons

- Divide the total distance by the fuel efficiency: 150 miles / 25 miles/gallon = 6 gallons

18. (C) 120

- Let 'x' be the original number
- Decreased by 30%: x - 0.3x = 0.7x
- 0.7x = 84
- Divide both sides by 0.7: x = 120

19. (A) 3/2

- Rearrange the equation into slope-intercept form (y = mx + b, where 'm' is the slope)
- 3x - 2y = 6
- -2y = -3x + 6
- Divide both sides by -2: y = (3/2)x - 3
- The slope (m) is 3/2

20. (B) 154 cm²

- Area of a circle = π * r^2
- Area = 3.14 * 7^2
- = 3.14 * 49
- = 153.86 cm² (approximately 154 cm²)

21. (B) x > 5

- Add 3 to both sides: 2x > 10
- Divide both sides by 2: x > 5

22. (B) 5/15

- Total number of marbles: 3 + 5 + 7 = 15

- Probability = (Favorable outcomes) / (Total possible outcomes)

- Probability of blue marble = 5 / 15

23. (C) √5

- An irrational number cannot be expressed as a simple fraction.

- √5 is a non-terminating, non-repeating decimal.

24. (C) 4

- Substitute the values of 'a' and 'b' into the expression

- $ab + b^2 = (4)(-2) + (-2)^2$

- $= -8 + 4$

- $= -4$

25. (A) Yes

- This triangle satisfies the Pythagorean theorem ($a^2 + b^2 = c^2$), which is a characteristic of right triangles

- $6^2 + 8^2 = 10^2$

- $36 + 64 = 100$

- $100 = 100$

26. (B) 17

- This is an arithmetic sequence with a common difference of 3

- Add 3 to the last term: 14 + 3 = 17

27. (C) 144

- $2^4 = 2 * 2 * 2 * 2 = 16$

- $3^2 = 3 * 3 = 9$

- $16 * 9 = 144$

28. (A) $60

- Calculate the discount amount: 25% of $80 = (25/100) * $80 = $20

- Subtract the discount from the original price: $80 - $20 = $60

29. (B) x = 3

- Subtract 3 from both sides: 7x = 21

- Divide both sides by 7: x = 3

30. (C) 40 cm²

- Area of a parallelogram = base * height

- Area = 8 cm * 5 cm = 40 cm²

31. (B) 11

- Let the original number be 'x'

- Triple the number: 3x

- Increase by 12: 3x + 12

- The result is 45: $3x + 12 = 45$
- Subtract 12 from both sides: $3x = 33$
- Divide both sides by 3: $x = 11$

32. (C) 120

- 5! (5 factorial) = $5 * 4 * 3 * 2 * 1 = 120$

33. (A) 6 and 8

- We know:
  - $a * b = 48$
  - $a + b = 14$
- You can solve this either by trial and error with the answer choices or by substitution.
- **Trial and Error:**
  - Try the pairs in the answer choices and see which one satisfies both equations.
  - (A) 6 and 8:
    - $6 * 8 = 48$ (Correct)
    - $6 + 8 = 14$ (Correct)
- **Substitution:**
  - Solve the second equation for one variable (let's solve for a): $a = 14 - b$
  - Substitute this into the first equation: $(14 - b) * b = 48$
  - Expand: $14b - b^2 = 48$
  - Rearrange into a quadratic equation: $b^2 - 14b + 48 = 0$
  - Factor: $(b - 6)(b - 8) = 0$
  - This gives us two possible solutions for b: $b = 6$ or $b = 8$
  - Substitute these back into $a = 14 - b$ to find the corresponding values of 'a'
  - If $b = 6$, then $a = 8$
  - If $b = 8$, then $a = 6$
  - Either way, the two numbers are 6 and 8

34. (B) 36

- The Least Common Multiple (LCM) is the smallest number that is a multiple of both 12 and 18
- Find the prime factorizations of 12 and 18
  - $12 = 2 \times 2 \times 3$

277

- 18 = 2 x 3 x 3
- The LCM is found by taking the highest power of each prime number that appears in either factorization and multiplying them together
- LCM = 2^2 x 3^2 = 4 x 9 = 36

35. (A) 5 cm

- Volume of a cube = $side^3$
- 125 = $side^3$
- Take the cube root of both sides: side = $\sqrt[3]{125}$ = 5 cm

36. (A) 16 cups

- The ratio of sugar to flour is 3:4
- Set up a proportion: 3/4 = 12/x (where 'x' is the number of cups of flour)
- Cross-multiply and solve for x: 3x = 48 => x = 16

37. (C) x = 3

- Subtract 3x from both sides: x + 7 = 10
- Subtract 7 from both sides: x = 3

38. (C) 8 cm

- Perimeter of a square = 4 * side
- 32 = 4 * side
- Divide both sides by 4: side = 8 cm

39. (B) 2/10

- Total number of balls: 5 + 3 + 2 = 10
- Probability = (Favorable outcomes) / (Total possible outcomes)
- Probability of yellow ball = 2/10

40. (B) 7x + 1

- Combine like terms: 4x + 3x - 5 + 6
- Simplify: 7x + 1

41. (C) 8

- Multiply both sides by 2: 3x - 4 = 10
- Add 4 to both sides: 3x = 14
- Divide both sides by 3: x = 14/3 or 4 2/3

42. (C) 11

- Substitute x = 4 into the function
- f(4) = 2(4) + 3
- f(4) = 8 + 3
- f(4) = 11

43. (B) 21

- The median is the middle value when the numbers are sorted in ascending order.
- The numbers are already sorted.
- The middle value is 21

44. (C) 29

- A prime number is a whole number greater than 1 that has only two divisors (factors): 1 and itself
- 29 is only divisible by 1 and 29

45. (A) y = 2

- Subtract 3 from both sides: $y = 2$

46. (C) 3/4

- 0.75 is the same as 75/100
- Simplify by dividing both numerator and denominator by their greatest common divisor, which is 25
- $75/100 = (75 \div 25) / (100 \div 25) = 3/4$

47. (C) 28

- 35% of 80 = (35/100) * 80
- = 28

48. (B) 45 mph

- Average speed = Total distance / Time
- Average speed = 180 miles / 4 hours
- = 45 mph

49. (B) 1/4

- Simplify the fraction by dividing both numerator and denominator by their greatest common divisor, which is 16
- $16/64 = (16 \div 16) / (64 \div 16) = 1/4$

50. (B) 32

- This is a geometric sequence where each number is double the previous one
- 16 x 2 = 32

51. (C) 12

- The Greatest Common Factor (GCF) is the largest number that divides both 36 and 48 without leaving a remainder
- Find the prime factorizations:
  - 36 = 2 x 2 x 3 x 3
  - 48 = 2 x 2 x 2 x 2 x 3
- The GCF is found by multiplying the common prime factors, each

raised to the lowest power it appears in either factorization.

- GCF = 2 x 2 x 3 = 12

52. (B & D)

- A triangle with angles of 45°, 45°, and 90° is both:
    - **Isosceles:** It has two equal angles (45° and 45°)
    - **Right:** It has a right angle (90°)

53. (C) 5

- Subtract 2 from both sides: 3x = 15
- Divide both sides by 3: x = 5

54. (B) 6x^3

- Multiply the coefficients and add the exponents of the variables
- $(2x^2)(3x) = (2 * 3) (x^2 * x^1)$
- $= 6x^3$

55. (C) 9 cm

- Area of a square = side²
- 81 = side²
- Take the square root of both sides
- side = √81 = 9 cm

56. (D) 17

- Substitute the values of 'a' and 'b' into the expression
- 2a² + b²
- $= 2(2)^2 + 3^2$
- = 2(4) + 9
- = 8 + 9
- = 17

57. (C) x = 6

- Subtract 2x from both sides: 7 = 2x - 5
- Add 5 to both sides: 12 = 2x
- Divide both sides by 2: x = 6

58. (B) 12

- The Greatest Common Factor (GCF) is the largest number that divides both 24 and 60 without leaving a remainder
- Find the prime factorizations
    - 24 = 2 x 2 x 2 x 3
    - 60 = 2 x 2 x 3 x 5
- The GCF is found by multiplying the common prime factors, each raised to the lowest power it appears in either factorization
- GCF = 2 x 2 x 3 = 12

59. (B) $4.00

- Find the cost of one pen: $1.50 / 3 pens = $0.50/pen

- Cost of 8 pens: 8 pens * $0.50/pen = $4.00

60. (A) x ≤ 4

- Add 2 to both sides: $5x \leq 20$

- Divide both sides by 5: $x \leq 4$

61. (C) 12

- The square root of 144 is 12 because 12 * 12 = 144

62. (B) 4

- In the set {2, 4, 4, 6, 8}, the number 4 appears twice, which is more frequent than any other number

63. (B) 4.5

- Multiply the original amount of sugar by 3: 1.5 cups * 3 = 4.5 cups

64. (C) 6

- Add 8 to both sides: $3x = 18$

- Divide both sides by 3: $x = 6$

Made in the USA
Middletown, DE
23 November 2024

65304511R00157